Active Directory Best Practices:

Migrating, Designing, and Troubleshooting

24seven

Active Directory® Best Practices:
Migrating, Designing, and Troubleshooting

24seven™

Brad Price

SYBEX®

San Francisco
London

Associate Publisher: Joel Fugazzotto

Acquisitions Editor: Elizabeth Peterson

Developmental Editor: Tom Cirtin

Production Editor: Lori Newman

Technical Editor: David E. Brown

Copyeditor: Kathy Grider-Carlyle

Compositor: Maureen Forys, Happenstance Type-O-Rama

Graphic Illustrator: Happenstance Type-O-Rama

Proofreaders: Laurie O'Connell, Nancy Riddiough

Indexer: Ted Laux

Cover Designer: Ingalls + Associates

Cover Illustrator: Hank Osuna

Library of Congress Card Number: 2003115669

ISBN: 0-7821-4305-9

Manufactured in the United States of America

10 9 8 7 6 5 4 3 2 1

To the three most important people in my life—
my beautiful wife DeAnn and equally beautiful
daughters Jami and Becca.

I cherish your love and am thankful for all of your
support.

Acknowledgments

I WOULD NOT HAVE been able to complete this project without the support of my family. DeAnn—once again I find myself thanking you for all that you sacrifice so that I can complete these demanding schedules. Thank you for standing beside me, believing in me, and taking the time to allow me to complete these projects. You are truly my soulmate, and I love you very much. Jami and Becca—your compassion, humor, and beautiful smiles make every moment I spend with you the most fulfilling moments of my life. I have watched you both grow into smart, caring, beautiful women, and I am very proud of you. I love you both!

I have to thank my brother, John, for his contributions to the book. He took time out of his own busy schedule to write Chapter 19, "Securing the Base Operating System," and Chapter 21, "Patch Management." He has collaborated with me on each of the books that I have written and has been an invaluable asset. Without him to bounce ideas off of and brainstorm with, I wouldn't have been able to maintain my sanity.

To the rest of my family—I couldn't have done this without your understanding. Dad and Mom—you two are the best. You gave me the confidence to believe that I could do anything I put my mind to. Your support has always meant the world to me. To the rest of this ever expanding, slightly insane cast of characters that I call my family—even though I rarely get the chance to say it, each and every one of you means so much to me. Thank you all for supporting these ventures of mine.

I also work with a fantastic group of people who allow me to bounce questions and ideas off them: Bill Davis, Martin Deutsch, Penny Morgan, Randy Muller, Ron Smiley, and Scott Fenstermacher. I want to give Michelle Ingram a special thank you for your Novell expertise. I just hope I didn't depress you too much when you read my take on migration! And to Jason Oldham, Dan McCain, Susan Kunz, Margaret Teague, Chris and Connie Kelly, Mark Smith, Eros DeSouza, Terry Sikkema, Steve Denger, Dawn Oltmanns, Diane Silveri, Karen Gill, Krista Stellar, Courtney Simpson, Leon Hedding, Todd Smith, Adam Corsaw, Chad Price, Roxanne Gaskins, Yannick LeBoulch, and all of the other characters in my life—thanks for supporting my efforts.

As for the Sybex staff that I worked with on this runaway train, thank you for believing in me enough to ask me on for another project. Elizabeth Peterson—we've worked on two together now. Ready for another? Tom Cirtin—you were a great DE to work with. Thank you for all of your help and guidance. Lori Newman—I know I had you scared at the start, and the middle, and at the end as we fought to keep things on track, but we did it. I hope I didn't cause you to pull too much of your hair out! David E. Brown, technical editor—thanks for keeping my head straight in a couple of places and handing out suggestions as we went along. Kathy Grider-Carlyle, editor—thank you for making my words resemble English instead of gibberish! Your polish makes the manuscript shine. And to everyone else who assisted on the book—bravo!

Contents at a Glance

Contents

Introduction

This book was an interesting departure from the study guides that I have written in the past. Gone were the nights of trying to come up with hundreds of sample questions and simulations.

If you look at the information contained in these pages, you will find that I did not include basic introductory information about Windows 2000, Windows Server 2003, or Active Directory. I approached this book at the intermediate and advanced level. I assumed that this book's readers would have a basic understanding of Windows server operating systems and would know how to use and manipulate the Active Directory tools that ship with the operating systems.

With that assumption in mind, I broke the topics into four parts:

◆ Design

◆ Deployment and migration

◆ Maintenance and administration

◆ Securing Active Directory

These are four areas that administrators need to face and understand if they are going to have a sound, functional, and efficient Active Directory.

Part 1, "Design," covers the important issues that you will need to address as you prepare to roll out Active Directory. Forest, domain, and DNS design issues are addressed so that you will have a thorough understanding of the criteria and interoperability requirements that you need to have in place. Without a sound plan, you may be required to rework your design.

Also in Part 1, we cover the topics of sites, Flexible Single Master Operations, Global Catalog, Organizational Units, the effects of Exchange on your design, and hardware-sizing recommendations. Even though this information will probably be used only once during the lifecycle of your Active Directory infrastructure, it takes up a fair amount of the book. You should treat Active Directory like a child. If you nurture it and treat it right during its infancy, you will probably end up with a healthy child.

Part 2, "Deployment and Migration," addresses three topics:

◆ Deployment

◆ Domain migration and consolidation

◆ NetWare migration

Deployment takes into consideration the different methods of rolling out the operating systems and Active Directory. Tips and methodologies for manual and automated installation are covered. Domain migration and consolidation addresses what you should expect when moving from a Windows NT–based infrastructure to Active Directory, as well as moving from Windows 2000 to Windows Server 2003. NetWare migration takes a look at some of the stumbling blocks you may encounter when you are moving from "that other network operating system" to Active Directory.

Part 3, "Maintenance and Administration," is probably where a majority of readers will dog-ear the pages of this book. This part covers:

♦ Backup and Disaster Recovery

♦ Maintaining the Active Directory Database

♦ Troubleshooting Active Directory and File System Replication

♦ Maintaining DNS

♦ Troubleshooting Logon Failures

♦ Controlling the Flexible Single Master Operations

♦ Working with Group Policy

A lot of information is contained in this part, and I hope you find that it is a good reference when you have problems with your Active Directory infrastructure.

Part 4, "Securing Active Directory," presents tips on securing your domain controllers and Active Directory from many different types of attacks, from physical attacks to attacks on the database itself. Due to the sheer number of attacks that are occurring on all computer platforms, many companies have created security initiatives so that they can protect their assets. In this part, I tried to present some of best security tips for:

♦ Securing the Underlying Operating System

♦ Preventing Problems through Patch Management

♦ Securing the Underlying DNS

♦ Securing Active Directory Itself

Why Should You Read This?

This book is designed to give you the solutions you need fast and give them to you without a lot of wasted verbiage. I tried to put together information that will help you maintain your Active Directory infrastructure in the most efficient manner. I did not add fluff to this book. It is as concise as possible, yet it brings together some of the most important topics that you will have to face. If you are looking for a book about day-to-day operations, such as creating users and groups, working with group management, and using Computer Management to create shares or look at Event Viewer, you will need to look for another one. *This book is meant for the administrator who already understands the standard tools and is looking for more.*

Have you seen tools such as DSAStat, ADSI Edit, FRSDiag, and ReplMon? They are covered here. Other utilities that will help you maintain Active Directory replication, perform FRS replication, perform disaster recovery, work with Group Policy, and secure your system are also covered.

Not everyone can be an expert on all facets of Active Directory. Many people understand Active Directory well, but they do not have the additional knowledge to maintain some of the underlying technologies that allow it to function. Some have a love/hate relationship with Active Directory and want to know what they can do to alleviate some of their problems, while others will want to know the logic behind the design decisions. The topics covered in this book will help you with some of the more obscure and misunderstood topics. You should consider adding this book to your administrative toolkit.

Design

part I

In this part:

chapter I

Active Directory Forest Design

How DO YOU OPTIMALLY design a database that replicates only parts of itself to as many as thousands of domain controllers at differing intervals? Therein lies the need for this book. Active Directory may very well become the largest database implementation within your organization. If you talk to very many database administrators, you will see them cringe when you mention that you would like to replicate a database to multiple servers. But that is exactly what you are going to do with Active Directory and your domain controllers.

Throughout the first section of this book, I am going to discuss design criteria that you should consider when designing your Active Directory infrastructure. The chapters in Part I are organized simply. To do an Active Directory design, go through the chapters in order. By doing so, you will end up with a good understanding of the building blocks for a design that allows for efficient administration and control of the entire Active Directory environment.

Active Directory is a technology that is unlike most directory services in that it is an integral part of the operating system (OS). The many other directory services out there "sit on top" of the OS. Netware Directory Services (NDS), for example, can be easily upgraded independent of an OS upgrade. Not so for Active Directory. To update the directory service on the Microsoft platform, you currently need to upgrade to the latest Server OS or service pack. Each service pack brings a host of bug and security fixes for Active Directory, as well additional functionality; therefore, you should apply the latest service pack on all of your domain controllers within a month of its release—although that is easier said than done.

Take note that Active Directory enhancements, features, and functionality are greatly upgraded by Windows Server 2003. The move from Windows 2000 to 2003 requires very little planning. The two databases are built on the same underlying technologies, but Microsoft learned a lot after the initial rollout with Active Directory under Windows 2000. Consider Active Directory in Windows Server 2003 as version 2.0 to the 1.0 Active Directory version in Windows 2000—this is an unofficial versioning that's included just for illustrative purposes. New administrative tools have been added and additional functionality has been included. However, for most of the added functionality, you will need to retire all of your Windows 2000 domain controllers. I'll discuss more on that later in this chapter as we review the functional levels for domains and forests.

You should consider moving to Windows Server 2003 for a myriad of reasons, not the least of which is the support timeline expiration of Windows 2000. Mainstream product support expires five years after a product release. Many in the IT industry will take the conspiracy theorist's stance and accuse Microsoft of retiring products in order to keep companies on the purchasing side of the table. However, in our industry, you must admit that the technologies that develop over the course of five years tend to make operating systems and applications obsolete. For those of you who have left Windows NT 4 for the greener pastures of Windows 2000 and Active Directory, could you even imagine trying to perform some of the administrative tasks on Windows NT 4 that you can perform with the newer technologies?

TIP   *For more information on the lifecycle of operating systems and applications, peruse the article on Microsoft's website* `http://support.microsoft.com/default.aspx?pr=lifecycle`

In the following sections, we are going to look at the criteria you should consider when developing your Active Directory design. Most of the information included comes from working with Active Directory over the past few years and the methodology that has proven to work the best. While some of the information may seem like it is common sense to you, there are times when common sense seems to take a back seat to the desire to implement technology.

Active Directory Forest Design Criteria

Active Directory design is both technically and operationally driven. It requires compromise among diverse groups that may be used to doing tasks their own way—DNS admins can use Unix for DNS, NetWare admins have a different architecture of directory services that they want to implement, ERP packages use their own directory service, proxy/firewall/internet access might use its own directory service, mail uses its own directory service.... You get the idea. How do you please everyone in your design? You probably won't. Start by developing the ideal design by yourself, if possible, and then let each group have its turn telling you what modifications they would like to see or, in a worst case scenario, why your design won't work. If you let each group try to design Active Directory, you'll never get done.

Get executive sponsorship in the design phase. I cannot stress this point enough. In other words, find an executive to approve the design phase of Active Directory with input from other groups (afterward). If you make an executive ally within the organization and they trust and like your plan, you will find that getting the design approved and moving on to the planning stages will be much easier. A college professor of project management once told me that executive sponsorship of projects is the number one indicator of whether a project will get done. He actually buys stock in companies that have good project management business processes. He says he does well with his stock picks.

Active Directory design is about putting structure around a chaos of unorganized objects. It's about administrative control and separating the service owners accountable for maintaining Active Directory and the services that support it from data owner administrators who are responsible for maintaining the objects within the directory. It is about architecting a solution that takes into account the limitations of the technology you are working with (Windows Server and Active Directory) and designing around the organizational day-to-day business. Your design needs to take into consideration speed/latency, name resolution, availability, security, disaster/recovery, hardware, etc.

Forest Design should be your first architectural element when designing Active Directory. A forest is the smallest instance of Active Directory. The forest is the topmost container in Active Directory. It is scalable beyond 5,000 domain controllers, 5,000 sites, and millions of users according to Microsoft's Branch Office Deployment Guide. Even the largest organizations should be able to contain all of the necessary objects within a single forest. You will find that other considerations will come into play when developing your design. Legislative, political, or organizational reasons may force you to move to a multiple forest design, but make sure there is a valid reason to do so. Later in this chapter, I will discuss the pros and cons of single and multiple forest implementations.

Although a forest is almost insanely easy to build, it is far, far more complex to design. Several options are available, and you need to know what roles forests and domains play within your organization. As you will see in the next section, the domain is no longer the security boundary, as it was under Windows NT 4. I will discuss the differences and the new technologies that make up the security boundary, replication boundary, administration boundary, schema, and Global Catalog.

Schema

A forest shares a single *schema*, which can be defined as the rules of what can go into a directory service. Active Directory is made up of *objects*, which are instances of an object class that have been defined by combining attributes to form what can be allowed within the directory. These rules also define where objects can be created and used within the directory service. Because all of the objects within the forest have to follow the same rules, there can be only one schema per forest.

Due to the important nature of the schema, you should not take its existence lightly. While you may not have to think about it on a daily basis, you will need to make sure that you do not allow anyone to have access to the schema. If changes are enacted within the schema, the results could be disastrous. Your organization may be one of the lucky ones that never have to modify their schema, but very few organizations are so lucky.

Many organizations will modify their default schema so that it will support directory-enabled applications. One such example, and probably the most popular, is the need to implement Exchange. Both Exchange 2000 Server and Exchange Server 2003 add many additional attributes and object classes to the schema. Prior to implementing an Active Directory–enabled application within your production environment, make sure you understand the ramifications of altering your schema. Test the application first in a test environment. Later, in the "Best Practices for Forest Design" section, I will discuss the need to change management. You should read this section if you want to control how changes are made to your infrastructure.

NOTE *If you would like to see the schema extensions that are installed with Exchange 2000/2003, check out the information at* `http://msdn.microsoft.com/library/default.asp?url=/library/en-us/e2k3/e2k3/e2k3_ldf_diff_ad_schema_intro.asp`.

Schema Considerations

If you are extending the schema for an in-house application, consider contacting an Object Identifier (OID) issuing authority for the proper classification. Failure to do so could cause problems with other applications when they are installed within your environment. If an application needs to use an OID that is already in use, the application will fail the install. Windows Server 2003 will allow you to reclassify an attribute; however, Windows 2000 will not. As a best practice, you should contact one of the following organizations to verify that the OID is not in use:

◆ Internet Assigned Numbers Authority (IANA) hands out OIDs for free under the "Private Enterprises" branch.

◆ American National Standards Institute (ANSI) hands out OIDs under the "US Organizations" branch for USD 1,000.

◆ British Standards Institute (BSI) hands out OIDs under the "UK Organizations" branch.

◆ Visit http://www.iso.ch for information on your country's National Registration Authority.

While you are at it, register the OID so that no one else can use it for their commercial applications. Microsoft will validate all applications that you want to be certified for use within Active Directory. If you register your OID and someone else tries to use it, Microsoft will fail the application and the software vendor will have to change their application accordingly.

For information on registering OIDs for the ISO or if you are registering an OID under Microsoft's branch, see the following websites:

◆ http://msdn.microsoft.com/library/en-us/ad/ad/obtaining_a_root_oid_from_an_iso_name_registration_authority.asp

◆ http://msdn.microsoft.com/library/en-us/ad/ad/obtaining_an_object_identifier_from_microsoft.asp

Security Boundary

The rules have changed since Windows NT 4. Under NT, the domain was the security boundary. If you were a member of the Domain Admins group, you had full control of your domain and were isolated from Domain Admins from other domains. Now with Active Directory, the forest is the security boundary in Active Directory (AD), not the domain. I get a kick out of clients who want to argue this point with me. Any Domain Admin on any domain controller throughout the forest can bring down the entire AD forest—either on purpose or by mistake. There are some simple ways to do this:

◆ Impersonate any user in the forest (in any domain).

◆ Read, change, or delete any Windows-secured resource or configuration setting on any machine (especially domain controllers) in the forest.

◆ Modify service accounts that run in the *system context*—that means operating system privileges.

◆ Run code in system context.

◆ Hide (bury) domain administrator–equivalent accounts for later use. I participated in an audit that found a hidden Admin account named GOD.

◆ Cause changes to replicate to other DCs. This is not a problem with database corruption; but it is for a denial-of-service (DoS) attack, which would be easy with a simple script that added users endlessly.

◆ Take ownership of files, folders, objects, attributes, and, thereby, breach privacy.

These are just a few of the many ways to bring down the Active Directory forest.

NOTE *See Chapter 2, "Active Directory Domain Design," for more information on what Active Directory domains are used for and the design drivers behind them.*

When you are creating your Active Directory design, you must account for who will become the forest owner. The forest owner is any account that has full control access to every domain within the forest. Any domain administrator in the root domain of the forest (the first domain created in the forest) is automatically made a member of the Enterprise Admins and Schema Admins Groups in Windows 2000. You should be thinking like the rest of us and take users/Admins out of this group immediately.

Replication Boundary

Active Directory forests provide for a complete replication boundary. Two Active Directory partitions, the configuration and schema partitions (or naming contexts), replicate on a forest-wide basis. Every domain controller within the forest will share identical data for these two partitions. Even if you have domain controllers from different forests within the same physical location, they will not share configuration and schema partition data; only those from the same forest will.

Another partition type, the application partition, can be configured to replicate to all domain controllers within the forest, but it is not mandatory that it do so. With an application partition, you have the ability to choose which domain controllers the partition will replicate to, thereby giving you a means of controlling some of the replication traffic within your organization. Later, in Chapter 3, "Domain Name System Design," we will look at how the application partition works and the benefits of using this new partition type.

You can see the naming contexts upon opening Active Directory Services Interface (ADSI) Edit, which is provided in the Support Tools on the Windows 2000 (W2K) or Windows 2003 (W2K3) CD under \SUPPORT\TOOLS. Figure 1.1 shows ADSI Edit with the naming contexts opened.

FIGURE 1.1

ADSI Edit and the Naming Contexts

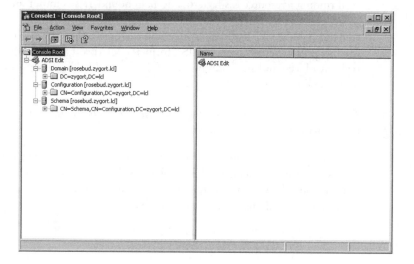

As you will see in the following chapter, the domain partition, or domain-naming context, is replicated only to other domain controllers within the same domain. Although this does improve performance by restricting the amount of replication throughout the organization, it does cause issues when users are trying to locate objects within other domains. To alleviate some of the problems associated with partitioning the forest into separate domains, a Global Catalog was introduced.

A Common Global Catalog

A forest also provides for a common Global Catalog (GC) within the forest. A Global Catalog is a domain controller that hosts objects from every domain-naming context within the forest. At first you might think that could be a lot of data for a domain controller to host. If the Global Catalog server were to hold all of the attributes from every domain within the forest, you would be correct. However, to keep network traffic at a minimum, only around 200 of the 1,700+ available attributes for each object are copied into the GC. The GC is like a giant cache of directory objects and attributes that keep you from needing to query beyond a single domain controller. For example, you could easily take a laptop from domain to domain, country to country inside the same forest and authenticate immediately because your user object (and every user object in the forest) is cached in the Global Catalog, which replicates forest-wide.

You can control which attributes populate the Global Catalog with the Schema Management MMC snap-in. Be warned though, in Windows 2000, when you make a change to what values get put into the GC, you cause a full GC replication throughout the forest. This is not a big deal in an office of 200 people, but it is very much a concern when you have a 9GB GC such as Microsoft. This does not happen in W2K3; instead, only the changed or added attribute is replicated throughout the forest.

Later, as we determine the placement of domain controllers, we will come back to the Global Catalog server. There will be specific locations where you should place Global Catalog servers so that users and applications have access to the GC. For instance, the GC is Exchange 2000/2003's Global Address List (GAL), so you need to provide constant access to the GC for all of your Exchange servers.

If finding a resource easily across domain boundaries is important, without additional software services, consider a single forest. A single forest will allow all of the objects from every domain to be seen through the GC. If you must use multiple forests, there are applications, such as Microsoft Identity Integration Server 2003 (MIIS), formerly Microsoft Metadirectory Services (MMS), that can replicate objects and attributes between forests and differing directory services such as Novell's NDS to Active Directory.

TIP *For more information concerning Microsoft Identity Integration Server 2003, visit Microsoft's website at* `http://www.microsoft.com/miis`.

When you have multiple domains within your forest, you need to have a method to gain access to the resources in each domain. The Global Catalog servers need to have the ability to pull data from domain controllers in each of the other domains. In order to do so, trust relationships are used to determine which domains can contact each other.

Kerberos and Trusts

Under the Windows NT 4 model, every domain was its own security boundary. To allow users to access resources within another NT domain, you had to create a trust relationship between the two domains. When you created a trust relationship, only one domain was allowed to trust users from the other domain. If you wanted to allow both sets of users to access each other's resources, two trust relationships needed to be created. To make matters worse, there was no sharing of trust. In other words, the trust relationships were not transitive. If DomainA had a trust relationship with DomainB, and DomainB had a trust relationship with DomainC, DomainA was still restricted from accessing DomainC until an explicit trust was set up between DomainA and DomainC. Needless to say, planning and maintaining the correct trust relationships in a large NT infrastructure caused many administrators to lose sleep.

Windows 2000 and Windows Server 2003 have changed the trust relationship game. Within a forest, all of the domains are interconnected through two-way transitive trusts. This allows every user within the forest to access resources within any domain within the forest so long as they have been granted permissions to access the resource. All of this is accomplished using the fewest trust relationships possible. Take a look at Figure 1.2. This is a typical forest that has two trees and several domains within each tree. In a Windows 200x forest, you will need only the trust relationships shown in the graphic. If you were to implement the same number of domains within a Windows NT 4 environment, you would need 20 trusts.

In order for the trust relationships to work within our forest, the Kerberos authentication service is used. With Kerberos, each of the domains and all of the security principles within each domain are identified and given access to the resources through a process known as *delegation*. As we look at domain design within Chapter 2, we will take a closer look at Kerberos and how it works across domain boundaries.

FIGURE 1.2
Active Directory
trusts within a forest

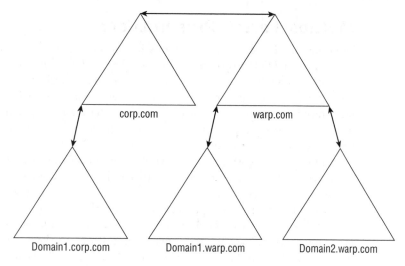

Political and Administration Boundary

These two topics, political and administration boundaries, are tied together due to the fact that there is usually an underlying political reason that separate forests are created. As I mentioned before, the forest is the security boundary. Administrative accounts from the root domain of the forest have the ability to become the forest owners and, as such, can control all of the objects within the forest. Although there are other reasons why you may want to create separate forests, doing so to appease a faction within your organization might end up being the deciding factor. Some divisions simply do not like allowing other administrators to be able to access their data. The only way that you can isolate their data is to create a separate forest and assign them as the forest owners.

The drawbacks to giving them their own forest are that you will have additional administrative overhead and you will need to make sure that they are properly trained to use Active Directory. If you can get by with a single forest, do so. You will reduce the total administrative costs. Later in this chapter, we are going to review the advantages and disadvantages associated with single and multiple forests.

The key to deciding where the administrative boundaries should be drawn will be dictated by whether you need to isolate services or data from other portions of the organization. Creating a separate forest is the only way you can isolate the directory services and data from groups of users. Before you make the decision to create a separate forest, review the arguments from all sides. You may be able to create a separate domain in order to give autonomy over services and data. Autonomy allows the administrators of certain resources to control them, while at the same time limiting the access to those resources from the other domains. Weigh the cost of a separate forest where isolation can be granted against the ease of administration with a single forest where you can apply autonomy. Of course, the political battles will ensue, as each division wants to have complete control over all of their resources. Don't forget what I mentioned earlier about executive sponsorship. If the battles rage on and you need to settle the disputes, there is nothing like having someone with lots of clout in your corner.

Multiple Forests Pros and Cons

Seeing multiple forests within a medium-sized client is not uncommon. One of my Active Directory clients had about 2,000 people and six forests. They used one for production, one for development, two for extranet applications, and two for development that mimicked the extranet production forests. This was a good, secure design for them. While not every organization will need to go to this extreme, I often recommend that you have a separate forest in which to test changes to Active Directory and software interaction. Creating a miniature version of your production environment will allow you to test changes before they are implemented within your production environment. Most companies that have a test environment have far fewer problems within their infrastructure than those that "shoot from the hip." I can't tell you how many times a service pack or hotfix has caused instability within a network.

I also like to recommend using a development forest if an organization has developers who need to test their software prior to implementing it within the production forest. Developers need their own forest if they require excess privileges or if they touch Active Directory. Often developers feel like they need Domain Admin access and a domain controller under their desk. I would never give developers this much power over my forest. As I mentioned within the "Schema" section, changes to the schema are not easily undone. Although Windows Server 2003 is a great deal friendlier when it comes to modifying the schema, you should never make any changes without first testing the implementation to determine what the ramifications will be. I always recommend that developers do their work in a separate forest or, if possible, on virtual machine technology. Running a virtual system on an existing system is an easy way to mimic the production environment. The drawback is that the computer on which you are running the virtual system needs to have enough horsepower to run multiple operating systems at the same time. Two premier virtual system software applications are available. Microsoft sells their version, Microsoft VirtualPC (`http://www.microsoft.com/virtualpc`), which was originally marketed by Connectix, and EMC markets their own version called VMWare (`http://www.vmware.com`).

I also briefly mentioned a forest used for extranet applications. This is one area where you will need to determine the level of security you will need for users who access your infrastructure across the Internet. Some organization will implement a completely different forest for their perimeter network than they use within their internal network. This adds an additional layer of security to your design. If you were to use the same forest in both locations, you could run the risk of exposing information about your internal network if someone were able to hack into your perimeter network.

Figure 1.3 is a flowchart that will assist you in making decisions for your forest design. Within this flowchart, I take into account isolation and autonomy needs and choose the best forest design based upon the needs of the organization. In Table 1.1, you will find the advantages and disadvantages to using a single forest. Table 1.2 compares the multiple forest pros and cons.

TABLE 1.1: SINGLE FOREST PROS AND CONS

SINGLE FOREST PROS	SINGLE FOREST CONS
Easier to administer.	Less secure for multiple business units with unknown/untrusted administrators.
Easier to troubleshoot.	Forests cannot be merged or split.
A single security boundary.	Domains cannot join other forests.
Single schema.	Schema differences are sometimes needed between business units.
Easier to support.	Cannot agree on change control within a domain.
	Users cannot search GCs of other forest without additional software.

TABLE 1.2: MULTIPLE FOREST PROS AND CONS

MULTIPLE FOREST PROS	MULTIPLE FOREST CONS
More secure.	More administration.
May have different schema in each forest (e.g., one business unit uses Exchange and another doesn't want its schema extended with the Exchange attributes).	Difficult to remember what schema extensions have been added and from which application they were added.
More control over outside trusts.	Don't have complete transitive trusts.
Trusts between forests in W2K3 are transitive Kerberos secured.	Trusts between two forests are one-way, nontransitive NTLMv2 in W2K.
	Certain Exchange 2000 mailbox features are not available when users exist in a different forest than their user object.

FIGURE 1.3
Flowchart to determine isolated or autonomous control

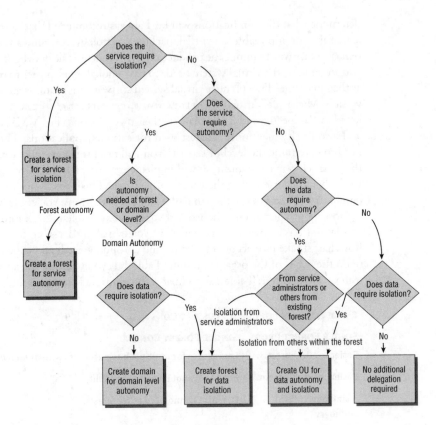

Most small and medium-sized companies will correctly opt for a single forest. Possible exceptions could be when:

◆ Extranet application(s) use Active Directory.

◆ Acquisitions and/or businesses break off into their own entities.

◆ Pilot deployments are needed to roll out application or new systems.

◆ Network administration is separated into autonomous groups that do not trust one another.

◆ Business units are politically separated.

◆ Business units must be separately maintained for legal reasons.

◆ There is a need to isolate the schema or configuration containers.

NOTE *If part of your organization needs to have additional schema attributes and objects, and those attributes and objects are specific to an application, you could be able to use an Active Directory Application Mode (ADAM) partition, sometimes referred to as an* application partition, *instead of creating a separate forest. Note that if the objects are used for security purposes, they will have to be stored within Active Directory and not as an ADAM partition.*

- There is a need to limit the scope of trusts between domains.

If you are considering a multiforest implementation, realize that you will need to do special planning for:

- DNS name resolution. Your solution is easy in W2K3 because you can use *conditional forwarding,* forwarding to preferred DNS servers depending on the domain name.

- Resource sharing. This includes things like printers, Global Catalog, certificate synchronization, trust relationships, and access control. The solution here is simply MIIS Server, a free download for W2K3 Enterprise Server users.

- Network infrastructure. It doesn't permit communication in a single forest (sites, subnets).

WARNING *If you plan to use Active Directory in an outward-facing mode (extranet application), use a separate forest. If you need to synchronize accounts, download the free version of MIIS (formerly MMS) from* `http://www.microsoft.com/miis`. *You must be using W2K3 Enterprise Server to run it.*

To get the most functionality from your Active Directory implementation, you will want to move to one of the higher *functional levels.* A functional level is a mode in which you can run Active Directory that allows it to utilize new tools that are not available if you have domain controllers from other operating systems within your infrastructure. Depending on what operating systems are running on your domain controllers, you will have the ability to change Active Directory's functional level to suit your needs.

Forest Functionality Mode Features in Windows 2003

Native mode in W2K is expanded into *forest functionality* and *domain functionality* in W2K3. Each of these two modes buys you extra AD functionality. Your goal in any migration, upgrade or clean install, is to get to *Forest Functionality level,* a term used with Windows Server 2003, as soon as possible. This is known as native mode in Windows 2000.

Your goal, in any upgrade, migration, or install, is to get to Windows 2000 native mode or Windows Server 2003 Forest Functionality mode as soon as you can. Forest Functionality means that you are no longer backward-compatible with Windows 2000 servers. In return, because all of the domain controllers are at their highest level, you can take advantage of all of the advanced feature sets of Windows Server 2003. Enterprise Admin rights are needed to upgrade to Forest Functionality level. As you can see in Figure 1.4, you will find the Forest Functionality choice in Active Directory Domains and Trusts. You can, however, also manually edit the functionality levels in ADSI Edit, and/or LDP.EXE, although I don't recommend doing so unless Microsoft support tells you to manually edit them.

FIGURE 1.4
Forest Functionality
level

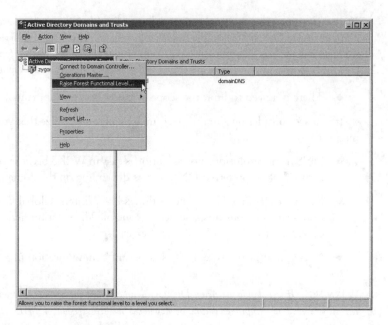

When going to Windows Server 2003 Forest Functionality level, you gain the following features:

◆ Domain Rename, through the `netdom` command line utility.

◆ Link Value Replication. This is the ability, for example, for a group to replicate a single member when a change is made instead of the entire group being replicated each time (which is what Windows 2000 does). This also removes the 5,000-member limit on groups.

◆ The ability to convert a user in Active Directory to INetOrgPerson on-the-fly; plus gain the ability to put a user password on the InetOrgPerson LDAP object.

◆ Schema Redefine. This is not deletion, though it is the next best thing.

◆ Dynamic Auxiliary Classes. Use this when you need to have a departmental schema extension that doesn't affect the rest of the forest. For example, use it when a department needs to put employee IDs put into Active Directory and you, as the forest owner, don't want to extend the schema for this small department's needs.

◆ Basic and Query Group Types.

◆ Improved KCC (Knowledge Consistency Checker) algorithms and scalability. This feature is a big deal. In Windows 2000, you were told to turn off the KCC for implementations where you had about 100 DCs in a domain. Now, the KCC can scale to more than 4,000 DCs in a domain, although you'd probably never want to have a domain that big.

◆ Additional attributes automatically added to the Global Catalog.

- ISTG (Inter-site Topology Generator) ability to stop replicating with an "off-line" domain controller automatically.

- Constrained Delegation. This allows you to control the service principle names of the service accounts that another service account can be delegated.

- Application Groups. This is a method of controlling the accounts that have access to an application.

- Cross Forest Trusts. These are perfect for Exchange clients that exist in one forest, but have their Exchange mailbox in another forest. They eliminate the need to relogin. Windows 2000 has NTLMv2 cross-forest trusts. Windows Server 2003 uses Kerberos trusts. (Can you say single sign-on?)

- Update logon time stamp as a fast synching replicated attribute.

- Universal groups (same as in native mode for Windows 2000).

- Group Nesting (same as in native mode for Windows 2000).

- Switching distribution groups to security groups and vice versa (same as in native mode for Windows 2000).

- SID History as an attribute of a user object (same as in native mode for Windows 2000). This is a very important part of migrations that happen over time. An NT4 or Windows 2000 SID can be brought over during migration so that authentication against resources and objects in the NT4 or Windows 2000 domain/forest that have not been migrated will still work.

Best Practices for Forest Designs

As with any technical topic, you should follow best practices when you are designing. Active Directory is no different. You will want to make sure you follow each of the best practices described in the following sections in order to design an efficient and functional Active Directory forest.

Keeping It Simple: Start with a Single Forest

Review your current infrastructure and determine what works. Then review it again and look at what doesn't work. If you are moving from a Windows NT 4–based network, you will want to look at how you have your domains implemented and determine if you will need to create separate forests to isolate the data or consolidate them into a single forest. Simple designs are easier to maintain over the long run. Start with a single forest—one forest, one domain. Work from there to justify additional forests and domains. Having a single forest is like consolidating your environment; it saves money and time. You save duplication of administration efforts and expertise, thereby reducing your administrative overhead.

A single forest may contain several name spaces. Remember that name spaces are a function of domain design, not forest design; each name space requires a separate domain, but not necessarily a separate forest. Each of the name spaces will become its own tree within the forest. An organization that has multiple identities could utilize a single forest to facilitate sharing of resources. For example,

Microsoft is known for all of its diverse business ventures; `microsoft.com`, `msnbc.com`, `xbox.com`, and `msn.com` can all exist in the same forest.

Aiming for the Ideal Design

Aim for the absolute best design scenario based upon the requirements and priorities of your organization. Be open, though, to evaluate several alternatives. Once you have created what you determine to be an optimal design, let others within the organization review your design and allow them to have input. Not every design will fall neatly into specific categories, so be flexible. If you based your design on best practices, little structural change should need to be implemented. Also remember that the design process is always in a state of flux. Businesses change, sometimes on a daily basis.

Designing with Change Control Policies in Mind

This is an often overlooked planning step. Realize that extending the schema later (to implement or upgrade to Exchange, for instance) affects the entire forest, every object, and the domain controller. Have a Change Control policy in place that emphasizes proper operational processes. I know this is boring and a pain, but it is sorely needed. Everything you do should be verified in a lab first, monitored, rolled out to a pilot group, verified, and then deployed in a systematic approach. Anticipate change, reorganizations, politics, etc.

Before deciding to make any type of change, make sure you verify that the change that will be implemented is required. If you are simply adding an attribute to an object class, make sure none of the existing attributes will support your needs. There are 15 custom attributes that can be used for any purpose. Using these attributes will only cause replication traffic to the domain controllers in the domain where the object exists. If the change needs to be added to the Global Catalog, the change will replicate throughout the forest. Be aware of the additional replication you will be introducing.

If you do add an additional attribute or attributes to an object class, the new object class will need to replicate to all domain controllers within the forest. If you have WAN links where replication is controlled through a schedule, you could introduce inconsistencies between your domain controllers until the replication has completed. You will also cause additional replication across those WAN links, which could pose other problems for the users who are trying to use them. Make sure you know how you are going to roll out the changes and the schedule you will enforce.

A well-defined Change Control policy will reduce the problems associated with making changes to your infrastructure. Debates will rage among the administrators of the domains within the forest. The battles that need to be fought to prove the change needs to be put into place are hard enough without having to decide on all of the criteria to include within your policy. The criteria should include the following:

◆ Planning and testing. The planning documents that must be completed and the types of tests that the change will need to pass.

◆ Who is able to make the change. The appropriate parties that will be able to enact the change within the schema.

◆ The rollout schedule. Project guidelines for how the change will be made.

◆ Where the change can be made. The systems that will be used to change the schema.

Prior to implementing Active Directory, decide who will make up the approval committee. Meet with the administrators of all of the domains within the forest to gain approval of the policy. Everyone who will be affected needs to buy in. Getting them to do so may not be a simple task, especially in an environment where you have service or data autonomy. Some administrators may not have a great deal of trust in other administrators. As mentioned before, make sure you have the appropriate allies so that you can get approval from the highest-level stakeholder.

Separating Extranet Applications into Their Own Forest

I can't stress enough that security is too important to take administrative shortcuts. Don't allow an extranet application in your DMZ to use the same forest as your production users. Simple hacks (such as enumeration, denial-of-service [DoS], and elevated privileges attacks) against your extranet could cause catastrophic damage to your internal network Active Directory structure if the two are linked with a single forest.

If you are running Windows Server 2003 as the operating system upon which Active Directory is operating, you will have options, such as conditional forwarding, that will make implementing separate forests easier. Even if you are still running Windows 2000, you should take the time to design a secure foundation for your Active Directory infrastructure, even if it will take additional administration and time.

Building a Design Based on the Standard Forest Scenarios

There are three basic forest design scenarios: the organization-based forest, the resource forest, and the restricted-access forest. Each of them is used for specific design goals.

Organization-Based Forest   Organization-based forests are the most common type of forest. Using this design, an organization's resources are placed within the forest and organized so that the appropriate groups have control over the resources they need. While companies will choose the decentralized model for several reasons, one of the primary reasons is autonomy of control. If autonomy is required, a department or division could have a domain created for them, or OUs could be built within a domain.

Resource Forest   If certain resources need to be isolated from the rest of the organization, then a resource forest can be created. A resource forest is one in which the resources (such as shared folders, printers, member servers, etc.) are located within their own forest so that the owners of the resource can control them. Usually, the resource forest will not have any user accounts within the forest with the exception of the service administrator accounts that are required to maintain the forest. Using this type of forest, an organization can make sure that the resources contained within the resource forest are not affected by the loss of services in any other forest.

Restricted-Access Forest   A restricted-access forest creates complete separation of service administrators. While trust relationships can be built to allow users to access the resources within the remote forest, the service administrators from the two forests will not be allowed to administer the other forest services. If there is any need for isolation of services, this is the type of forest structure that will need to be built.

ADDITIONAL RESOURCES

The following are white papers and websites that will help you familiarize yourself with some of the important Active Directory topics:

Multiple Forest Considerations Whitepaper `http://www.microsoft.com/downloads/details.aspx?displaylang=en&familyid=B717BFCD-6C1C-4AF6-8B2C-B604E60067BA`

Design Considerations for Delegation of Administration in Active Directory `http://www.microsoft.com/technet/prodtechnol/windows2000serv/technologies/activedirectory/plan/addeladm.mspx`

Best Practice Active Directory Design for Managing Windows Networks `http://www.microsoft.com/technet/prodtechnol/windows2000serv/technologies/activedirectory/plan/bpaddsgn.mspx`

Active Directory Information `http://www.microsoft.com/ad` and `http://www.microsoft.com/technet/ad`

How to Create a Cross-Reference to an External Domain in Active Directory in W2K `http://support.microsoft.com/?id=241737`

Next Up

You should have a good understanding of the elements that go into a forest design. However, before you can actually create the forest, you must make sure you have the appropriate domain design criteria in place. The forest is created as soon as the first domain is built. But before you jump into promoting a Windows 2000 or Windows Server 2003 system to a domain controller, you will need to make sure that the domain design for your forest is well thought out and will support your organization's needs. The next chapter will assist you in making good design decisions based upon the administrative and support needs of your organization.

chapter 2

Active Directory Domain Design

IN THE LAST CHAPTER, we looked at what goes into a forest design. The criteria that I introduced for forests will flow over into this chapter, which will discuss domain design. You are still going to base your design decisions on one major design criteria: administrative control. Keep this in mind as you work through this chapter. All of your decisions will have administrative control as the primary priority, and then group policies and security policies will help you refine your design.

As many administrators will tell you, designing the domain structure can be troubling. If you have separate administrative teams within your organization, you will probably find that they do not trust outside influences and will demand that they have their own forest so that they can have complete control over their resources. Although there may be cases where you will give in and allow them to have their own forest, you should try to avoid creating an additional forest under most conditions. For more information about having multiple forests, including the pros and cons, see Chapter 1, "Active Directory Forest Design."

To create a forest, you must first promote a stand-alone server to a domain controller. During that promotion, you will specify the details that will control the very destiny of the forest. Think about that for a moment, because that statement does imply the gravity of the design decisions you are making. Creating an Active Directory infrastructure takes planning and understanding of the options you have available to you. That is where this chapter comes into play. We are going to look at the design decisions for domains, which ultimately will affect the forest structure as well.

We are going to start with the design criteria that you should take into consideration and then move into a discussion of the administrative and replication issues that pertain to domains. From there we will go through a quick rundown of the benefits and drawbacks when you have a single domain design as compared to a multiple domain and multiple tree design. We will examine trust relationships within the context of this chapter, and we will look at the different trusts that can be built, as well as alternatives to creating additional trust relationships. Because some domains will need to support previous versions of Windows domain controllers, the functional modes of Windows 2000 and Windows Server 2003 domains will be studied. Finally, a look at best practices and additional resources will round out the chapter.

Active Directory Domain Design Criteria

I'm going to say it again, and you are probably going to tire of hearing this, but administrative control will become the primary domain design criteria. As you remember from Chapter 1, the forest is the security boundary. Due to the fact that you cannot guarantee that a domain cannot be affected by an account from outside of the domain, the forest becomes the security boundary within Active Directory. So then, the domain becomes the autonomous administrative boundary. This means that administrators for a domain have control over the resources within their domain, but no other domain. The reason I state that they have autonomy over their domain is that they are responsible for the resources, but those same resources can be controlled by members of the forest root high-level group Enterprise Admins.

However, before planning multiple domains, you should think about the ramifications of having multiple domains within your environment. Later in this chapter, I am going to spell out the advantages and disadvantages of having multiple domains and trees. Always start simple—single forest, single domain—and work from there. You will encounter plenty of political battles as you design your domain structure, so plan your battles well. Create a design that you think will work, and just as with the forest structure, let others review it so that you can refine it to fit their needs.

Defining Domain Requirements

Effectively, a domain can host millions of objects. Theoretically, you are restricted only by the hardware limitations of your domain controllers. With that being said, you will find that other factors will force you to limit the size of your domain in order to make your Active Directory infrastructure efficient. If all of the accounts that you have created within your domain are within a large well-connected network where you have plenty of available bandwidth for all of your network traffic to flow upon, you could probably get by with a single domain. Problems start to crop up when you start working with locations that are separated by wide area network (WAN) links that may not have enough available bandwidth to support the replication traffic.

Domain Boundaries

As we mentioned before, the forest is the administrative boundary for Active Directory. Because the Enterprise Admins group has the ability to affect any domain within the forest, administrators will not have complete isolated control of their domain. However, account policies that consist of password, lockout, and Kerberos policies are defined for an individual domain. The same can be said about the replication boundary. The schema and configuration naming contexts are replicated throughout the forest. Application mode partitions can also be replicated throughout the forest. The domain naming context on the other hand, only replicates between domain controllers within a single domain. In this section, we are going to look at how this can affect your domain design.

ACCOUNT POLICY BOUNDARY

An account policy is enforced at the domain level and will not affect other domains within the forest. Account policies are not inherited from domain to domain, so a parent domain's policy will not affect any child domain. At the same time, you cannot override the account policy within the domain by using another policy that is linked elsewhere within the domain. In other words, you cannot set differing password policies at the domain and OU levels; the domain policy will override the OU policy.

Domain account policies consist of three policy sections: password, lockout, and Kerberos restrictions. If you look at Figure 2.1, you will see the sections as found in the Default Domain Policy. When the domain is created, a security template is imported into the Default Domain Policy. Every domain member will then be affected by the policy. For a better look at domain policies, check out Chapter 22, "Securing Active Directory."

FIGURE 2.1

Default Domain Policy security options

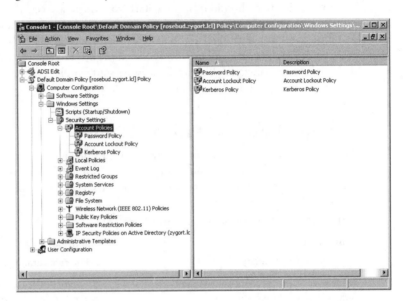

Even though every account within the domain will have to follow the rules as set forth under the Default Domain Policy, you can programmatically enforce some options on users. For instance, if you want to ensure that administrative accounts are forced to change their passwords on a 30-day cycle, but the account policy for the domain is set so that users will not have to change their password until 60 days have lapsed, you can write a script that checks when the administrator's password was last changed. If 30 days have passed, the script can force them to update their password.

REPLICATION BOUNDARY

Domain controllers within a domain will share their domain naming context with one another, but will be selfish with domain controllers from other domains. There is a perfectly good reason for this though. The domain naming context will usually be the largest of the Active Directory partitions and is the one that changes the most frequently. To reduce the amount of replication traffic that has to be sent to each of the domain controllers within your forest, the domain boundary was defined.

Defining Tree Requirements

Every domain within a tree shares the same DNS namespace. A majority of organizations will only need to use a single namespace to define all of the units within their organization. If you need to support two namespaces within your organization, and you do not want to support multiple forests, creating another tree within your existing forest will provide you will additional administrative advantages over the multiple forest design. Every tree within the forest will still use the same schema and configuration naming contexts. They will also be under the same Enterprise Admins control. Every Global Catalog will contain the same information so that users will be able to search for resources anywhere within the forest.

At the same time, the administrative staff from the new tree will have only autonomous control over their resources. This can become a political issue if you are working with separate companies all under the same organizational umbrella. However, the administrative costs of maintaining a single forest with multiple trees will usually outweigh the need to complete isolation of resources between divisions of an organization. Remember, always start simple, and then add complexity to your design only if you have a valid reason to do so.

Multiple Domains Pros and Cons

Any time you add additional domains, whether the domains exist within the same tree or if there are multiple trees hosting the domains, you will have additional administrative requirements. Table 2.1 details some of the advantages and disadvantages to having multiple domains.

TABLE 2.1: MULTIPLE DOMAINS PROS AND CONS

ADVANTAGES	DISADVANTAGES
Account policy boundary	Additional administrative overhead
Centralized GPOs, account policies, and administrative delegation	Separate GPOs, account policies, and administrative control at each domain
Active Directory database size reduced	Increase in Global Catalog size
Reduced domain naming context replication traffic	Increase in Global Catalog replication
Less file replication service traffic	Moving user accounts to other domains more difficult than moving them within domain

NOTE   If you add several layers of domains within your forest, the resources required to process resource access through the transitive trusts could hinder performance of your domain controllers.

DNS Requirements

The Domain Name System (DNS) design criteria will be discussed within the following chapter; however, any discussion of domains must mention DNS. Active Directory relies on DNS to function, and the domains that make up Active Directory have a one-to-one relationship with DNS. Each of your domains will share a name with a DNS zone. Whenever a domain controller is brought online, SRV records are registered within the DNS zone that supports the Active Directory domain. Figure 2.2 shows the correlation between Active Directory domains and the corresponding DNS zones.

FIGURE 2.2
Active Directory
and DNS domain
correlation

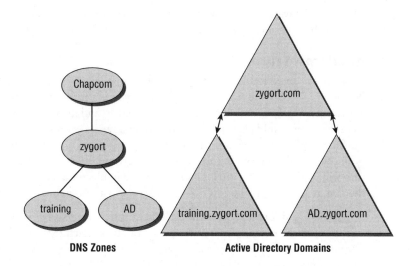

DNS Zones   **Active Directory Domains**

Authentication Options

When a domain is in mixed mode, the authentication options are limited. You will have the ability to use only the standard logon method. Once you have cleansed your environment of the Windows NT backup domain controllers, you can let your remaining Active Directory domain controllers expand their horizons and start taking advantage of some of the new features they have wanted to enjoy. For user authentication, this means that the User Principle Name can now be used when authenticating.

Standard Logon   Most users are now familiar with the standard logon method where you enter your username and password, and then choose the domain to which you are authenticating. Using this method, your username and password are taken and used to create a hash that is sent to the nearest domain controller from the domain that was chosen from the dropdown box.

UPN   If you choose to use your UPN instead of the standard logon method, after you enter your UPN and password, a Global Catalog server is contacted to determine to which domain your logon request should be sent. There are several advantages to this. If your users become familiar with their UPN, they do not have to be concerned about which domain the workstation is a member of when they sit down at a workstation. As a matter of fact, at that point the user doesn't really need to know in which domain their account is a member.

Using either of the two logon methods produces the same results when the user is authenticated. Kerberos builds the appropriate tickets for the user so that the user can be authenticated and authorized to access all of the resources for which they have been given permission. The only difference is that a Global Catalog server is required when using the UPN in order to determine which domain the user belongs to, or when the domain is in native mode. As we look at Global Catalog servers in

Chapter 4, "Sites, Flexible Single-Master Operations, and Global Catalog Design," we will discuss some of the pros and cons of locating a Global Catalog server within a site.

Interforest Trusts

Between domains within a forest, you will find trust relationships that define how the users within the domains can access resources within other domains in the forest. By default, when a domain is created, a trust relationship is built between the new domain and its parent. In a single tree, the trust relationships are parent-child trusts. When a new domain tree is created, a tree-root trust is created between the forest root and the root of the new tree. You cannot control this behavior. The Active Directory promotion tool, Dcpromo, is responsible for creating the trust relationships and configuring how they will work. When the trust relationships are in place, each domain will allow requests to flow up the tree in an attempt to secure Kerberos access to a resource.

Parent-Child Trust   A parent-child trust is the most basic of the two trust types due to the fact that all of the domains share the same namespace. Each trust relationship is configured to allow two-way access to resources and is also transitive in nature so that users within every domain can access resources anywhere in the tree structure, if they have been given permissions to do so.

Tree-Root Trust   Tree-root trusts also share the same behavior as the parent-child, but they are used to allow communication between the two namespaces. Due to their two-way transitive nature, users from any domain within the forest are allowed to access resources anywhere within the forest, assuming that the administrative staff has given them the permissions to do so.

Another interforest trust relationship type exists: the shortcut trust. A shortcut trust is available to reduce the network traffic that is incurred when a user attempts to gain access to a resource within the forest. By default, when a user attempts to connect to an object, and that object resides within another domain, the user's account has to be authorized to access the object. This process has been nicknamed "walking the tree" due to the fact that the trust path that the user needs to be authorized through could take the user to multiple domains within the forest. A domain controller from each domain within the trust path will be contacted to determine if the user is allowed to access the object in question. If you look at Figure 2.3, you will see that for John, whose account is located in the domain `hr.north.bloomco.lcl`, to access a printer in the `hr.east.zygort.lcl` domain, domain controllers from `hr.north.bloomco.lcl`, `north.bloomco.lcl`, `bloomco.lcl`, `zygort.lcl`, `east.zygort.lcl`, and `hr.east.zygort.lcl` will need to be contacted in order for John's account to receive the appropriate Kerberos authentication and authorization to the printer.

There are a couple of options that you can implement that will reduce the amount of Kerberos traffic as John tries to access the printer. The first is to place domain controllers from each of the domains within the trust path into the same site as John's account. This will alleviate the need to send the traffic across WAN links. However, you will incur additional costs because you will need additional hardware, and you may also incur additional administrative overhead at that site due to the addition of the domain controller hardware at that location. This scenario has a serious drawback. If you have users who frequently access resources from the other domain, yet those users are located in different sites, you may be forced to locate domain controllers at each of the sites to optimize your traffic.

FIGURE 2.3

Trust path

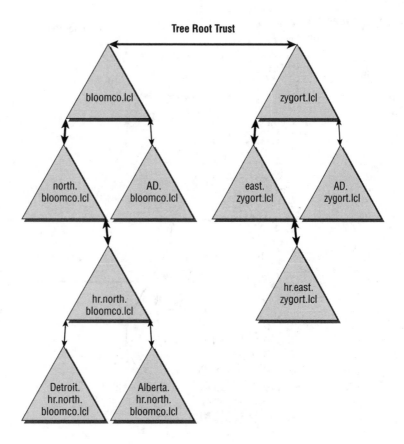

As an alternative, you can create a shortcut trust between the two domains. In doing so, you are essentially cutting a path from one domain to another, thereby allowing the two domains' Kerberos subsystems to work together instead of having to pass the data through intermediary domains. Figure 2.4 shows the shortcut trust created between `hr.north.bloomco.lcl` and `hr.east.zygort.lcl`.

There is an advantage to creating a shortcut trust; you have the ability to dictate how the trust will be used. As long as you have the appropriate credentials, you can create the shortcut trust between the two domains so that it is a two-way trust; in other words, both domains can then utilize the trust path. You can also create the trust as a one-way trust, which will allow only users from one domain to access resources in the other, but not vice versa.

Remember the last line of the opening paragraph for this section; when the trust path is used, the trust path flows up the domain hierarchy. In Figure 2.4, users from `hr.north.bloomco.lcl` and any child domain beneath it can take advantage of the trust path, but the parent domains will still have to take the original trust path.

FIGURE 2.4
Shortcut trust path

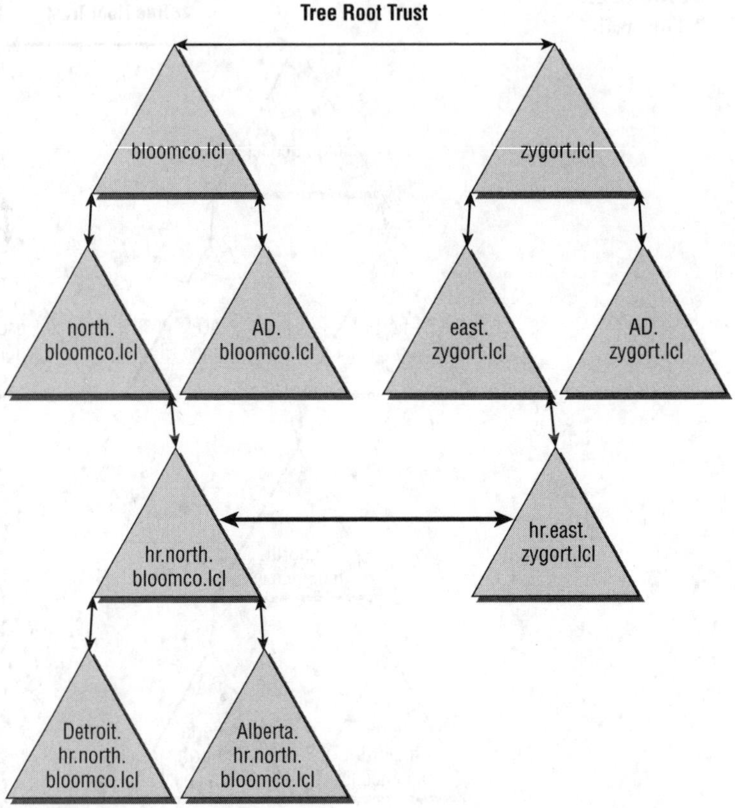

Domain Controller Placement

Domain controllers host the database that is Active Directory. In order for users to log on to the domain, they need to be able to connect to a domain controller. The rule of thumb is to locate a domain controller near any user so that the user can log on even if wide area network connections fail. There are instances when you will not want to place a domain controller at a specific location. In the following sections, we are going to look at the options for placing domain controllers within your infrastructure, and in some cases, the reasons why you would not.

PHYSICAL ACCESS TO DOMAIN CONTROLLERS

It is rare to meet a developer who doesn't believe he needs to be a member of the Domain Admins group. As a matter of fact, many developers have rogue domain controllers under their desks to use for testing. This is a bad practice because any domain admin can bring down the entire forest. A simple power off on the domain controller immediately causes replication problems in Windows 2000, although Windows Server 2003 has a mechanism for just such an occurrence. The solution is to use a separate forest for any developer who either develops on Active Directory or needs elevated privileges. Yes, this increases administrative costs, but it will help secure your forest.

No matter how much time or money you spend securing an environment, it is for naught if someone can physically get to your servers. All bets are off if your server is physically accessible. If someone is in front of your server, it is not *your* server anymore. Especially take this into account if you have branch offices that may not have a room to lock up the domain controller. Protecting your directory service database should take precedence over making sure that the users will be able to log on if the WAN link fails.

TIP   *See Part IV, "Security in Active Directory," for more information concerning security.*

SITE AWARENESS

Active Directory–aware clients (such as Windows 2000 and Windows XP), along with operating systems that have Active Directory client software available (such as Windows 98 and Windows NT 4) are able to determine whether or not a domain controller is within the same site as the client. If a domain controller is not located in the same site, the client will connect to a domain controller that is located in a nearby site.

If you have several users within a site, it may be in your own best interests to include a domain controller within the site. Of course, you should take the previous section into consideration; you want to make sure you can physically secure the domain controller. After users authenticate and receive an access token and the appropriate Kerberos tickets, they will be able to access resources until the Kerberos ticket expires. However, if the user logs off during the time a domain controller is unreachable, they will be logged on using cached credentials and will not be able to regain access to resources using their domain account.

If the users require uninterrupted access to network resources within the domain, you should also consider adding two domain controllers. Although this is an added expense, you have the peace of mind of knowing that if one domain controller fails, the other will still allow users to authenticate. You also gain the added advantage of having an additional domain controller to take on part of the client load.

GLOBAL CATALOG PLACEMENT

Global Catalog servers are domain controllers that take on the additional load of hosting objects from every domain within the forest. Chapter 4 contains a discussion on Sites and Global Catalog servers, and it details the specifics of both. With that in mind, you should also be familiar with the placement of Global Catalog servers within your network. The same basic rule applies to a Global Catalog server as does a domain controller; one should be placed within every site. Of course, this could be easier said than done. Budget limitations and security practices may prohibit you from placing Global Catalog servers everywhere you want. Follow these guidelines for tradeoffs:

◆ If the Global Catalog cannot be physically secured, do not place it in the unsecured location.

◆ If an Exchange 2000 or Exchange Server 2003 system is within a site, place a Global Catalog server within the same site.

NOTE   *For more information about Exchange and its relationship to Active Directory, check out Chapter 6, "Exchange Design Considerations."*

- If you have only a single domain, make all of your domain controllers Global Catalog servers.

- If you have multiple domains, you will need to make sure that the Infrastructure Master role is not on a Global Catalog server and the Domain Naming Master is on a Global Catalog server.

Domain Functional Levels

As the engineers behind Active Directory build new and better features, administrators are given more efficient and easier tools with which to work. At the same time, the new features in one operating system are not always supported in legacy operating systems. Windows NT 4 had some serious limitations when it came to secure and efficient administration. Windows 2000 addressed many of the limitations and presented Active Directory as the next generation of directory services.

Moving from the original Security Accounts Manager–based directory service within Windows NT 4 to Active Directory was embraced by thousands of organizations once they realized the level of control and security that was built in. The only problem was that the thousands and thousands of Windows NT 4 installations could not simply roll over to Active Directory overnight. There had to be a means of interoperability between the directory services. To complicate matters, some of the features introduced with the Windows Server 2003 version of Active Directory are not supported under the Windows 2000 version of Active Directory.

To help with the interoperability issues between the differing directory services, Microsoft created functional levels that essentially put restrictions in place on the newer versions of Active Directory so that they play by the rules of the earlier operating systems. These functional levels come in various flavors: Windows 2000 Mixed Mode, Windows 2000 Native Mode, Windows Server 2003, and Windows Server 2003 Interim.

Windows 2000 Mixed Mode   If you need at least one each of Windows NT 4 and Windows 2000 domain controllers within your domain, you will need to maintain a mixed mode environment. In mixed mode, the domain controllers work under the NT 4 rules for backward compatibility. This is the most restrictive mode, and you do not get all of the functionality of Active Directory. However, you can still utilize your Windows NT 4 Backup Domain Controllers (BDCs) to authenticate users until you have a chance to upgrade all of the BDCs.

NOTE   *Note that the functional levels apply only to domain controllers. You can still have Windows NT 4 member servers within domains of any functional level.*

Windows 2000 Native Mode   When you decide that you are ready to move to native mode, you manually set off the update through the appropriate Active Directory snap-ins. How do you know if you are ready? You are ready if you no longer need to have NT4 BDCs as part of Active Directory. This could mean application needs, political needs, or timidity from moving from NT4. Basically, if an NT4 BDC has to be a part of an Active Directory domain, then you are not ready to go to Windows 2000 Native Mode. Moving to Active Directory Native Mode is a one-time, permanent move. Once you are here, replication to Windows NT BDCs no longer occurs and you cannot add any new BDCs to the network.

Windows Server 2003   This is the utopia for Windows Server 2003 domain controllers. Once you have raised the domain to this level, they no longer need to share their databases with any of the

Windows NT–based or Windows 2000–based domain controllers. As with native mode, once you have set the functional level to Windows Server 2003, there is no going back and you cannot install a Windows 2000–based domain controller into your Active Directory infrastructure.

Windows Server 2003 Interim   The Interim functional level assumes that you are migrating directly from Windows NT 4 to Windows Server 2003 without ever introducing Windows 2000–based domain controllers into the mix. You can still implement a Windows 2000–based workstation or server into the infrastructure; they will work perfectly. The major advantage to moving directly from Windows NT 4 to Windows Server 2003 is that the Windows Server 2003 Interim functional level allows you to take advantage of linked value replication (LVR) when replicating the membership of groups. This means that every member of a group is seen as a separate attribute. If you do not choose the Windows Server 2003 Interim level during the upgrade of the PDC to the forest root, or you do not have the forest root domain at the Windows Server 2003 Interim level when you upgrade PDCs to their own domain within the forest, group membership values will be replicated as a single attribute. LVR also removes the 5,000-member limit on groups.

Depending on the version of Active Directory you are currently running, you will have different methods of changing the functional level of the domain. If you are running Windows 2000's Active Directory, meaning that you have not added any Windows Server 2003 domain controllers, you can change to native mode as seen in Figure 2.5. If you have added a Windows Server 2003 domain controller, you can change to native mode by raising the functional level within Active Directory Users and Computers by right-clicking on the domain and selecting Raise Domain Functional Level, as seen in Figure 2.6. The same procedure can be performed through Active Directory Domains and Trusts. The screen seen in Figure 2.7 will appear after you have chosen to raise the functional level of the domain. Notice that you do not get an option to change to any other levels except for Windows 2000 Native Mode and Windows Server 2003.

FIGURE 2.5

Changing to Windows 2000 Native Mode

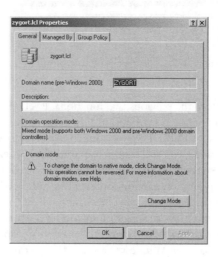

FIGURE 2.6
Choosing to raise the
functional level in a
Windows Server
2003 Active Direc-
tory domain

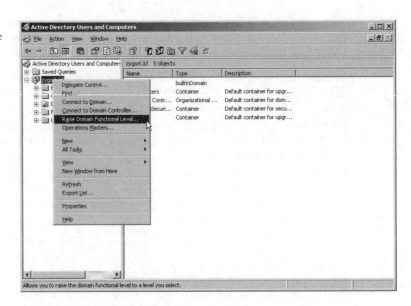

FIGURE 2.7
Changing to Win-
dows 2000 Native
Mode functional
level

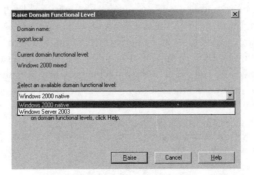

You may have noticed from the previous two functional level options that you cannot raise the functional level to Windows Server 2003 Interim. You do have the option to set the functional level when you upgrade the domain's PDC. To set the functional level to Windows Server 2003 Interim after the PDC has been upgraded, you will have to use either the LDP.exe tool or the ADSI Edit MMC snap-in. Using either of these tools, connect to the domain controller that holds the Schema Master role and connect to the configuration naming context. The fully qualified path is CN=Partitions, CN=Configurations, DC=*ForestRootDom*, DC=*tld* object, where *ForestRootDom* is the name of the root domain for your forest and *tld* is the name of the top-level domain that you are using within your forest. The attribute you need to change is the msDS-Behavior-Version attribute. Setting this attribute to a value of 1 will place the forest in Windows Server 2003 Interim. Figure 2.8 shows the ADSI Edit utility being used to change the msDS-Behavior-Version attribute.

FIGURE 2.8

Using ADSI Edit to change the functional level to Windows Server 2003 Interim

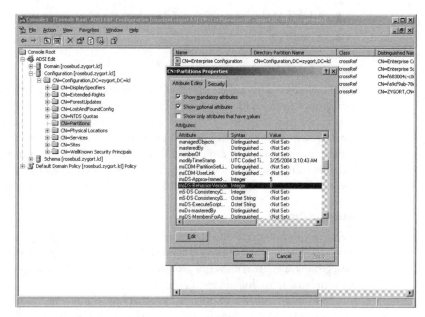

SETTING THE FOREST FUNCTIONAL LEVEL

You can set the forest functional level to any of the three levels by using LDP.exe or ADSI Edit. When you attach to the msDS-Behavior-Version attribute, you have the ability to set the level by entering one of the following values:

◆ Value of 0 or not set=mixed level forest

◆ Value of 1 = Windows Server 2003 Interim forest level

◆ Value of 2 = Windows Server 2003 forest level

BENEFITS OF NATIVE MODE

Native mode gives you the best options that Windows 2000 has to offer. Once at this level, you will have the ability to use security groups to your advantage. Global and domain local groups can be nested and universal security groups are available to make administering large organizations easier. Native mode and higher allows for the following group functions and features:

◆ Domain local groups

◆ Universal groups

◆ Group nesting

◆ Switched-off NETLOGON synchronization

◆ SIDHistory

◆ ADMTv2

Domain Local Groups

All of the servers within a Windows NT 4 domain, and member servers within Active Directory, have local groups to access local resources. Using local groups became cumbersome to use because you had to re-create the group on every server where you wanted to allow users to access similar resources. Now you can share local groups across the entire domain in Windows 2000 Native Mode. Domain local groups membership can include universal groups, global groups, user accounts, and computer accounts from any domain within the forest, in trusted forests, or in trusted Windows NT 4 domains. Domain local groups are able to grant permissions only within their own domain.

Universal Groups

Universal groups were created to address the limitations of global groups within a large environment. Just as local groups had the negative side effect of duplicate groups on multiple servers, which domain local groups alleviated, universal groups alleviate the need to manage several global groups when adding membership to domain local groups.

For instance, consider an organization that has 10 domains. Each of these domains has printers for which users from every domain will need to have print permissions. Creating domain local groups and assigning print permissions to the domain local groups is the logical starting point. Then you need to create the global groups and add user accounts that have the same resource access needs to the global groups. For simplicity's sake, let's say you have 20 domain local and 20 global groups. If you were to then add the global groups to the domain local groups, the users would have the ability to print, but if you added one more domain local group, you would have to add in all 20 of the global groups to the new domain local. Inversely, if you created a new global group, you would have to add it in to 20 domain local groups.

The universal group would simplify your administrative overhead by minimizing the number of groups with which you would have to work. After you have assigned permissions to the domain local group and added the users to the global groups, you can create a universal group and add all of the global groups to it. Then by adding the universal group to the domain local group, all of the users will have access to the printers. If you add another printer and create a domain local group for access, all you would have to do is add the universal group to the domain local group's membership and all of the users will have access. Of course, the inverse works. If you create a new global group, you can add it to the universal group to give the users access to all printers.

There are a couple of caveats to using universal groups. First, you should make sure all domains in the forest are in native mode. Native-mode functionality is controlled on a domain-by-domain basis. Users logging on to domains that are in native mode will have their universal group membership enumerated before they log on, but if they log on to a computer in a mixed-mode domain, the universal group membership is ignored. This can cause problems with the access token when accessing resources because a user could be denied access to a resource due to their universal group membership.

Another caveat is the universal group membership replication that occurs. Global catalog servers within the forest will receive the universal group's membership through replication. Whenever there is a change to the group's membership, the changes have to be replicated to all of the other global catalogs throughout the forest. Within a Windows 2000 Active Directory domain, the group membership is a single attribute within the Universal Group object. Unfortunately, if you change a single member of the group, all of the members have to be replicated, and a group with a large number of members will cause a considerable amount of replication. Your best bet is to include global groups as the only members of a universal group. Doing so will allow you to add and remove members from the global group, thus not directly affecting the universal group.

Group Nesting

Nesting groups is immensely helpful. Putting global groups into other global groups can really simplify matters for an admin. This feature is available once you have moved to Windows 2000 Native Mode. Windows 2000 has a group limitation of 5,000 members—Windows 2003 has no such limitation. Using nested groups in Windows 2000 helps alleviate the 5,000-member limit by allowing a single group object (which may contain thousands of members) to count as one object in the group in which it is put.

Group nesting also allows you to apply the "most restrictive/most inclusive" nesting strategy to make administration of resources easier. In most organizations, you will find that there are employees who need access to the same resources. These employees may have different levels of authority within the organization, yet they have similar resource access needs. After you determine what resources they will need to access, you can develop a nesting strategy that will allow you to control the resource access easily.

Take for instance the typical accounting division. Within the division, you usually have at least two departments, Accounts Payable and Accounts Receivable. Within each of these departments, you usually find employees who have differing job responsibilities and different resource access needs—yet there will be those resources to which they will all need access. Managers from all of the departments will need to have access to resources that the other employees need to access, such as employee performance reviews. If you create a global group for the Accounts Payable managers and another for the Accounts Receivables managers, you can add the appropriate user accounts into the groups so that they can access the confidential resources.

Because Accounts Payable employees have different resource access needs than Accounts Receivables employees, global groups should be created for each and the appropriate user accounts should be added to the global groups. Now, this is where group nesting and the most restrictive/most inclusive method of group creation comes into play. Instead of adding all of the managers from each department to the employees global groups, simply add the managers' global group to the employees' global group. This has the same effect as adding the managers' accounts into the employees' global groups, but it simplifies group administration later. If you hire a new manager, you simply add the new manager's account into the managers' global group and the new manager will have access to all of the resources from both global groups. Taking this one step further, if there are resources that all of the users from both Accounts Payable and Accounts Receivable need, you could create an All Accounting global group and add the Accounts Payable and Accounts Receivable global groups to it.

TIP *See Chapter 19,"Securing the Base Operating System," later in this book for more information on Active Directory groups.*

NETLOGON *Synchronization Is Switched Off*

Don't worry about this; it isn't as bad as it seems. It just means that you will not be able to add additional Windows NT 4 BDCs to your domain. Once you have made the commitment to move to Active Directory, you should not need to install additional Windows NT 4 domain controllers to your network. There are always cases where this may not be true, but if you have eliminated all of the Windows NT 4 BDCs from your domain, you can safely make the move to native mode. Windows NT 4 member servers can still be part of the Windows 2000 Active Directory domain.

SIDHistory

Moving user accounts between organizational units (OUs) is a relatively painless operation. Because they are still within the same domain and retain the same security identifier (SID), you only need to be concerned about the effects of group policy objects (GPOs) during the move. Moving the user between domains is another issue altogether. A special utility needs to be used to move the user accounts, and when the account is moved, the SID is changed. In order for the user to continue accessing the same resources they had access to within the original domain, you would need to rebuild the access control for every resource.

Active Directory accounts within native mode have an additional attribute, SIDHistory. When an account is moved from a domain, Windows NT 4 or Active Directory, to a native mode or higher Active Directory domain, the SIDHistory attribute is populated with the SID from the previous domain. Almost as if by magic, the user has access to all of the resources that were granted to the user's previous account. Every time you move the account to another domain, the previous SIDs are included in the SIDHistory to make the move easy on administrators and users alike.

WARNING   There is a catch to the SIDHistory attribute; it is deemed as a security risk in some environments. See Chapter 22, Securing Active Directory," for more information on how you can limit the use of the SIDHistory attribute.

ADMTv2

The Active Directory Migration Tool version 2 is the best free migration tool around. You can find it on the Windows 2003 CD under the i386 directory or as a free download from the Microsoft website. This is the tool you want if you are moving users between domains. It will allow you to migrate users from a Windows NT 4 domain as well as move users between Active Directory domains. It is also the tool that populates the SIDHistory attribute, but you need to be in native mode in order to do so. Make sure you get version 2. It has lots of upgrades, including password migration.

Best Practices for Domain Designs

As a quick summary of domain design, you should consider each of the following options:

Keep it simple; start with a single domain.   A single domain will allow you to have both centralized and decentralized administration, as well as allowing collaboration between administrators within the domain.

Add domains for security purposes.   If there is a need to have different password, account lockout, or Kerberos policies between user accounts, you will need to have multiple domains to support the differences in account policies.

Consider replication costs when designing your domains.   If your network uses WAN links between locations, consider how much traffic replication will cause. You may be better served to create a separate domain for the location.

Create trees within the forest instead of an additional forest.   If you need to have an additional namespace, but you don't need administrative isolation, create a new tree within your forest. This will allow you to use the same schema for all of your domains and keep the domains and trees interconnected through interforest, two-way transitive trusts.

Next Up

Designing the domain structure will force you to have a good grasp of how the organization administers resources. But in order to implement your domain design, you will need to make sure that the network infrastructure will support Active Directory.

Everyone's favorite topic, DNS, will be tackled in the next chapter. Specifically, we are going to discuss the design options when using DNS, Microsoft or otherwise, within an Active Directory environment. Due to the tight integration between Active Directory and DNS, you should understand the design options that are available for DNS servers, as well as some of the new configuration options that can be used with Windows 2000 and Windows Server 2003 DNS servers.

chapter 3

Domain Name System Design

YOU CANNOT HAVE Active Directory without having the Domain Name System (DNS) in place. I know that is a blunt way to open the chapter, but it is the fundamental truth with this chapter. DNS is required when you implement Active Directory. Although you do not have to run Microsoft's version of DNS, there are many reasons why you would want to do so.

As with all services that are used within a network, you have many options as to how you will implement the service. However, you should follow some general guidelines if you want to make sure you are taking advantage of the best way to use DNS. Throughout this chapter, we are going to look at why DNS is required and how you can implement an efficient and secure DNS infrastructure. Later, in Chapter 14, "Maintaining DNS," I will cover troubleshooting DNS.

Tied Together

If you are looking to implement Active Directory within your environment, DNS is required. Active Directory cannot exist without DNS. If you haven't immersed yourself in the finer details of DNS, now is the time. If you think you understand how DNS works, you should still go back and review all of the new options that have been added to Windows Server 2003 DNS. Where Windows 2000 added some fancy new features into the Microsoft DNS world, such as support for dynamic updates and SRV records, Windows Server 2003 upped the ante even more with support for stub zones and the ability to use directory application partitions for Active Directory–integrated zones.

As I mentioned in the introduction to this chapter, you are not required to use Microsoft's implementation of DNS; UNIX BIND DNS will work just fine as long as it meets certain criteria. We will look at using BIND within your infrastructure later in the chapter.

Looking at the correlation between your Active Directory and DNS, you will find the two will share the same zone naming conventions. If your Active Directory domain name is going to be `zygort.1c1`, the DNS namespace will also be `zygort.1c1`. This is due to the fact that Active Directory needs to register records within the DNS zone in order for the Active Directory clients to locate domain controllers. The records in question are service locator records, more commonly referred to as *SRV records*.

As a domain controller comes online, part of its startup routine is to attempt registration of the SRV records that identify the services that are running on the domain controller. If the SRV records are not listed within the zone, the client will not be able to locate the domain controller. If the SRV records are listed, the host name of the server that is providing the service is returned to the client. The client will then query the DNS server for the A record of the domain controller in order to resolve the IP address.

How to Resolve

Windows 2000 DNS servers introduced *forwarders* to the Microsoft DNS world. Using forwarders, you can specify another DNS server that will attempt to resolve queries when the local DNS server cannot. By default, a DNS server will use the DNS servers that are configured within the Root Hints tab of the DNS server properties. However, there may be instances when your DNS server cannot reach the root servers defined there or when you want to control the servers that perform the iterative queries from your organization.

There is one interesting configuration setting that you will find with a Windows 2000 DNS server: if you allow the DNS server to be created when you promote your first domain controller, it will become the root of your DNS infrastructure. All of the queries from clients will result in internal resolution only; you will not be able to resolve external zone information without additional configuration. If you do not want to isolate yourself, you will need to manually configure the DNS server with a zone that will be used to host Active Directory. In doing so, the DNS server will automatically configure itself to use the root hints.

NOTE   *For more information on root hints and forwarders, see the TechNet article 229840 at* `http://support` `.microsoft.com/default.aspx?scid=kb;EN-US;229840`.

Another item to note, if a DNS server is configured as the root server for the organization, you cannot configure it to forward requests to another DNS server. If by accident this has happened to you, you can simply delete the root zone from the DNS server, which is specified by the dot (.), as seen in Figure 3.1. In the case of a Windows 2003 Server, the root zone is designated by `.(root)`, as seen in Figure 3.2. Once the root zone is deleted, you can enter external root servers into the root hints, as well as configure forwarders.

This behavior does not occur within a Windows Server 2003 DNS server when you promote the first domain controller. This doesn't mean that you should let Dcpromo install the DNS service; instead, you should configure the DNS zone first, and then promote the domain controller. Doing so will allow you to configure the zone the way you want and then allow the domain controller to register. Make sure that you configure the zone for dynamic updates, however. Otherwise, you will receive an error message stating the domain is not configured.

Windows Server 2003 introduced another method of forwarding, *conditional forwarding*. Using conditional forwarding, you can specify a DNS server that will be used to resolve queries based on the domain name in question. For example, if a user needs to resolve an address for `zygort.com` and if a conditional forwarder is created for the `zygort.com domain`, the DNS server will send a recursive query to the server specified within the forwarder setting. Figure 3.3 shows conditional forwarders configured for the zones `zygort.com` and `bloomco.org`. Notice the All Other DNS Domains entry. Configuring DNS addresses within that setting specifies which servers will be used as standard forwarders if no conditional forwarders meet the query needs.

FIGURE 3.1
Root zone in Windows 2000

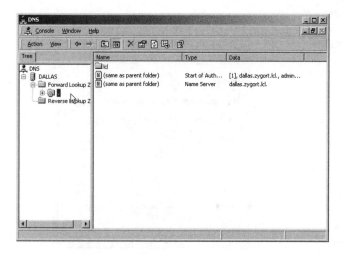

FIGURE 3.2
Root zone in Windows Server 2003

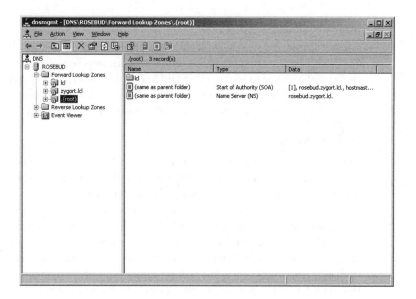

NOTE   *For more information on conditional forwarding, see the TechNet article 304991 at* http://support .microsoft.com/default.aspx?kbid=304491&product=winsvr2003.

FIGURE 3.3
Conditional
forwarders

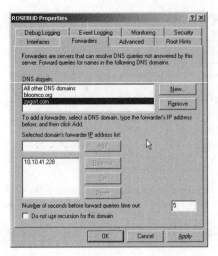

So Many Zone Types

For every zone that you use, you will need to determine how you will configure the DNS servers to use them. There are basically three zone types: primary, secondary, and stub. Of the three zone types, you have the choice of making standard and stub zones Active Directory–integrated, but secondary zones cannot be Active Directory-integrated. Each of them has their place within your infrastructure, but knowing when to choose one over the other can be confusing.

PRIMARY ZONES

Primary zones have traditionally been held on a single system and are known in the Microsoft world as *standard primary zones*. The limitation to these zones is their inherent single point of failure. Although the zone data can be transferred to another server that acts as the secondary zone, if the server holding the primary zone fails, you no longer have an update point. In order to make updates to the zone while the server holding the original primary zone is unavailable, you have to change a secondary zone to a primary.

Another limitation to standard primary zones also stems from the single update point. When using clients that support dynamic DNS updates, the only server in the zone that can receive the updates is the server holding the primary zone. Whenever a dynamic DNS client comes online, it queries its preferred DNS server for the Start of Authority (SOA) record for the zone in which it is preparing to register. The SOA record informs the client of the server that is authoritative for the zone. The client then sends the dynamic DNS registration information to the server holding the primary zone. This is not a problem unless the server with which the client is registering is across a slow or over-consumed WAN link. The additional DNS registration traffic may become too cumbersome. In addition, the same data then has to travel back across the WAN link if a server holding the secondary zone requires a zone transfer.

This has led administrators to create subdomains within the DNS hierarchy to support the remote locations. In this manner, the remote locations have their own DNS servers to hold their primary zones, with the parent domain holding delegation records to the subdomain. Clients within the zone register locally, and the only data that needs to be sent across the WAN link are the queries for zone information and zone transfers if a secondary zone is configured on another server.

However, this scenario has two problems: you may not have an administrative staff in place at the remote locations, and query traffic could consume more bandwidth on the WAN link than the registration traffic would. So what is an administrator to do?

Besides evaluating the traffic that would be generated from either of the two scenarios to determine which will be the lesser of two evils, you could break away from the archaic DNS methodologies and start using the new and improved Microsoft DNS technologies. Using Active Directory–integrated zones greatly enhances your DNS infrastructure. Gone are the days of having one update point and tedious zone transfers. (Do I sound like a salesman yet?)

Active Directory–integrated zones boast the benefit of being able to share the responsibility of updating the zone, whether it is from dynamic DNS clients or manually entered records. The single point of administration and single point of failure disappear. There are limitations to using Active Directory-integrated zones, however.

First, you can create an Active Directory–integrated zone only on a DNS server that is also a domain controller. If you have a location where you do not want to place a domain controller, you will not be able to take advantage of Active Directory–integrated zones on a DNS server at that location. Of course, if you do not have enough clients to warrant placing a domain controller at that location, you probably will not have dynamic update client issues either.

The second limitation is only a limitation of Windows 2000 domain controllers and not typically a problem with Windows Server 2003 domain controllers. The zone data is replicated to every domain controller within the domain. As you will see in the section "Propagating the Changes," Active Directory replication is far more efficient than zone transfers, but there are still some problems with replicating changes. Windows 2000 domain controllers will only replicate changes to other domain controllers within the same domain, and that replication goes out to all domain controllers, not just those that are DNS servers.

Windows Server 2003 made Active Directory–integrated zones more efficient, but at the same time, using the zones gave the administrators a little more to think about. Active Directory–integrated zones within a Windows Server 2003 environment do not hold the zone data within the domain partition; instead, a separate partition, a directory application partition, is used. An application directory partition does not rely on any specific domain within Active Directory, it can be replicated to any domain controller in the forest. If you look at the partitions within a Windows Server 2003 domain controller, you will find the typical partitions (Schema, Configuration, and Domain), and you will also find directory application partitions for the forest and domain.

When you create an Active Directory–integrated zone on a Windows Server 2003 domain controller, you have the option of determining the scope of replication for the zone. Four options are available:

◆ Replicating to all DNS servers in the forest

◆ Replicating to all DNS servers within a domain

◆ Replicating to all domain controllers within the domain

◆ Replicating to all domain controllers defined in the replication scope of a DNS application directory partition

If you choose the first option—replicating to all DNS servers within the forest—every DNS server within the forest will receive the DNS zone information. The zone information will be held within an application partition. This will cause the most replication because every DNS server within the forest will hold the records for the zone, but the only domain controllers that will receive the data will be those that host the DNS service. You cannot have any Windows 2000–based domain controllers in this scenario.

The second option—replicating to all DNS servers within the domain—will reduce the amount of replication traffic because only the domain controllers that are DNS servers for the domain in question will hold a copy of the domain records. As with the previous option, the zone is stored in an application partition. Again, as with the previous option, you cannot have any Windows 2000–based domain controllers within the domain.

The third option—replicating to all domain controllers within the domain—essentially makes all of the domain controllers within the domain behave as if they are Windows 2000 domain controllers. Every domain controller, whether or not it is a DNS server, will hold the data for the zone. If you still have some Windows 2000–based domain controllers that are DNS servers, this is the option you will choose.

The final option—replicating to all domain controllers defined in the replication scope of a DNS application directory partition—is also an option that is only available to Windows Server 2003 domain controllers. Using an application directory partition, you can choose which of the domain controllers will host a copy of the partition. In this manner, you can control exactly which domain controllers, that are also DNS servers, will host the zone data. If you do not want to replicate the zone to a server that is across a WAN, you will not have to replicate it.

NOTE *For more information about controlling the replication scope by creating application partitions, also known as Active Directory Application Mode (ADAM), see Chapter 14, "Maintaining DNS."*

SECONDARY ZONES

Secondary zones still have their place within an organization. If you have a remote location where you do not want to support a domain controller but want to provide local resolution to the clients, you can create a secondary zone on a server within that location. This will reduce the amount of query traffic that has to pass across the WAN link, but you will be required to send zone transfers from a master server across the WAN link to the secondary. Typically, there will be more queries sent by clients than there will be dynamic updates from clients. Even so, you should monitor the traffic that is passing across the WAN link to determine if you are using the link appropriately.

STUB ZONES

New to Windows Server 2003 is the stub zone. Although the name may sound a little strange, it does perfectly describe this zone type. Stub zones do not contain all of the resource records from the zone, as the primary and secondary zones types do. Instead, only a subset of records populates the zone, just enough to provide the client with the information necessary to locate a DNS server that can respond to a query for records from the zone.

When you create the stub zone, it is populated with the SOA record along with the NS records and the A records that correspond to the DNS servers identified on the SOA record. All this is done automatically. The administrator of the zone is not required to create the SOA, NS, or A records. Instead, as the zone is created, the DNS server will contact a server that is authoritative for the zone and request a transfer of those records. Once populated, the DNS server holding the stub zone will contact the authoritative server periodically to determine if there are any changes to the SOA, NS, and A records. You can control how often the DNS server requests updates by configuring the Refresh Interval on the SOA record for the zone.

As a client queries the DNS server to resolve the IP address for host, the DNS server is going to attempt to locate the A record for the hostname. If the DNS server is configured with a stub zone for the domain name contained within the query, the DNS server will send an iterative query directly to an authoritative DNS server for the zone. In Figure 3.4, you will find the common query path that is taken when a client is trying to resolve an address. In this case, the client is trying to locate `server1.dallas.bloomco.com`. When the client in `chicago.zygort.com` sends the recursive query to its DNS server, the DNS server will "walk the tree" by sending iterative queries to DNS servers along the path to eventually get to a DNS server that is authoritative for `dallas.bloomco.com`.

In Figure 3.5, we have configured the same server with a stub zone for `dallas.bloomco.com`. When the client sends the recursive query to its DNS server, the DNS server has a zone listed within its database that lets it know which servers to contact when trying to locate `dallas.bloomco.com`. The DNS server can then send a single iterative query to the authoritative server and then send the result back to the client, thereby making the resolution process far more efficient.

FIGURE 3.4

Standard name resolution

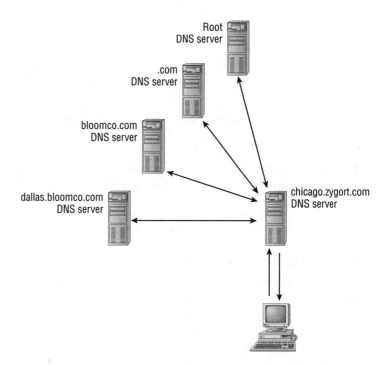

FIGURE 3.5
Name resolution
using a stub zone

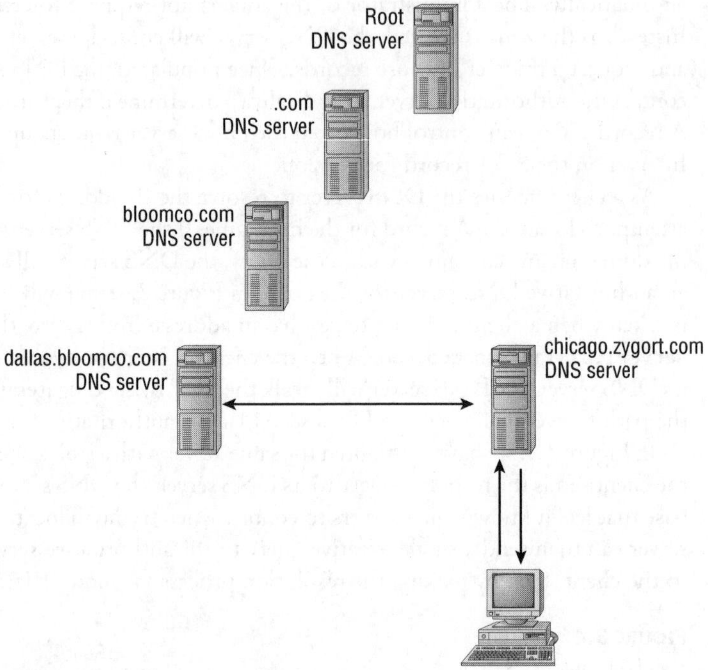

So the question on your mind is "Why not use a conditional forwarder instead of the stub zone?" There are two reasons why you would want to use a stub zone over a conditional forwarder. First, the stub zone has automatic updating features. When the refresh interval on the SOA record is reached, the server holding the stub zone will contact an authoritative server for the zone and update the list of name servers and their associated addresses. Conditional forwarders rely on administrative staff to keep them updated. Secondly, conditional forwarders will require more processing power to perform the logic of evaluating the conditions to determine which one matches. Stub zone information is held within the DNS database and can be parsed far more quickly.

NOTE *For more information on conditional forwarding and stub zones, see the Microsoft webcast at* `http://support.microsoft.com/default.aspx?kbid=811118&product=winsvr2003`*.*

How to Name a Zone

Trying to determine what you are going to name your zone can be one of the more difficult things you will do. The name should be descriptive enough so that it can be easily remembered while at the same time short enough so that it is not too difficult to type. If you are using any other DNS servers within your environment besides Windows DNS server, you should follow the DNS naming guidelines, as set forth in RFC 952. This document spells out the characters that can be used within a DNS implementation. Any character within the ANSI character set is legal to use.

However, if your network uses only Windows-based DNS servers you can use extended characters from the UTF-8 character set. This includes the underscore (_) character that is so popular amongst Windows NT administrators. During migration from Windows NT to Windows 2000 or Windows Server 2003, you will not have to rename computers that use an underscore in their name in order for them to be added to the DNS zone. Be wary, however. If you have any DNS servers that cannot handle the extended character set, you will receive errors during zone transfers.

TIP   You must register your Internet presence with an Internet registration authority so that you are ensured of owning your domain name. If you do not register your domain name, another company could register it and use it. Even if you do not plan to use the name on the Internet, register it so that it is reserved in case you ever do need an Internet presence.

Internal and External Name Options

Basically, you have two options when you are choosing internal and external namespaces for your organization: using different namespaces or using the same namespace. Each of the options presents its own trials and tribulations for administrators, so you should take the time to plan which method you will implement.

Keeping Them Separate

If you have determined that your organization will need an Internet presence, you need to determine the name with which you will be identified. Your name should identify your company. Users who are accessing your external resources should find your name easy to understand. One guideline is to make your name short, yet understandable. The easier it is to remember and type, the easier it will be for users to return to your site. The name `zygort.com` is much easier to remember and type than `zygort-manufacturing-inc.com`. Plus, if you are using a subdomain as your internal name, the longer the external DNS name is, the longer the internal namespace will be as you append the subdomain. Users will not appreciate having to enter `accountspayable.accounting.corp.zygort.lcl`.

To keep your internal resources hidden from external users, you should keep the internal namespace different than the Internet namespace. If you want to keep the two namespaces separate, you have the option of making the internal domain name a child domain from the Internet namespace or having two completely different namespaces.

Even if you never add any delegation records to the Internet domain so that the internal domain name is available from the Internet domain, you will still be using a domain name structure that will make sense to your users. If you decide to make the internal domain accessible, you can add a delegation record to the DNS servers that are used for your Internet presence or create a subdomain to allow specific servers to be accessed.

Identical Confusion

Using the same name for your internal infrastructure that you are using to identify your organization on the Internet can be very time consuming and confusing. While users will not have any problem remembering just a single namespace, the administrative staff will have the burden of allowing users the ability to access both internal and external resources.

One of the basic rules for protecting your resources is not allowing external entities to discover your internal resources. If you want to use the same namespace internally as well as externally, you will have to use two completely different zones with the same namespace, in order to guarantee that they will not share any zone information. Otherwise, zone transfers or Active Directory replication will populate the DNS servers that the external clients use with information about your internal network. Letting anyone outside of your organization access this information is not a good thing.

Therein lies the problem. How do you allow your internal clients the ability to access resources outside of your internal infrastructure? For each of the web servers, SMTP servers, and any other server that is part of your Internet presence, you will have to manually enter the records into your internal DNS zones. If anything changes, you must make sure that you update the records accordingly. Missing any updates or forgetting to enter records for resources that the users need to access will cause plenty of phone calls to come your way!

Understanding the Current DNS Infrastructure

DNS has been around for many years, and chances are you will already have DNS within your infrastructure. Whether or not your current DNS implementation will support your needs will have to be determined. After all, what works for the Unix or Novell side of your network may not work the best for Active Directory. Case in point, DNS is normally a single master database. This means that updates and entries into the database can only be made on one server—the server holding the primary zone. Every other DNS server that holds a copy of the zone will use secondary zone types that contain read-only copies of the zone database. In order for clients that support dynamic update to enter their resource records within the database, they have to be able to contact the DNS server that hosts the primary zone. As mentioned earlier in the chapter, this is an inefficient method of utilizing DNS.

Unix and Novell DNS solutions that are already in place may not support the Active Directory requirements. At the very least, your DNS has to support SRV records as recorded in RFCs 2052 and 2782. If it doesn't, Active Directory domain controllers will not be found by Active Directory–aware clients. The best environment would be to have a DNS server that not only supports SRV records, but also support dynamic updates as recorded in RFC2136. If the DNS server does not support dynamic updates, you will have to manually enter the correct information for the domain controllers, which will include all of the SRV records that are found within the NETLOGON.DNS file that is created when the domain controller is promoted. Doing so could be a time-consuming, boring task.

After determining if the current DNS servers will support Active Directory, take a look at where the DNS servers are located and the client population that they serve. You probably retain DNS functionality at those locations. You should also determine whether or not you want to place DNS servers in locations that are not supported by local DNS servers. Ask yourself if the clients would be better served to have a local DNS server. The answer will be based on the difference between the queries made by the clients and the zone replication between DNS servers. In a large zone, you may have a large amount of zone transfer data, so you need to weigh that against the number of queries the clients are making. Use a network monitoring tool, such as Microsoft's Network Monitor or McAfee's Sniffer, to analyze the data that is traveling through your network links to determine where the majority of the data is coming from.

That Other DNS Server

What are you supposed to do if another division is responsible for the DNS infrastructure? Some companies have a complete division of responsibilities, and the DNS servers may not be under your control. People are very possessive of the things they manage, and you may find yourself fighting a battle to get the support you need in order to implement Active Directory.

The Windows-based DNS service was designed to interoperate with the latest DNS standards. It was also designed to support additional features that are available only to a Microsoft DNS implementation. These additional features are beneficial to administrators who want to have easier administration and additional security options.

Due to Windows Server 2003's compliance with DNS standards, it will interoperate with Berkley Internet Name Domain (BIND) DNS servers running versions 9.1.0, 8.2, 8.1.2, and 4.9.7. Windows Server 2003 DNS is also fully compliant with Microsoft Windows NT 4's DNS service.

As you will note in Table 3.1, Windows Server 2003's DNS service and BIND 9.1.0 support some important DNS features. Other versions of DNS do not support all of the options.

TABLE 3.1: DNS FEATURES SUPPORTED ON MULTIPLE PLATFORMS

	SRV RECORDS	DYNAMIC UPDATES	INCREMENTAL ZONE TRANSFER	STUB ZONES	CONDITIONAL FORWARDING
Windows Server 2003	X	X	X	X	X
Windows 2000	X	X	X		
Windows NT 4			X		
BIND 9.1.0	X	X	X	X	X
BIND 8.2	X	X	X		
BIND 8.1.2	X	X			
BIND 4.9.7	X				

Additional features are present in a Windows Server 2003 DNS environment that are not supported by other DNS servers. A list of additional features is presented in Table 3.2.

When attempting to integrate Windows Server 2003 DNS into an existing environment, take the previously mentioned interoperability into account. If the existing infrastructure does not support some of the features, you may be forced to upgrade the current infrastructure to Windows Server 2003 DNS so that all of the features that you need for your design are met.

In many companies, a DNS infrastructure is already controlled by a DNS group. If this group is unwilling to relinquish control of DNS or will not allow you to implement your own Windows Server 2003 DNS server, you may be forced to use the existing DNS services. Some organizations do have separate divisions that are responsible for specific portions of the network infrastructure. If your organization is one of them and you are not allowed to implement DNS due to departmental standards and regulations, you will be forced to use what the DNS administrative staff dictates. Be aware of the requirements for Active Directory, however. You may need to force them to upgrade their existing servers to handle the service locator (SRV) records and dynamic updates that Active Directory uses.

TABLE 3.2: DNS FEATURES NOT SUPPORTED ON NON-WINDOWS PLATFORMS

	SECURE DYNAMIC UPDATES	WINS INTEGRATION	UTF-8 CHARACTER ENCODING	ACTIVE DIRECTORY INTEGRATED ZONES	APPLICATION DIRECTORY SUPPORT	OBSOLETE RECORD SCAVENGING
Windows Server 2003	X	x	x	x	x	x
Windows 2000	X	x	x	x		x
Windows NT 4		x				
BIND 9.1.0						
BIND 8.2						
BIND 8.1.2						
BIND 4.9.7						

Propagating the Changes

In order to have an effective DNS solution, you will want to make sure that the clients have access to a local DNS server. In order to have DNS servers close to the clients, you will probably need to propagate the zone data to DNS servers in several locations.

Zone transfers come in two flavors: *authoritative zone transfers (AXFRs)* and *incremental zone transfers (IXFRs)*. An AXFR, sometimes referred to as a complete zone transfer, transfers the entire zone database when the zone transfer is initiated. An IXFR, as defined in RFC1995, only transfers the changes in the zone since the last zone transfer. As you can probably guess, the amount of data that is transferred during an IXFR transfer could be substantially less than that of an AXFR.

The choice to use zone transfers is usually made because the DNS servers in your environment are not Windows 2000– or Windows Server 2003–based. Third-party DNS servers do not participate in Active Directory replication, nor can they read the Active Directory database to determine the resource records that are used. To keep the network usage as low as possible, you should make sure the DNS servers all support IXFR. Otherwise, every time a zone transfer is initiated, the entire zone records will be passed to all of the appropriate DNS servers.

Active Directory–integrated zones can take advantage of Active Directory replication to propagate the changes made to resource records. When you use Active Directory replication, not only do you have the additional benefit of only having one replication topology, but a smaller amount of data is usually passed across the network. For instance, take a record that changes a couple of times before the replication or zone transfer occurs. In the case of a zone transfer, if the record changes twice before the transfer is initiated, both changes have to be sent, even if some of the data is no longer valid. In the case of Active Directory replication, only the effective changes are replicated. All of the erroneous information is discarded.

You also gain the advantage of the built-in functionality of replication. In an environment where you have multiple sites, many of which could be connected through WAN links, if there is considerable amounts of zone information to be transferred, the replication traffic that is sent between domain controllers in different sites is compressed to reduce network overhead.

DNS Design Best Practices

DNS is often met with a grimace, but it doesn't have to be that way. If you understand how DNS functions, you will be able to manage it easier. The following list is a quick set of best practices to follow when working with DNS in an Active Directory environment.

- ◆ In a Windows 2000 infrastructure, create the zone prior to promoting your first domain controller.

- ◆ Use conditional forwarding to control sending queries to DNS servers that will be responsible for performing the iterative queries for specific zones.

- ◆ Use stub zones to ease the administrative burden of updating the DNS servers that are responsible for the zone.

- ◆ Place DNS servers on the same side of a WAN link to the users and close to the clients that need resolution in order to reduce the bandwidth-hungry query traffic and zone transfers passing across WAN links.

Next Up

Now that we have covered the design options for a successful DNS implementation that will support Active Directory, we need to look at some of the other requirements for our Active Directory infrastructure. We are going to look at a plethora of topics in the next chapter. First, we will look at site design, and then we'll move on to Global Catalog servers and the master operations, also referred to as flexible single master operations. A well-organized infrastructure will allow you to use all of these services efficiently. A good understanding of these topics will aid you in designing your infrastructure so that you will not have to make many changes in the future.

Sites, Flexible Single Master Operations, and Global Catalog Design

AT THIS POINT, YOU have had a chance to take a good look at designing some of the more common aspects of Active Directory. As we move on, we are going to be working with some of the important technologies that make up our Active Directory infrastructure but sometimes go ignored until they start causing issues within the organization.

This chapter is going to cover Active Directory sites and some of the criteria you should consider when creating sites, as well as the services that can reside on only one domain controller at a time (the Flexible Single Master Operations roles). We will finish with a discussion of Global Catalog servers and the placement of these servers so that you have efficient access to the services they provide.

Determining the Site Topology

Active Directory employs a multi-master replication technology that allows nearly every aspect of the directory service to be modified from any of the domain controllers within a domain. Changes that are made to one domain controller within the domain are replicated to all of the other domain controllers within the domain. This replication allows all the domain controllers to act as peers and provide the same functionality. However, this same replication can cause issues when you are trying to keep WAN traffic to a minimum.

To reduce the amount of WAN traffic generated by replication, you will need to create sites within Active Directory that define the servers that are well connected. The domain controllers that are all members of the same site will update quickly, whereas replication to domain controllers in other sites can be controlled as to when and how often the replication will occur.

Another advantage to using sites is that client traffic can be contained within the site if there are servers that provide the service that the user needs. User authentication will occur with domain controllers that are located in the same site as the computer that the user is logging onto if there is a domain controller for the appropriate domain in that site. In addition, you can make queries to a Global Catalog server and access the *Distributed File System (DFS)* shares within the same site as the user's computer.

Within a site, the *Knowledge Consistency Checker (KCC)*, a background process that runs on all domain controllers, creates connection objects that represent replication paths to other domain controllers within the site. These connection objects are created in order to produce an efficient replication path to all of the domain controllers within the site. An administrator can also create connection objects manually. If a manual connection is created, the KCC will build other connections around the manual connection to allow for replication redundancy. Do note, however, if you create a connection object that does not allow for efficient replication, the KCC will not override your efforts. As domain controllers are brought online or sites are created, the KCC is responsible for creating the connection objects to allow replication to occur. If a domain controller fails, the KCC will also rebuild the connection objects to allow replication to continue.

The KCC is also responsible for generating the intersite connection objects. When a site connector is created to allow replication between two sites, one domain controller is identified as the *Intersite Topology Generator (ISTG)*. The ISTG is responsible for determining the most efficient path for replication between sites.

Domain controllers that are placed in different sites do not automatically replicate to one another. To give them the ability to replicate objects to one another, you have to configure a site connector. Once the site connector is created, the domain controller that is defined as the bridgehead server for the site will poll the bridgehead server from the other site to determine if there is any data that needs to be replicated. Because data that is replicated between sites is compressed to conserve network bandwidth, you may want to designate a server to be the bridgehead server. Bridgehead servers should have enough available resources to perform the compression and decompression of data as well as send, receive, and redistribute the replicated objects.

NOTE *A new feature of Win2K3 is that intersite replication compression can be toggled in order to favor WAN utilization versus CPU overhead on the bridgeheads. See Chapter 13, "Troubleshooting Active Directory Replication," for more information.*

Bridgehead servers are chosen according to their *globally unique ID (GUID)*. If you do not select a domain controller to be a preferred bridgehead server, then the domain controller with the highest GUID is selected. The same holds true if you have multiple domain controllers that are configured to be preferred bridgehead servers; the one with the highest GUID is selected. The remaining domain controllers will wait until the bridgehead server goes offline, and then the ISTG will appoint one of the remaining domain controllers according to the GUID value.

Only one domain controller in each site will become the ISTG. Initially, it is the first domain controller within the site. As systems are added to the site, rebooted, and removed from the site, the ISTG will change. The domain controller with the highest GUID in the site will become the ISTG for the site. It is responsible for determining the bridgehead server and maintaining the connection objects between bridgehead servers in each of the other sites.

In the following section, we are going to look at the options and strategies that you need to consider when designing the site topology to support your Active Directory design. You will need to be comfortable and knowledgeable about all aspects of your current infrastructure before you can implement a stable Active Directory infrastructure.

Understanding the Current Network Infrastructure

Very few organizations will be starting fresh with Windows Server 2003. Unless it is a brand new business, some type of network will already be in place. To build an effective site topology for the Active Directory design, you will also need to know how the current infrastructure supports the user and computer base. Once you have identified the current network infrastructure, you can create the site and site link design.

Identifying the Current Network Infrastructure Design

Networks are made up of well-connected network segments that are connected through other less-reliable or slow links. For a domain controller to be considered "well connected" to another domain controller, the connection type will usually be 10Mbps, or greater. Of course, that is a generalization. Some segments on your network may have 10Mbps or higher links between systems, but if the links are saturated, you may not have enough available bandwidth to support replication. The inverse is also true; you may have network connections that are less than 10Mbps that have enough available bandwidth to handle the replication and authentication traffic.

Look over the existing network and draw out a network map that defines the subnets that are well connected. Some organizations have a networking group that is responsible for the network infrastructure and a directory services group that is responsible for the Active Directory infrastructure. If this is the case, you have to make sure that the two groups work closely together. From the group that is responsible for maintaining the network infrastructure, find out the current physical topology of the network. Gather information about the location of routers, the speed of the segments, and the IP address ranges used on each of the segments. Also note how many users are in each of the network segments and the types of WAN links that connect the locations. This information will prove useful as you design the site topology.

As an example, consider a company that has a campus in Newark with four buildings and two remote locations: Albuquerque and New Haven. All of the buildings in Newark are connected via a Fiber Distributed Data Interface (FDDI) ring. The two remote locations are connected to Newark via T1 connections. Figure 4.1 shows the network map, which also lists the user population at each location.

For those organizations that have more than one domain, you will need to determine where the user accounts reside. A site can support users from multiple domains as long as those domains are members of the same forest. On your network map, if you have more than one domain, designate the number of users from each domain. In our previous example, if the Research and Development department has its own domain for security purposes, the network map may look like Figure 4.2.

NOTE   *Don't confuse the logical representation of your network with the actual physical entities. You could still have domain controllers from multiple forests within the same physical subnet, but the Active Directory objects that define them can exist only within one forest.*

FIGURE 4.1
Network map

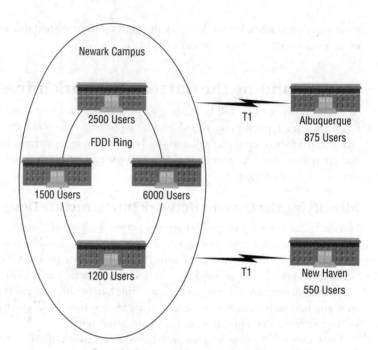

FIGURE 4.2
Multiple-domain
network map

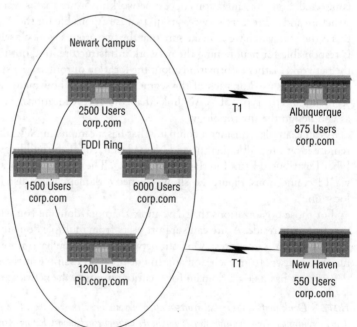

Setting Your Sites to Support the Active Directory Design

Once you have created the network map, you can begin designing the required sites. Sites are collections of well-connected subnets that are used to control Active Directory replication or manage user and application access to domain controllers and Global Catalog servers. As with every other Active Directory object, you should determine a naming strategy for sites and site links. A site's name should represent the physical location that the site represents. The location could represent a geographic location for organizations that have regional offices (the buildings within an organization's campus or distinct portions of a building). Once you have defined the naming strategy, make sure all of the administrators who have the ability to create sites understand the strategy and follow it.

You need to create a document that details the sites that will be used within the design. This document should include the name of the site, the location that the site represents, the IP subnets that are members of the site, and the WAN links that connect the sites.

If you look at Figure 4.2, you can see that the information that was gathered about the current infrastructure is shown in the network map. You need to use this information to create the site design, as shown in Figure 4.3. Notice that the primary locations are identified as sites within the design. Newark, New Haven, and Albuquerque are all identified as sites. Each of the IP subnets from the buildings at the Newark campus is shown as included within the Newark site; the IP subnets from the office in Albuquerque are included in the Albuquerque site; and the IP subnets from the office in New Haven are included in the New Haven site.

FIGURE 4.3

Site design layout

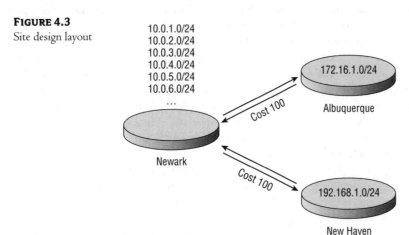

The WAN links that connect Albuquerque and New Haven to the Newark campus are shown on the site design layout. But because the Newark campus is considered a single site, the FDDI connections between the buildings are not considered WAN links at this point. Later when you address the replication needs, this may change.

You should also consider including information about the WAN links on the site layout. This information should include the locations that the WAN link connects, the speed of the link, the available bandwidth on the link during normal operation and how reliable the link is. You may also want to consider including information concerning when the link is used the most, when the off-peak hours are, and whether the link is persistent or a dial-up connection. This information will help you to determine the replication schedule.

Once the initial site choices are made based on the network requirements, you will need to determine if you should create sites to support user and application requirements. Users sitting at workstations that are Active Directory–aware will authenticate to a domain controller from their domain if there is one within their site. If their site does not have a domain controller for their domain, they will authenticate with a domain controller within another site. All domain controllers determine if any sites exist that do not contain domain controllers from their domain when they are brought online. If some sites match these criteria, the domain controller then determines if it is located within a site logically near the site without a domain controller. The domain controller determines this based on the cost of the site link or site link bridges that connect the two sites. If it is determined that the domain controller is close to the site, it registers a service locator (SRV) record for the site. Microsoft refers to this as *Automatic Site Coverage.*

TIP   For more information on how to configure domain controllers to register their services to other sites, see Knowledge Base articles 200498 and 306602.

As an example, Company G has two domains: `corp.com` and `RD.corp.com`. Five sites exist within their environment: A, B, C, D, and E. Figure 4.4 shows the site layout and the site links that connect them. Within the sites, there are domain controllers for each of the domains. Note that Site C does not contain a domain controller for `RD.corp.com`. In this case, as domain controllers start up, they will check the configuration of the domain to determine whether or not a site exists without a domain controller from their own domain. When domain controllers from `RD.corp.com` start up, they will recognize that Site C does not have a domain controller. They will then determine whether they should register SRV records for the site based on whether or not they are in a site that is considered to be the nearest. Because Site B has the lowest cost value over the site link to Site C, `RDDCB1.RD.corp.com` will register SRV records on behalf of Site C. When users from the `RD.corp.com` domain authenticate from a computer in Site C, they will authenticate with the nearest domain controller, `RDDCB1.RD.corp.com`.

Active Directory replication can consume a considerable amount of network resources within a site. Replication traffic is not compressed between domain controllers that exist within the same site. If the available network bandwidth will not support the replication traffic that you are anticipating, you may want to look into dividing up IP segments so that you can control the replication moving between the domain controllers. Once additional sites are created, site links can then be configured. Replication traffic that passes across site links is compressed to conserve bandwidth if the data exceeds 50KB.

Another consideration is application support. Applications such as Exchange Server 2003 require access to a Global Catalog server. If you want to control which Global Catalog server an Exchange server will use, you could create a site and place the two servers within the site to control the traffic between them. For example, within `corp.com` domain, the Exchange Server 2003 server is located within Building 1 of the Newark campus. We have specified that a domain controller within Building 2 is to be used by the Exchange server when it sends queries to a Global Catalog server. In order to control the requests, another site is created that includes Building 1 and Building 2. Figure 4.5 represents the site design once the change has been made to support the decision.

FIGURE 4.4
Determining the
nearest site

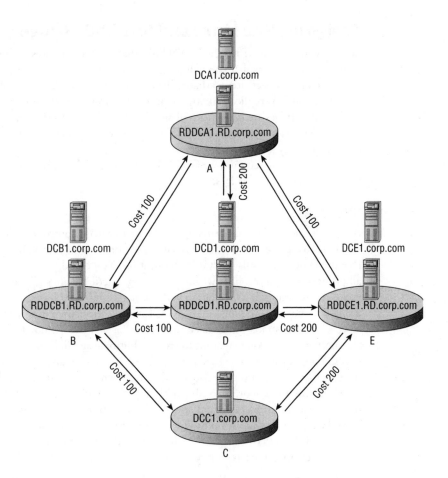

FIGURE 4.5
Site design to support application requirements

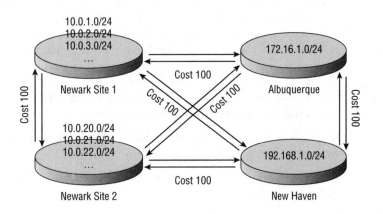

Designing Site Links and Site Link Bridges

Because you have identified the WAN links that connect the sites within your design, you can decide easily on the site links that you will need to support the design at this point. Site links are objects that are created to connect sites so that replication can be controlled. You also need to address other considerations such as replication, log-on authentication control, and application support.

Site link bridges are collections of site links that allow replication traffic from domain controllers in one site to pass to domain controllers in another site when no explicit replication partners exist in the intermediary site that connects them.

In the following sections, we are going to spend some time reviewing the options that are available for sites and site link bridges.

Site Links

By default, one site link is created when the first domain controller is installed. This site link is called DEFAULTIPSITELINK, but it can be renamed to conform to your naming strategy. This site link uses Remote Procedure Calls (RPC) for replication. You could take advantage of using this site link for all of the sites that you have within your infrastructure if they all have the same replication requirements. For example, if all of the sites are connected by WAN links that have approximately the same available bandwidth and they all use RPC for replication, then simply rename this site link to conform to your naming strategy and make sure all of the sites are included.

Another reason you may want to create additional site links is to control when the replication can occur. You may have some sites that need to have objects updated at different schedules. Using site links, you can create a replication schedule between sites. You cannot define which physical connection a site links uses in order to control the replication traffic over specific network links. For instance, if you have a T1 connection and an ISDN connection to a branch office and the ISDN connection is used only as a backup communication link if the T1 goes down, you cannot create two site links with two different costs, one for each of the communication links.

When creating the site link, you can choose between the following options:

Protocol Used for Replication   Two protocols (IP and SMTP) can be used for replicating objects. When selecting IP, you are really specifying that you want to use RPCs to deliver the replicated objects. You can select SMTP if the domain controllers that you are replicating data between are not within the same domain. If the domain controllers are within the same domain, the file replication service (FRS) has to use RPCs to replicate the Sysvol data. Because FRS requires the same replication topology as the domain partition, you cannot use SMTP between the domain controllers within a domain. You can use SMTP if you want to control the replication between Global Catalog servers or domain controllers that are replicating the schema and configuration partition data between domain controllers.

Name of the Site Link   The name should follow your naming strategy and should define the sites that are connected using the link.

Connected Sites   These are the sites that will explicitly replicate between bridgehead servers in each listed site.

Schedule   The schedule consists of the hours when replication can occur and the *interval*, how often you want to allow replication to occur during the hours that replication data is allowed to pass between the bridgehead servers.

Cost of the Connection   A value that determines which link will be used. This cost, or priority, value is used to choose the most efficient site link. You will use the combination of site links with the lowest total cost to replicate data between any pair of sites.

Note the replication patterns when you are trying to determine the schedule. You could cause a good deal of latency to occur if the schedule is not compatible. For example, a company may have a central office that acts as the hub for the regional office. The regional offices are responsible for replication to the branch offices in their region. Figure 4.6 shows the schedule for the Atlanta central office, the Sydney and Chicago regional offices, and the Exmouth, Peoria, and Bloomington branch offices. Because all of the domestic U.S. links have approximately the same bandwidth availability, you could create a single site link that uses a 15-minute interval. You could then create a separate site link between Atlanta and Sydney for which the replication interval is set to every two hours so that replication does not adversely affect the WAN links. Between the Sydney and Exmouth sites, another site link uses a one-hour interval to control traffic. Depending on the connection objects that are created by the KCC, the total propagation delay for an update in Chicago to reach Exmouth could be three and a half hours—and that is only considering the replication interval. The schedule on the site link could be configured to allow replication traffic to flow only during the evening hours. If you have a schedule that is closed off for a portion of time, the propagation delay will increase even more. You need to make sure that this will be acceptable within your organization.

FIGURE 4.6
Replication schedules based on site links

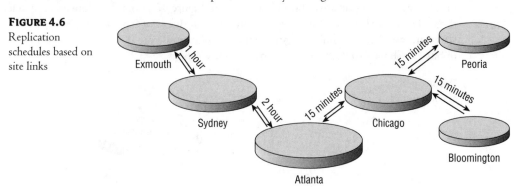

You should also plan the cost of site links carefully. The default site link cost value is 100. If all of the communication links have the same available bandwidth, you could leave the default cost on all links. However, if different bandwidth constraints occur on any of the communication links, you will need to adjust the cost values. One method of determining a valid cost for site links is to divide 1,024 by the base 10 logarithm of the available bandwidth as measured in kilobits per second (Kbps). In doing so, you will find cost values that correspond to the entries in Table 4.1.

TABLE 4.1: EXAMPLE OF COSTS FOR AVAILABLE BANDWIDTH

AVAILABLE BANDWIDTH IN KBPS	COST VALUE
4,096	283
2,048	309
1,024	340
512	378
256	425
128	486
64	567
56	586
38.4	644
19.2	798
9.6	1,042

Site Link Bridges

In Windows Server 2003 Active Directory, site link bridging is enabled for all site links by default, making replication transitive throughout sites. In Figure 4.7, note that domain controllers are in all three sites from corp.com. Site B is the only site that does not have a domain controller from RD.corp.com. With site link bridging enabled, replication from domain controllers for RD.corp.com in Site A will pass to RD.corp.com domain controllers in Site C.

FIGURE 4.7
Site link bridge

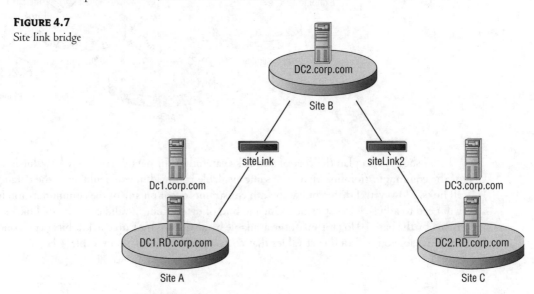

If you have a network infrastructure that is fully routed and all of the locations can communicate directly with one another, then you can leave this default setting turned on. However, if you have locations where not all of the domain controllers are able to communicate directly to one another—for instance, if they are separated by firewalls—you may want to turn off the site link bridging. You may also want to turn it off if you want to manually control where it is allowed. If you have a large, complex network, you could turn off the bridging and create your own site link bridges by defining which site links will be included in a bridge.

Firewalls that exist within your organization's network infrastructure could also pose challenges. There could be rules in place that will only allow specific servers to communicate with internal resources. If you do have a firewall in place, you may need to turn off site link bridging so that you can control the site links that will pass replication traffic from site to site.

Remember that the site link does not define any physical network links. The physical connections are determined by how the domain controllers are connected to one another. A site link cannot detect if a physical link is down and, therefore, will not reroute the traffic immediately. Determine your site link's costs based on the paths on which you would like replication to occur when using bridging.

The following sections cover the placement of Global Catalogs, as well as the Flexible Single Master Operations roles. Each of these technologies should be placed where they will be most effective within the organization.

Choosing Global Catalog Placement

Global Catalog servers provide functionality to users as well as applications within the domain. Global Catalog servers are responsible for collecting information about the objects that exist in the domain partition of other domains in the forest. Although this is just a subset of the attributes for the objects, this could still be a considerable amount of information. Once a domain controller is specified as a Global Catalog server, additional replication will occur so that information from the other domains will populate the database. You need to determine if this additional replication is going to affect the performance of the network links.

One of the new features of Windows Server 2003 is universal group membership caching. This feature is available only when the domain is in the Windows 2000 Native Mode or a higher functional level, and only Windows Server 2003 domain controllers provide this functionality. The benefit of using universal group membership caching is that a domain controller does not have to be made a Global Catalog server in order to provide the user with their universal group membership, which is required to log on. As users authenticate, the domain controller contacts a Global Catalog server from another site to retrieve the required information. The group membership is then cached on the domain controller and is ready to be used the next time the user logs on. Because the domain controller does not have to provide Global Catalog services, replication across the WAN link is reduced.

Universal group membership caching is not meant for sites with large user populations, nor is it meant to be used where applications need to access a Global Catalog server. A maximum of 500 users is supported using this caching method. Also, the cached data is only updated every eight hours. If you are planning on performing group membership changes on a regular basis, your users may not receive those changes in a timely manner. You can reduce the timeframe for updating the cache, but in doing so you will be creating more replication traffic on your WAN link. Make sure you weigh the trade-offs before you decide where you will place a Global Catalog server.

When determining if you should have a Global Catalog server placed within a site, you should consider how much the Global Catalog server will be used and whether applications within the site need to use a Global Catalog server. The following questions should be asked to determine whether or not a Global Catalog should be placed within a site:

Are any applications, such as Exchange 2000 Server or Exchange Server 2003, located within the site? If this is the case, you will want to locate a Global Catalog server within the same site as the application, because the LDAP queries being posted to the Global Catalog server will probably consume more bandwidth than replication. Test the network requirements to determine which will consume more bandwidth. If the WAN link is not 100 percent reliable, you should always have the Global Catalog server local; otherwise the application will not function properly when the link goes down.

Are more than 100 users located within the site? If more than 100 users within a site, you will need to determine if stranding them without having the ability to access a Global Catalog server if the WAN link goes down is an acceptable option. You will also need to determine if the query latency is worth the cost savings of keeping the Global Catalog server at another location and not dedicating hardware for the site in question.

Is the WAN link 100 percent available? If you need application support and the user base is less than 100 users, you could have those users access a Global Catalog server in the remote site if the WAN link is reliable. Although no WAN link will ever be 100 percent available, the higher the reliability of the link, the better your chances of being able to support the user base from a remote site. If the WAN link is not always available and there are no other applications that rely on the Global Catalog server, you could implement universal group membership caching to alleviate some of the problems associated with user authentication

Are there many roaming users who will be visiting the site? If many roaming users will be logging on at the site, you will want to locate a Global Catalog server within the site. Whenever a user logs on, the user's universal group membership is retrieved from the Global Catalog server. However, if the user population at the site is relatively static, you may be able to implement universal group membership caching on a domain controller.

Another Active Directory technology whose location needs to be determined is the Master Operations roles. Because only specific servers support the Master Operations functions, you should know the criteria for their placement.

Choosing Flexible Single Master Operations Placement

Due to the importance of the Flexible Single Master Operations (FSMO) or Master Operations roles, you should carefully choose where the domain controllers holding each of these roles are placed. The following sections discuss what guidelines you should take into consideration.

Operations Masters in a Single Domain Forest

Within a single domain forest, the infrastructure master does not play a very important role. As a matter of fact, its services are not used at all. Because you will not have any remote domains for the infrastructure master to compare domain information to, it will not matter if the domain controller is a Global Catalog server or not. In fact, in a single domain environment, all domain controllers could be enabled as Global Catalog servers because there will be no additional replication costs.

By default, the first domain controller within the domain will hold all of the Master Operations roles and will also be a Global Catalog server. You should also designate another domain controller as a standby server. You do not have to configure anything special on this domain controller. Just make sure that all administrative personnel are aware of your preference to use a specific server as the standby in case the first fails. Then, if a failure of the first server does occur, you can quickly seize the master operations on the second server. Make sure that the two systems are located close to one another and connected via a high-speed connection. You could even create connection objects between the two systems so that they replicate directly to one another, ensuring that their directories are as identical as possible.

Operations Masters Site Placement in a Multiple-Domain Forest

The five Master Operations roles will have to be placed on domain controllers where they will be the most effective. You should take certain criteria into consideration when you are deciding, which site these domain controllers will be placed.

SCHEMA MASTER

The Schema Master role is not one that is used very often. Typically, the only time the Schema Master needs to be online after the initial installation of Active Directory is when you are making changes to the schema. When you are planning the placement of the Schema Master, place it in a site where the schema administrators have easy access to it. Also consider the replication that will be incurred when a change is made. For this reason alone, you may want to place the Schema Master within a site that has the most domain controllers within the forest.

DOMAIN NAMING MASTER

As with the Schema Master, the Domain Naming Master is not used very often. Its role is to guarantee the uniqueness of domain names within the forest. It is also used when removing domains from the forest. For the Domain Naming Master to perform its function, you should locate it on a Global Catalog server, although with Windows Server 2003 this is not a requirement as it was in Windows 2000.

The Domain Naming Master and the Schema Master can be located on the same domain controller because neither of the roles will impact the way the domain controllers function. As with the Schema Master, it should be located close to where the administrative staff has access.

RELATIVE IDENTIFIER (RID) MASTER

The RID Master is responsible for generating and maintaining the RIDs used by the security principles within the domain. Each domain controller will contact the RID Master to obtain a group of

RIDs to be used as the accounts are created. If your domain is in native mode or higher, you should place the RID Master in a site that has domain controllers where administrators are creating a majority of the accounts. This will allow the RID Master to efficiently hand out allocations of RIDs to the domain controllers. If your domain is in mixed mode, consider placing the RID Master on the same server as the PDC emulator. The PDC emulator is the only domain controller that can create accounts within the domain when the domain is in mixed mode.

INFRASTRUCTURE MASTER

The Infrastructure Master holds a very important role within a multiple-domain forest. If users from one domain are added to the membership of groups from a second domain, the Infrastructure Master is then responsible for maintaining any updates when changes occur within the remote domain.

For instance, if a user from Domain A is added to a group in Domain B, and the user's name changes because she gets married, the user account name in Domain A will not match the entry within the group membership of Domain B. The Infrastructure Master is responsible for reviewing the information from Domain A and checking for discrepancies. If it finds that a change has been made, the Infrastructure Master updates the information in Domain B so that the new name information within the group can be replicated to all of the domain controllers.

If the Infrastructure Master is located on a Global Catalog server, it will check for differences between Domain A and Domain B, but it will not notice any discrepancies because the Global Catalog server hosts information from Domain A. Other servers that are not Global Catalog servers in Domain B will not have the correct information for the group, and the Infrastructure Master will not update the other domain controllers. So, in a multiple-domain forest, move the Infrastructure Master to a domain controller that is not a Global Catalog server. Of course, if you make every domain controller a Global Catalog server, you will not have to worry about the Infrastructure Master placement because every domain controller will host information from every domain and replicate changes whenever they are made.

When you are choosing the placement of the Infrastructure Master, place it within a site that also contains domain controllers from the other domains. This ensures that the queries and updates performed are local.

PRIMARY DOMAIN CONTROLLER (PDC) EMULATOR

The other Master Operations role that you need take into consideration is the Primary Domain Controller (PDC) emulator. Whenever Windows NT 4 Backup Domain Controllers (BDCs) exist within the domain, the PDC Emulator is responsible for keeping the Windows NT 4 BDCs and all other Windows 2000 Server or Windows Server 2003 domain controllers updated. The PDC emulator is also responsible for accepting password change requests from pre–Active Directory clients. If the domain is placed in Windows 2000 Native Mode or the Windows Server 2003 functional level, the PDC emulator becomes the clearinghouse for password changes within the domain. Any time another domain controller receives a password change from a client, the PDC emulator is passed the change so that the other domain controllers can be notified of the change. If a user has entered a bad password, the PDC emulator is passed the authentication request to validate that the user's password was not changed on another domain controller prior to the authentication request.

Another important function of the PDC Emulator is time synchronization. All members of the domain, whether they are running Windows 2000, Windows XP, or Windows Server 2003 as their operating system, will synchronize their clocks according to time on the PDC emulator and use the timestamp to authenticate clients. This timestamp is then used with the Kerberos service to authenticate clients.

When deciding the most appropriate site for the PDC emulator role, choose a site that is close to the majority of users within the domain. Also, make sure that domain controllers placed in other sites have reliable links and available bandwidth to support the traffic that will be used by the PDC emulator.

Best Practices for Site Design

To maintain an efficient replication strategy and control logon traffic amongst your domain controllers, you should carefully design your site layout. You should take into consideration where you want users to authenticate, then create sites and make sure there are domain controllers within the site to handle the authentication. Also, you do not want to consume your WAN links with replication traffic, so you will need to determine how you will build your sites to stifle the replication traffic. The following is a list of best practices that will help you reach your site design goals.

◆ Create subnet objects to represent your physical network segments, and sites that correspond to the well-connected subnets.

◆ Review the current replication topology before you manually configure a connection object.

◆ Create sites when you want to reduce the replication between subnets or control the domain controllers and global catalog servers that the users will connect.

◆ Configure the site link costs so that domain controllers register SRV records for sites that do not have domain controllers.

◆ In Windows Server 2003, turn off site link bridging if you want to control the site link bridges within your environment.

◆ If you have a small office and you do not have software that relies on a Global Catalog, turn on Universal Group Membership Caching.

◆ Place Global Catalog servers within the same site as Exchange servers.

◆ In a multiple-domain forest, if you do not configure all of your domain controllers as Global Catalog servers, move the Infrastructure Master to a domain controller that is not a Global Catalog server.

◆ Place the Primary Domain Controller emulator in the same site as the largest user population.

◆ Place the Schema Master in the site that has the most domain controllers from all domains within the forest.

◆ When the domain is in mixed mode, place the Relative Identifier Master close to the PDC emulator or on the same system as the PDC emulator.

◆ When demoting domain controllers, transfer any FSMO roles from that DC before demoting it. Although a demotion will "give away" all FSMO roles automatically, it makes no consideration for the suitability of the other DC that holds these roles in terms of connectivity, hardware specifications, and other FSMO location factors.

Next Up

No other application has as much impact on Active Directory as Exchange. When you are using an Active Directory environment, you can choose between two flavors: Exchange 2000 Server and Exchange Server 2003. There are some limitations to which version of Exchange you are going to use within your environment, and we are going to take a look at the limitations, as well as the effects implementing Exchange will have on Active Directory.

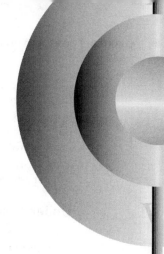

chapter 5

Organizational Unit Design

BEFORE WE START LOOKING at the organization unit (OU) design options, we should make one thing clear: the highest priority when designing OUs is the administrative control. OUs can be used for a myriad of purposes, but the basic design philosophy should be to ease the administrative burden. As we trudge through this chapter, you will find that it is divided into two main sections. The first section deals with designing for administrative control, and the second section discusses how to enhance the administrative design with Group Policy.

When you are determining how the organizational unit (OU) structure will be designed, you must understand how the organization is administered. If you do not understand how the organization is administered, the OU structure you create might not be as efficient as it could be and it might not remain effective over time. An unwieldy or faulty design could create more administrative problems than it helps alleviate.

Designing OUs for Administrative Control

To have complete control over an OU, you must first be delegated Full Control permission. This delegation is provided by the domain owner and can be granted to users or groups. For efficiency's sake, you should create a group that will manage the OU and delegate permissions to this group. You can then add user accounts that need to manage the objects, otherwise known as the OU *owners*, to the group with Full Control permissions.

OU owners control all aspects of the OU that they have been given authority over, as well as all of the objects that reside within the OU tree. Like the domain owner, they will not be isolated from outside influences, because the domain owner will have control if the need arises. However, this autonomy of control over the resources allows the OU owner to plan and implement the objects necessary to effectively administer their OU hierarchy. This includes delegating administrative control to those users who need to be OU administrators.

OU administrators are responsible for the specific objects within their OU. Usually, they will not have the ability to create child OUs. Their control will more than likely be limited to working with a specific object type within the OU. For example, the OU owner could delegate to the technical support staff. This would allow the technical support staff to create and delete computer objects within the OU, but they would not be able to control or modify user objects within the OU. Controlling user objects could be delegated to a Human Resources employee who is responsible for creating user objects when a person is hired and disabling and deleting objects when a person is discharged.

In the following sections, we will look at some of the design options that are available when creating OUs. These include the choices that should be made so that changes within the organization will not adversely affect the OU structure.

Understanding the OU Design Options

The OU design should be predicated on the administrative structure of the organization, not the departmental organization as seen on the company's organization chart. Most companies do not base the administration of resources on the organization chart. Usually, the IT department is responsible for objects within the company no matter which department is using the resource.

Although this centralized approach is the most basic method of controlling the objects within Active Directory, some organizations cannot utilize one single administrative group that has power over all of the objects. Other organizations will not have a centralized administrative team; instead they will have decentralized control over objects. In such cases, design decisions will have to be made that will dictate where the objects will reside within the OU structure. Microsoft has identified five design options when developing the OU design. These five allow the OUs to be designed by location, organization, business function, location then business function, or organization then location.

OUs Based on Location

If an organization has resources that are centralized, but the administrative staff is based at different geographic locations, the OU design should take on a location-based strategy. Using this strategy, the OU structure is very resistant to reorganizations, mergers, and acquisitions. Because all of the objects are located beneath the top-level OU, which is based on company location as seen in Figure 5.1, the lower-level OUs can be modified and the objects moved within the OUs to accommodate the changes. Consider the alternative: having domains that are used to host the objects. Moving objects between domains has many more implications because the security ID of the objects will have to change as will the domain owners.

However, some disadvantages to the location-based strategy exist. Unless the inheritance of permissions has been blocked, administrative groups that are granted authority at an upper-OU level will have the ability to affect objects in the lower-level OUs.

The location-based strategy works well within organizations that are using the departmental model but have geographically dispersed resources. In this manner, administrators located at the site where the resources are will have control over the objects that represent them in Active Directory.

OUs Based on Organization

If the administrative structure has an administrative staff that reports to divisions and is responsible for the maintenance of the resources for that division, the OU structure can be designed so that it takes advantage of the departmental makeup of the company, as seen in Figure 5.2. Using this design strategy makes the OU structure much more vulnerable to change within the organization should a reorganization occur. However, it does allow departments to maintain autonomy over the objects that they own.

FIGURE 5.1
OU structure based
on Location

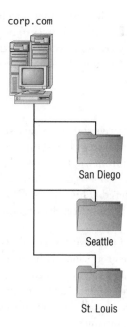

FIGURE 5.2
OU structure based
on Organization

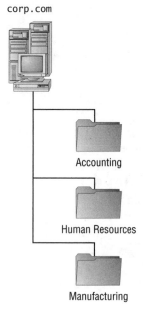

This strategy is usually employed whenever the cost center, product/service-based, or project-based business models are employed. This allows the resources to be grouped so that the cost centers are separate OU structures. The product, service, or project resources can likewise be isolated within an OU tree, and those administrators who are responsible for the resources can be delegated the ability to control the objects within Active Directory.

OUs Based on Function

Smaller organizations that have an administrative staff who have specific functions they provide to the organization typically use an OU design strategy based on job functions as seen in Figure 5.3. In these smaller organizations, the administrators will have several job responsibilities. Building the OU structure based on the job responsibilities allows the controlled objects to be grouped together based on the tasks that need to be administered. This type of OU deployment is resistant to company reorganizations, but due to the way the resources are organized, replication traffic may be increased.

This strategy can be employed with any of the business models. Because it is usually implemented in smaller companies, a single administrative group such as Information Technology is responsible for maintaining all of the objects. The functions can be broken out based on the staff responsible for maintaining user objects, group objects, shared folders, databases, mail systems, and so on. Of course, the administrative staff will have to be trusted by all divisions if this model is employed, but this is usually not as much of an issue in smaller companies.

FIGURE 5.3

OU structure based on Function

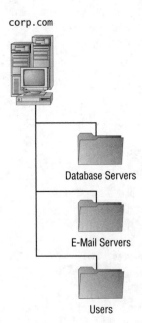

corp.com

Database Servers

E-Mail Servers

Users

OUs BASED ON LOCATION AND ORGANIZATION

Two hybrid methods of organizing resources exist. Each one is based on a combination of the location of resources and the method the company uses to organize the objects.

OUs Based on Location, Then Organization   When you use an OU design strategy that is first based on location and then organization, the upper-level OUs are based on the location of the objects within the directory, and the lower-level OUs are broken out by the organization's departmental structure as seen in Figure 5.4. This strategy allows the organization to grow if necessary, and it has distinct boundaries so that the objects' administration is based on local autonomy. Administrative staff will need to cooperate if administrative groups are responsible for the departments within the OU structure, because if this is the case, OU owners will have control over all of the objects within the OU tree.

Large companies that employ the departmental business model might have several locations within the company that have administrative staff controlling the resources. If this is the case, the OU owner for the location can control all of the accounts that are OU administrators for the individual departments within that location. This allows the OU owner to control users within the location for which they are responsible, while still maintaining control over their location. OU administrators would only be able to affect objects within their department at that location.

FIGURE 5.4

OU structure based on Location, Then Organization

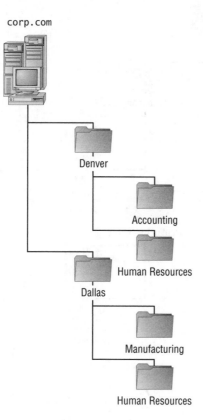

OUs Based on Organization, Then Location   With an OU design strategy that is first based on organization and then location, the OU trees are based on the organization's departmental makeup with the objects organized based on location, as seen in Figure 5.5. Using this strategy, the administrative control of objects can be delegated to administrative staff responsible for objects at each of the locations, whereas all of the resources can be owned by a department's own administrative staff. This allows a strong level of autonomous administration and security; however, the OU structure is vulnerable to reorganization because the departmental design of the company could change.

Very large companies using the cost center–based, product/service-based, or project-based business models may create an OU tree that is based on the organizational makeup of the company and then have a decentralized administrative staff that is responsible for the resources within different geographic regions. This allows more efficient control of the resources while still allowing the OU owners to have a level of autonomy over the objects that represent their resources within the company.

FIGURE 5.5

OU structure based on Organization, Then Location

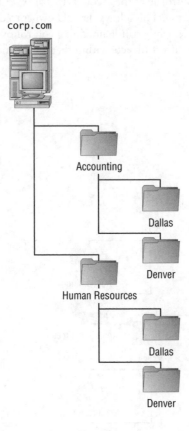

CHOOSING THE BEST OU DESIGN

You will notice that each of the design options has its own unique set of advantages and disadvantages. To choose the best design for your company, you will have to weigh the pros and cons of each strategy so that you come up with the design that is the best fit for your environment. If your company is not going to undergo many reorganizations or mergers and acquisitions, you may want to choose a design that makes the delegation of control easiest for your current administrative model. Company reorganizations could force a reevaluation of the departmental makeup within the organization, therefore forcing the OU hierarchy to change. Projects that are completed or abandoned will also force the OU structure to change. You might not want to rework the OU structure every time management decides they want to try running the business in a new fashion.

The adage "The only constant is change" will probably ring true no matter what strategy you employ, so try to employ the strategy that appears to be the least likely to change but reflects the way the administration is provided.

Understanding OU Design Criteria

As you build your organization's OU hierarchy, you will need to make sure that you design the OU structure so that it uses the most efficient layout possible. Designing the OU hierarchy can prove a very challenging endeavor. If you build too many OUs with several child OUs beneath them, you could create problems when trying to apply Group Policies. If you create too few, you may find that you have to perform special actions against the Group Policies so that you are not applying them to the wrong accounts.

OUs are built based on three criteria: autonomy over objects, control object visibility, and efficient Group Policy application. The following sections describe controlling the visibility of OUs and how to control autonomy over OUs. Once we finish this section, I will launch into a discussion of how you should design with Group Policies in mind.

OPTIONS FOR DELEGATING CONTROL

Object autonomy should be the primary criteria by which most organizations design their OUs. Giving the OU owners the ability to control the objects for which they are accountable allows them to perform their job functions. At the same time, they will feel comfortable knowing those objects are not controlled by other OU owners or administrators from outside their OU structure, with the exception of the forest's and domain's service and data administrators. Once a group is identified as the OU owner, they can control the accounts to which administrative control within the OU tree can be granted.

Users do not usually have the ability to view OUs. They use the Global Catalog to find objects that give them access to the resources within the network. OUs are designed to make administration easier for the administrative staff within the company. Keep this in mind when you are creating your OU structure. Build it with administration as the top priority; you can address other issues later.

Because so much power can be wielded when a user is allowed to become an OU owner, they should be trained on the proper methods of delegation. This means that anyone who is allowed to delegate control to another user should understand the two methods of delegating permissions—object-based and task-based—as well as how inheritance affects the design. If OU owners are not properly trained on how to delegate control, the OU structure could be at a security risk with users who have too much power or, on the opposite extreme, with users who do not have the proper amount of authority to administer the objects they are supposed to control.

The OU owners are responsible for making sure that the appropriate users and groups have the ability to manage the objects for which they are responsible. In the following sections, we will look at the options available to make sure those users and groups are properly configured for the access they need.

Understanding Delegation Methods

Object-based delegation grants a user control over an entire object type. Objects within Active Directory include users, groups, computers, OUs, printers, and shared folders. If a user needs to have control over computer accounts, you can use the Delegation of Control Wizard to allow Full Control permission only over computer objects within the OU. You might have another user who administers the User and Group objects within the OU. This level of control can be delegated as well.

Task-based delegation grants a user the ability to perform specific functions against objects within the OU. Controlling objects at this level is more difficult to manage and maintain, but sometimes you may find it necessary. Take for instance a case where a company has a Help Desk department and one of its job duties is to reset passwords for users. However, you don't want them to modify any of the user properties. If you delegate the ability to work with user objects, the Help Desk personnel will have too much power. Instead, you can delegate the ability to reset passwords at the task level, locking them out of having the ability to affect the objects in any other way.

As mentioned earlier, however, it is much more difficult to manage the permissions granted at the task level than it is the object level. You will need to make sure that you document the groups to which you are delegating permissions. Otherwise, you may find it problematic to try to track down where permissions are applied and troubleshoot access problems. As a best practice, try to design the OU structure so that you can take advantage of object-based delegation as much as possible.

Understanding Account and Resource OUs

In some Windows NT 4 directory service structures, the user accounts and resources are divided into their own domains, based on the administrative needs of the domain owners. Because the domain is the administrative boundary within NT 4, the user account administrators have control over the account domain. Resource administrators have domains that are made up of the resources they are responsible for maintaining—usually systems that provided database, e-mail, file, and print services, to name a few.

You must understand how the organization is administered when you are determining how the organizational unit (OU) structure will be designed. If you do not understand how the organization is administered, the OU structure you create might not be as efficient as it could be and it might not remain effective over time. An unwieldy or faulty design could create more administrative problems than it helps alleviate.

Depending on the administrative needs of the organization, delegation of the sublevel OUs should follow a few rules:

The OU owner will have full control.   The OU owner will have the ability to work with any object within the OU tree for which they are the owner. Once the domain owner delegates full control to the top-level OU for the OU owner, the OU owner will be able to take ownership of any object within that OU tree.

The OU admin can control only objects for which they have been granted permissions. The OU owner should only delegate the ability to work with the object types that the OU owner needs to modify. If the OU admin is an account admin, then only user and/or group object permissions should be granted. If the admin is a resource admin, only the appropriate object type should be delegated to them. OU administrators should not have the ability to affect OUs, but only the objects within them.

Account OUs and resource OUs can provide the same functionality that account and resource domains provided under NT 4. Account OUs will hold the user and group accounts that are used when accessing the resources. Resource OUs will host the resources that users will need to access within the domain. These could be computer accounts, file shares, shared folders, and contacts. You can build an OU structure that allows the user, group, and resource objects to be separated based on the staff that needs to have administrative control over them.

Understanding Inheritance

Inheritance allows the permissions set at a parent level to be assigned at each child level automatically. The inheritance of object permissions from the parent object to the child object eases some of the administration headaches. Permissions set at the parent level are propagated to the child levels by default. Any object created within an OU will inherit the applicable permissions from the OU. With this being the case, whenever an account is granted permissions at the OU level, all of the child OUs and objects within those OUs inherit the settings. OU owners have the ability to control all of the objects within their OU tree after the domain owner delegates the appropriate permissions to the top-level OU.

There will be occasions when the permissions set at higher levels within Active Directory are not the proper permissions needed at a lower level. If this is the case, inheritance can be blocked, which means that permissions set at the parent level will no longer pass to the child objects. When blocking the inheritance of permissions, the administrator who is initiating the block can choose whether or not to copy the inherited permissions to the object or remove them completely. If the inherited permissions are removed from the object, only the permissions that are explicitly set at the object level will apply. This could restrict an upper-level OU owner, OU administrator, domain owner, or forest owner from being able to perform actions against the object. If this happens, the OU owner, domain owner, or forest owner has the ability to reset the inheritable permissions on the object or objects that were affected.

The blocking of inheritance could be problematic for those users or groups who do not have the power to change the inheritable permissions setting. If inheritance is blocked to objects that a group needs to have control over, they will not be able to effectively maintain those objects. At this point, the OU owner could step in and change the inheritance on the OU or object, or change the effective permissions on the objects that the group needs to control. Trying to troubleshoot inheritance issues can be time consuming and difficult, so try to limit the amount of inheritance blocking you use within your design.

Creating an OU structure for a brand new design can be challenging. Developing a design that allows the administrative functions to be performed easily is of the utmost priority. However, very few organizations have the option of creating a brand new design. An existing infrastructure probably already exists. If the organization is using a Windows NT 4 domain environment, you need to consider several design options.

CONTROLLING VISIBILITY

When controlling object visibility, OUs can be used to hide objects from users when they are searching within Active Directory. By hiding the objects that users do not need to access, you can add a level of security to those objects. If users do not have the List Contents permission to an OU, they will not be able to view any of the objects within the OU. You can hide printers that they do not need to use and shares that should not appear in search results in this manner. You can also hide user and group objects from other administrators.

When you design the OU structure, you should always start with designing for administrative control, and then take visibility of objects into consideration. The primary goal of the OU design is to make administration of objects as efficient and easy as possible. Once you have completed the administrative design, you can address visibility requirements.

For example, take a company that has a printer that is restricted from users being able to print to it with the exception of a few authorized users. This printer is used to print accounts payable and payroll checks. Only a few Accounts Payable employees are allowed to send print jobs to this printer. Also, some shares on the Accounts Payable server are exclusive for use by the Accounts Payable staff. Because these resources need to be isolated from the rest of the organization, they should not show up when users from other departments perform searches within Active Directory.

The Accounts Payable department is part of the Accounting division of the company. Because the company has all of the accounting resources located at the corporate office, the corporate Information Technology department is responsible for maintaining the objects in Active Directory. Other departments have staff located at other offices, and each of those offices has administrative staff responsible for maintaining the resources.

During the design phase, the design team decides to use the Location, Then Organization design approach. This allows them to assign control over all resources to the administrative groups that need to be owners of the OU hierarchy, and then to grant other levels of control at the departmental level for those administrators who control a subset of resources. The initial design looks like Figure 5.6.

The objects that were initially identified as needing to be hidden from users need to be placed within an OU that will not allow users to view its contents. For a user to be able to "see" the objects within an OU, at the very least they will need the List Contents permission granted to them. If they do not have this permission, the objects contained within the OU will not show up in their searches. Because this permission is included in the standard Read permission, accounts with Read permission will be able to list the contents of the OU.

Because users need to view objects within the Accounts Payable OU, the permissions to that OU cannot be changed. Instead, a child OU is created to control visibility of the objects. The users within Accounts Payable department who need to work with the objects will be able to see them when they access Active Directory tools or perform searches, but no one else will. It should be noted that the AP Admins still need to be able to maintain the objects within the OU, so their permissions will either need to be re-added to the access control list, or the existing permissions will need to be copied directly to the OU with the unnecessary accounts and permissions then removed. The final OU design for Accounting will look like Figure 5.7.

FIGURE 5.6
OU design for
administrative
purposes

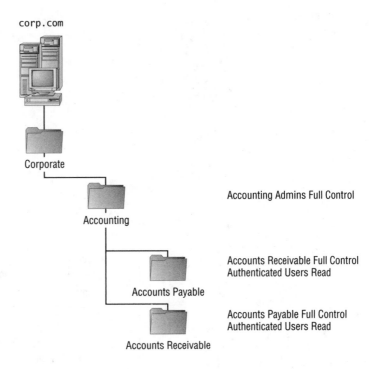

corp.com

Corporate

Accounting Admins Full Control

Accounting

Accounts Receivable Full Control
Authenticated Users Read

Accounts Payable

Accounts Payable Full Control
Authenticated Users Read

Accounts Receivable

As we have mentioned, the primary reason to create an OU structure is to have the ability to control administrative abilities and make administration of resources more efficient. Because there is only one way to delegate administration of resources and there are many options to control group policies, as you will see later in this chapter, the administrative design should take precedence.

Designing OUs for Group Policy

Group Policy has proven to be one of the most widely used Active Directory technologies and, at the same time, one of the most misunderstood and misused. Many administrators who have taken advantage of GPOs in order to control the security of systems and to distribute software to users and computers do not fully understand the options that are available when using GPOs. Understanding the settings that can control security, restrict user sessions and desktops, deploy software, and configure the application environment should be given top priority when you are using GPOs. Options that affect how the GPOs are applied need to be understood as well; some of the options we will discuss include blocking inheritance, enforcing settings, applying settings to specific users or systems, and filtering out the accounts that do not need to have settings applied to them.

FIGURE 5.7
OU design with OU created to control visibility

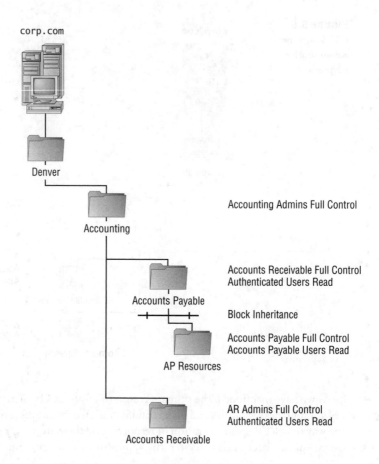

corp.com

Denver

Accounting — Accounting Admins Full Control

Accounts Payable — Accounts Receivable Full Control
Authenticated Users Read

Block Inheritance

AP Resources — Accounts Payable Full Control
Accounts Payable Users Read

Accounts Receivable — AR Admins Full Control
Authenticated Users Read

To make your job much easier, Microsoft has introduced a freely downloadable utility: the Group Policy Management Console (GPMC). The GPMC simplifies the task of administering the GPOs used within your organization. From one location, all of the GPOs from any domain in any forest of the organization can be controlled and maintained. You can download the utility from Microsoft's website. As you can see in Figure 5.8, once this utility is installed on a system, the Group Policy tab on the properties page of a site, domain, or OU will no longer show the GPOs linked at that object. Instead, a button to open the GPMC appears there. The GPMC is added to the Administrative Tools menu also.

NOTE   *For more information about the Group Policy Management Console and how to download your copy of this tool, go to* http://www.microsoft.com/windowsserver2003/gpmc/default.mspx.

FIGURE 5.8
The Group Policy
tab after the Group
Policy Management
Console is added

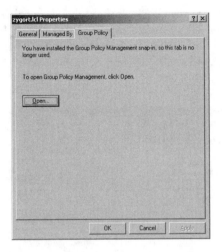

The GPMC will function only on Windows XP and Windows Server 2003 operating systems. Any administrators within the organization who needs to use this utility will need a workstation running Windows XP or else they will need to work from a server where the GPMC has been added. Figure 5.9 shows the GPMC. Notice how the group policies are all organized beneath the Group Policy container. This allows you to go to the container and work with any of the GPOs that you are using in Active Directory. Also note that the domain and all of the sites and OUs are organized within the console so that you can see at which level GPOs are linked.

NOTE *In order to run the Group Policy Management Console on a Windows XP–based system, you will need to load Windows XP Service Pack 1 and the .Net Framework 1.1 or later.*

FIGURE 5.9
Group Policy Objects within the
GPMC

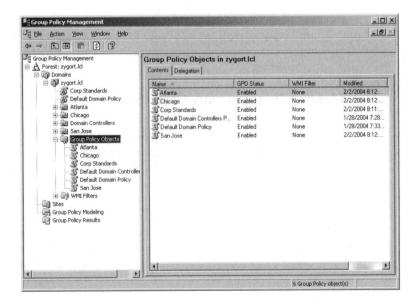

Of course, the real power to the GPMC is the ability to run sample scenarios and to determine which GPOs are being applied to a user or computer. As you design the GPOs that will be used within your organization, take the time to test the effects the GPO will have on users and computers when applied in conjunction with other GPOS. Figure 5.10 shows an example of the GPMC's Group Policy Modeling section.

FIGURE 5.10
Group Policy
Modeling

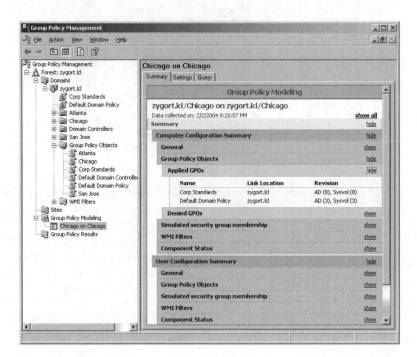

In the following sections, we will take a look at company uses for GPOs. These uses will include the security needs, software installation options, and user restrictions that will be used to control the user's environment.

Understanding Company Objectives

Before sitting down and designing the OUs that you will use for implementing GPOs, you need to understand the needs of the organization. Although every Active Directory rollout will have password requirements, lockout restrictions, and Kerberos policies applied, that is usually where any similarities between organizations end. The first thing you should do is document the administrative structure of your organization. This will give you a better understanding of how administration of resources is applied within the organization.

Base your Group Policy design on this administrative design as much as possible. Most organizations find that if they create their OU structure on the administrative functions, the Group Policy requirements follow along pretty well. Although you may still have to build OUs for special purposes, the basic design should already be put into place. The special purposes could include special software that a subset of users from a department need to use, or restrictions on the systems that temporary employees will have.

A good Group Policy design starts with defining exactly what actions GPOs will perform for your organization. Because GPOs are primarily an administrative tool, you can ease the administrative staff's load and allow the system to control users' environments. Some of the areas that can be controlled are security, software installation, and user restrictions.

IDENTIFYING SECURITY NEEDS

The security settings that will be enforced for users and the systems to which they connect will be the first types of settings that need to be determined. When Windows Server 2003 is configured as a domain controller, the security policy for the domain requires users to use *strong passwords*, which are password that do not use words that can be found in a dictionary and utilize several different types of characters. Microsoft has identified strong passwords as those that follow these guidelines:

- They are at least seven characters long.

- They do not contain your username, real name, or company name.

- They do not contain a complete dictionary word.

- They are significantly different from previous passwords. Passwords that increment (*Password1, Password2, Password3 ...*) are not strong.

- They contain characters from at least three of the following four groups:

- Uppercase letters, such as *A, B,* and *C.*

- Lowercase letters, such as a, *b,* and *c.*

- Numerals, such as *0, 1, 2,* and *3.*

- Symbols found on the keyboard (all keyboard characters not defined as letters or numerals), including the following: ` ~ ! @ # $ % ^ & * ( ) _ + - = { } | [ ] \ : " ; ' < > ? , . /

Training users on the proper methods of creating and using passwords can prove to be difficult. For instance, turning on the complexity requirements that force a user to have strong passwords usually ends up with the user writing their password down on a piece of paper or a sticky note and placing it close to their computer. You should implement corporate standards that identify how passwords should be protected and the ramifications of not following the policy. Of course, training the users and explaining the reason passwords are a vital defense mechanism can aid in the acceptance of the password policy.

Account lockout restrictions are another defense mechanism that should be used. Any time a brute force attack is made against an account, the account lockout policy prevents the attackers from being able to make too many attempts at discovering the password. Most companies have this setting configured to allow between three and five attempts before the account is locked. Once it is locked, the attacker does not have the ability to try any additional passwords against the account for as long as the account is locked. This brings us to the second part of account lockout restrictions: you should always leave the accounts locked until an administrator unlocks it. Although this increases the administrative load to some extent, and more times than not the lockout is due to the user forgetting their password or having the Caps Lock key turned on, at least the administrator is notified of the possible attack. Just to make sure that you are not allowing an unauthorized user access to another user's account, you will need to put procedures in place that will help you identify the user who needs their account unlocked. This is especially true if they call to have their account unlocked and they mention that they cannot remember their password. Before changing the password, you will need to authenticate the identity of the user.

Aside from the account policies that can be set, other requirements also need to be identified. For instance, you may have users who need access to servers that hold confidential information. If users need to use an encrypted connection when accessing the data, you can specify the Internet protocol security (IPSec) policies that will be enforced by using GPOs. For example, if a user within the Payroll department needs to modify the salary and bonus structure for an employee, and the employee data is hosted on a server that you want to make sure is only accessed when IPSec communication is used, you can create an OU, IPSec Servers, for the payroll departments server and any other servers that require IPSec communication. You can then create a Group Policy for the IPSec Servers OU that enforces the Secure Server IPSec policy and apply it to all servers in the IPSec Servers OU. Another OU, Payroll Clients OU, can be created for the workstations within the Payroll department. The Group Policy that is defined for the Payroll Clients OU could have the Client IPSec policy assigned to it, which would turn on IPSec communication whenever connecting to the Payroll servers.

IDENTIFYING SOFTWARE INSTALLATION NEEDS

Using GPOs to roll out software can drastically reduce the administrative efforts required to install and maintain software within the organization. At the same time, it can increase the load on the network to a point that is not acceptable. You need to determine if the benefits gained from having automated installation of software outweigh the network overhead required. Of course, no matter how much you may want to use GPOs to push software to client machines, some instances will occur when the network infrastructure will not allow it. This is especially true if you use wide area network (WAN) links between locations and the software distribution point is located on a server on the other end of the slow link.

A Service Level Agreement (SLA) could affect the rollout of software. SLAs are contractual obligations that dictate the amount of service availability that is required for servers or workstations. In some cases, software can take several minutes to install. If SLAs are in place and they restrict the amount of time that it takes to install an application, you may be forced to manually install the application for the user during times when they are not using the system. Another alternative is to link the GPO after hours and have the software installation assigned to the computer. Due to the fact that the software installation client side extension is not included in the periodic refresh of GPOs, any changes that you make to the software installation options within a GPO are not processed on the client. Using remote access tools, you could then restart the user's computer, which would initiate the installation of the software.

If you determine that you are going to assign or publish applications to users or computers, you need to identify which applications are required. Most applications written by commercial software vendors within the last few years take advantage of Microsoft's IntelliMirror technology and are supported by Group Policy. Make sure the software is stamped with Microsoft's seal of approval. If Microsoft has certified the software to run on Windows Server 2003, the application will support IntelliMirror.

Work with each department within the organization to determine their software requirements. Understanding the software needs of the organization helps you identify which software packages need to be rolled out through a GPO. You may need to make some trade-offs. If every user within the organization needs to have a specific application such as antivirus software, it may be easier to create a system image that includes that operating system and the software. Using a third-party disk imaging utility, you can create a generic image of a system that includes all of the software and the appropriate system settings for the organization. Whenever the tech staff builds a new client system, the image is placed on the hard drive of the new computer, and when the computer is rebooted, it is configured with the default settings and software. This is a very quick and usually painless method of getting systems online in short order. However, you will encounter some drawbacks.

If devices on the new hardware are not supported at the time the image was originally created, the new hardware may not start up correctly and you will be left trying to install the correct drivers. As new software packages are identified, as required for the organization, you may have to rebuild the image to support the software, which then brings us back to the advantages of Group Policy software deployment. Although operating systems cannot be deployed through a policy—that is, a function of Remote Installation Services (RIS)—new and updated software can be. Of course Microsoft Systems Management Server (SMS) will also roll out software to client machines and will do so with more efficient management options. One of the benefits of SMS that Group Policy has yet to implement is the ability to push the software package out at a predetermined time.

After determining which of the deployment options you are going to use, you then need to determine which software packages are going to be rolled out with Group Policy and how you are going to accomplish this.

IDENTIFYING USER RESTRICTIONS

User restrictions limit what actions a user can perform on their workstation or control the applications that are allowed to run. For some companies, not many settings are required. The users have control over their workstations and the administrators may only control the security policies that are put into effect with the Default Domain Policy, which is where the password requirements, account lockout settings, and Kerberos policy settings are configured. Other companies take full advantage of using GPOs to restrict their users from being able to access any of the operating system configuration options. Some companies even force all of the systems to have the corporate background.

As extreme as it may sound, the fewer configuration options that a user is allowed to access, the less the user can affect, and possibly change for the worse. Desktop restrictions can remove the icons for My Computer and My Network Places, or they can change what the user sees from the context menu when the right mouse button is used on these icons. The Display properties can be locked out so that the user cannot choose a monitor refresh rate or screen resolution that is not supported by the video subsystem. Start menu items can be restricted so that the user does not have the ability to open the Control Panel and modify settings within the operating system.

NOTE *For more information about Group Policy and the settings that you can use to control a user's environment, see the Group Policy section within the Windows Server 2003 Technical Reference on the Microsoft website,* `http://www.microsoft.com/ resources/documentation/WindowsServ/2003/all/techref/en-us/default.asp`.

You should identify which operating system configuration settings the users within the organization really need to work with, and how much power they need to wield over their workstations. Whereas it may take you a little longer to plan out the Group Policy settings that need to be applied to groups of users, the administrative headaches that these restrictions will alleviate will be worth the trouble. As you design the Group Policy settings that will be used to control and assist the administrative structure, remember the golden rule: keep it simple.

Creating a Simple Design

The underlying design goal, aside from supporting the organization's objectives, should be to create a Group Policy design that is as simple as possible. A simple design will allow more efficient troubleshooting and processing of Group Policy settings. The fewer Group Policy settings that need to be applied to a computer or user, the faster the computer will start up, the quicker the users will be able to log on to their systems, and because a small GPO can be 1.5MB in size, network traffic will also be reduced. If problems arise due to Group Policy conflicts or inappropriate settings, it is easier for an administrator to troubleshoot the problem if the design is simple.

When determining the best and most efficient use of GPOs, you should review the requirements of the users who will be affected and then try to consolidate settings into the fewest GPOs possible. Then make sure you are taking advantage of the natural inheritance of Active Directory and are not using too many options that change the inheritance state.

IDENTIFYING USER REQUIREMENTS

Determine what you need to provide for the users and their computers. Every company's requirements will be different. Understanding how employees function on a day-to-day basis and what they need in order to perform these functions will aid you in determining the Group Policy settings you need to enforce. You will need to determine which settings need to be applied based on employees' job functions and job requirements, and you will need to identify the corporate standards that should be put in place.

Corporate Standards

Corporate standards are usually the easiest settings to figure out. These are the settings that should be set across the board for every employee and computer. Corporate standards are settings that you define in order to control the environment so that no employee is allowed to perform actions that are prohibited. Settings that make up these standards include the password policy, account lockout policy, software restrictions, Internet Explorer Security Zone settings, and warning messages that appear when someone attempts to log on.

Corporate standards are settings that should be applied as high in the Group Policy hierarchy as possible. The Group Policy hierarchy consists of the three levels at which a GPO can be linked; site, domain, and organizational unit (OU). Because the GPO settings are inherited from each of these levels, by linking the GPO at the highest level within the hierarchy where it applies, you will be able to enforce the settings over a large number of objects with the fewest GPOs.

Most designs apply the corporate standards at the domain level so that every user logging on and every computer starting up will have the policy applied to it. To make sure that these settings are imposed on every user and system, the Enforced setting should be enabled on the GPO that represents the corporate standards. This way, if another administrator configures a GPO with settings that conflict with the corporate standards and links the new GPO to an OU, the corporate standards will still take precedence.

Don't modify the Default Domain Policy to include the settings for the corporate standards. Although this may seem like a logical place to enforce the settings because the Default Domain Policy affects all users and computers within the domain, the new Default Group Policy Restore Command (dcgpofix.exe) found in Windows Server 2003 will not retain the settings that have been modified since the domain was created.

NOTE *For more information about the Default Group Policy Restore Command utility (dcgpofix.exe), see the section "Options for Linking Group Policies" later in this chapter.*

If multiple domains exist within the organization, chances are the corporate standards will apply to them also. The GPMC will allow you to copy a GPO from one domain to another. Using this functionality, you can create a duplicate GPO that can be linked to a domain. This will alleviate having to link a single GPO to multiple domains. Whereas this is not an issue when you have domain controllers within a site that host the GPOs, if you have to pull the GPO from across a WAN link, you could increase the user's logon time considerably.

Job Function

Employees have specific functions that they provide for the company. An employee within the Human Resources department provides different functions than a temporary employee providing data entry for the Marketing department. Identify what the employees require to perform their jobs. Document your findings, and then compare what is the same among all employees within an OU and what is different. You may be able to create a single GPO for a department that applies to all of the users and computers and then link it at the parent OU for the department. Those settings that are specific to a subset of users or computers can then be added to a GPO that is linked to the child OU where the user or computer accounts are located.

Organize all of the setting required by employees within a department and create a GPO named after the department. That GPO can then be linked to the department. Other settings that are specific to a subset of the users within that department can either be linked to the OU and configured so that only those users receive the settings, or linked to a child OU if the users and computers are distributed for administrative purposes.

Job Requirements

There may be specific job requirements that must be met by users or computers that are different even though the job functions may be very similar. Whereas all members of the Human Resources department will need to access the training materials and benefits documents so that they can assist employees when necessary, a subset of Human Resources personnel may have access to the employee database. If this database resides on a server that requires IPSec-encrypted communication, only the appropriate Human Resources personnel should fall under the control of the GPO that provides the appropriate IPSec policy settings. By linking a GPO to the server's OU that enforces the servers to require IPSec for communication and another GPO linked at the Human Resource's client OU that uses the IPSec client policy, the Human Resources personnel will communicate securely with the servers.

System requirements may be different for users depending on their job requirements. You may have users who need to use modems to connect to remote systems. Other users may need to have access to administrative tools. Exceptions to restrictions that are applied at the domain or parent OU may need to be overridden for these users. Make sure you document the special needs of every user.

MINIMIZING GROUP POLICY OBJECTS

If you use as few GPOs as possible, you will be able to troubleshoot problems that arise much more easily than if several GPOs could affect users and computers. Policy settings that are related, such as software restrictions that affect a large group of users, should be added to the same GPO. By adding settings to a single GPO instead of using multiple GPOs to enforce the settings, you will reduce the GPO processing time.

SLAs are starting to become more widespread. As systems become more and more vital to company operations, having these systems online becomes mandatory. Although we think of SLAs controlling servers and server maintenance, SLAs that affect workstations are also being put into place. Some of these dictate the amount of time that a user will have to spend for applications to load and the amount of time spent waiting for logon to complete. This may sound picky to some individuals, but some financial institutions, brokerage firms, and other organizations require their workstations to be available at all times so that they can perform their duties.

If your organization falls under an SLA, you will need to determine how long it takes to process the GPOs you are planning. By combining settings into a single GPO, you will decrease the amount of processing time required to process the settings. If the settings are spread amongst several GPOs, all of the settings for each of the policies will have to be processed.

Try to determine if you can condense the settings into a single policy, and if you cannot, try to condense to the fewest policies possible. Of course, this is a practice that you should follow whether you are working under an SLA or not. Users do not like to wait to access their systems. The faster they are able to see their logon screen and access their desktops, the happier they are. The happier the users are, the better your day will be.

Another method of making your GPOs more efficient is to disable part of GPO from processing. Each of the two sections that you can configure settings in, computer and user, can be disabled. When you do so, you are essentially telling the system to ignore any of the settings in that section. Because the client side extensions do not have to parse through the GPO to determine what needs to be enforced or disabled, the GPO will process faster, thereby reducing the time it takes for the computer to reach the logon screen or the user to log on to their system.

IDENTIFYING INTEROPERABILITY ISSUES

Windows XP and Windows Server 2003 are the only operating systems that can take full advantage of the new Group Policy settings in a Windows Server 2003 Active Directory environment. Windows XP can take advantage of all of the new client specific settings, whereas Windows Server 2003 can take advantage of all of the new server-based settings. For users running Windows 2000 Professional or servers running Windows 2000 Server, over 200 possible settings will not be processed on those platforms. When you edit the settings for a GPO, make sure each of the settings specify to which operating system platform the setting will apply.

Windows Management Instrumentation (WMI) filters provide additional functionality to a Group Policy application. By specifying operating system or system options, you can control which computers a GPO will apply. For instance, if you want to make sure that a system has enough free space on a partition or volume in order to install software, you can specify that the free space must exceed the minimum requirement for the application. Figure 5.11 is an example of a WMI filter that is used to control the installation of software to partitions or volumes with enough free space. If the requirement is not met, the application installation setting is ignored. Again, Windows XP and Windows Server 2003 can take advantage of WMI filters, but Windows 2000 cannot. If a WMI filter is in place that controls whether a GPO is applied and the computer is running Windows 2000, the WMI filter is ignored and the settings are applied.

Other operating systems, such as Windows NT 4, Windows 95, and Windows 98, will not process GPOs. If you want to control computers running these operating systems, you will have to use System Policy Editor. This means that you will have to support two different technologies when trying to set user restrictions. Another drawback comes from the fact that only a small subset of settings is supported by System Policies. In order to efficiently control the systems and users within your environment, try to determine an upgrade path for the older operating systems.

FIGURE 5.11

WMI filter for detecting adequate drive space

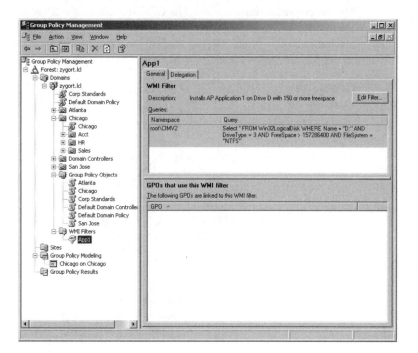

DESIGNING FOR INHERITANCE

Just as permissions are inherited from a parent OU to the child OU, Group Policy settings will also pass down through the hierarchy. Taking advantage of *inheritance*, you will be able to create a Group Policy hierarchy that allows you to efficiently apply GPOs to your organization and make it easy for your staff to troubleshoot issues arising from GPOs. You have several options when you are using inheritance. You should implement best practices that will allow inheritance to work as it should and then use the options that change the default behavior only when necessary. The more the options for enforcing (referred to as No Override if you are not using the GPMC), blocking, and filtering are used, the harder it is to troubleshoot the design.

Organizing OUs

Use the OU structure that is based on the administrative requirements as much as possible. Create additional OUs only if it makes the application of Group Policy easier to maintain and troubleshoot. For instance, if you look at Figure 5.12, an OU structure has been created that allows the Engineering department administration to be broken out into two departments: Graphic Design and Model Shop. Each of the departments has a different internal administrative staff responsible for maintaining the user and computer accounts. Within the Model Shop, some employees work with the Research and Development department to build prototypes. For users to access the plans from the Research and Development (R&D) servers, which are placed in an OU that has the require IPSec policy applied, they need to use IPSec-encrypted communication. The GPO that allows the IPSec client policy is applied to the R&D Model Shop OU, where the user accounts are located, giving them the ability to access the plans from which they need to build. The rest of the Model Shop employees' accounts are placed with the Users container.

FIGURE 5.12
OU structure enhanced for Group Policy application

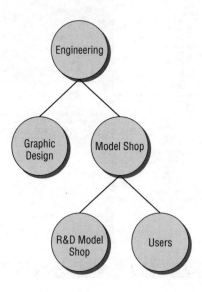

Define Corporate Standards

Once the settings for corporate standards have been identified and configured within a GPO, they should be linked high within the hierarchy, preferably at the domain level. Once linked, the Enforced option should be set so that lower-level GPOs do not override any of the standards. Figure 5.13 shows a domain with the Default Domain Policy and the Corporate Standards policy. Notice that the Corp Standards GPO has the Enforced option turned on. Figure 5.14 shows the inheritance of GPOs at the Accounting OU. Notice that the Corp Standards GPO is the GPO with the highest priority within the list due to its Enforced setting.

FIGURE 5.13

Corporate Standards GPO enforced at the domain level

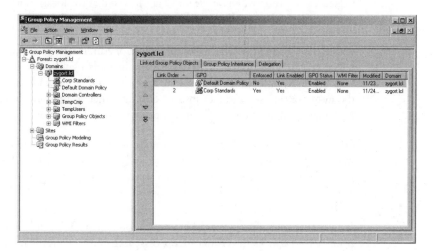

FIGURE 5.14

Corporate Standards affecting the Accounting OU

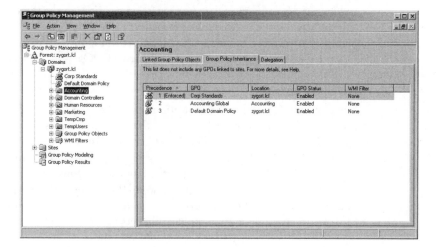

Use Blocking and Filtering Sparingly

The Block Inheritance option stops the natural inheritance of settings from GPOs higher in the hierarchy. When you use this option, you will block every GPO setting from any parent object with the exception of the domain account policies. Once blocked, the only way that a GPO's settings will override the Block Inheritance option is if you apply the Enforced option. The Enforced option takes precedence over any Block Inheritance option that it encounters, but it is only applied to an individual GPO. You will need to set the Enforced option for every GPO that needs to override the blockage.

Filtering is the process of specifying to which accounts the GPOs will apply. By default, the Authenticated Users group will have the GPO applied to it at the location where the GPO is linked. This may work in some instances, but for most applications, you will not want every account to be under the GPO's control. For instance, if the user account that has administrative rights to the OU is located within the OU and the GPO restricts the use of administrative tools, the administrative user will not have access to the tools they need to perform their job. Determine which accounts will need to have the GPOs applied to them and create a group based on that need. Do not add the administrative users to the group for the user accounts; instead, create another group so that the administrators can be members of it. Configure the Security Filtering option to include the group to which the GPO will be applied.

TIP   *If you are changing the permissions for a user or group so that the GPO is not applied to them, make sure you remove the Read permission if the accounts do not need to work with the GPO. If you simply remove the Apply Group Policy permission, the accounts will still process the GPO settings, resulting in longer logon delays.*

Prioritizing

If more than one GPO is attached to a site, domain, or OU, you will need to determine the processing priority for each. As the GPOs are processed, the GPO with the lowest processing number, which is the highest priority, will override any of the other GPO's settings that are linked to the same location (with the exception of those GPOs that have the Enforced options enabled). Compare Figure 5.12 to Figure 5.15. In Figure 5.16, the processing priorities of the three GPOs linked at the Accounting OU are set so that the Accounting Registry & File GPO has the lowest processing priority. Yet because the Enforced option is set, you can see in Figure 5.16 that the Group Policy Inheritance tab lists it with a higher priority than the other two GPOs.

Enabling Loopback

Some computers within an organization should be used only for certain purposes. Kiosks will have access to public information, but because they are usually accessible to the general public, you may not want such computers to have the ability to access sensitive corporate information. You may encounter other computers that need to have user settings applied to the computer no matter which user is logged on. To enforce these settings, the loopback feature is used. Once enabled, the settings from the User Configuration portion of the Group Policy object that is applied to the computer's OU will take precedence instead of the User Configuration settings at the user's OU.

There are two methods of applying the settings once loopback processing has been enabled. The first, Merge, consolidates all of the settings from the user's and computer's GPOs; if any settings conflict, the computer's setting will apply. The second is Replace. When Replace is chosen, the user's settings are not processed. Instead, the computer's settings are applied, thereby restricting the user account to just those settings that are allowed by the computer's GPO settings.

FIGURE 5.15
Priorities for GPOs attached to the Accounting OU

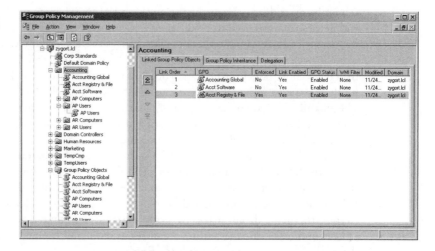

FIGURE 5.16
Processing order for GPOs at the Accounting OU

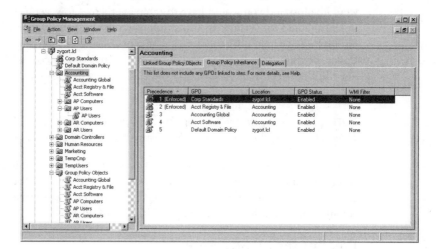

OPTIONS FOR LINKING GROUP POLICIES

At this point in your MCSE studies, you should know that GPOs can be linked at the site, domain, or OU level. Although you might want to link at the site or domain level, doing so is usually not suggested. Linking at the OU level allows you to efficiently control the GPOs and how they are applied to users and computers. Of course, there are always exceptions.

The primary exception is for the security settings that are applied at the domain level. You'll recall that the Default Domain Policy is where the password requirements, account lockout settings, and Kerberos policy settings are configured. These settings are then applied throughout the domain and cannot be overridden. This is the reason that a separate domain needs to be created if any settings within these options need to be different between user accounts.

As a general rule, you should not make changes to the Default Domain Policy, with the exception of setting the security policy options settings. If any settings will define corporate standards other than the security policy settings and you want to apply them at the domain level, create a new policy for these settings. Although this goes against the recommendation that you use the fewest GPOs possible, it will allow you to have a central point to access the security policies for the domain and separate any other policy settings that are applied. Another reason is that this gives you the ability to re-create the Default Domain Policy if it becomes damaged.

Included with Windows Server 2003 is a utility called `dcgpofix.exe`. This command line utility will re-create the Default Domain Policy and the Default Domain Controller Policy if necessary. It will not create either policy with any modified settings; it will only re-create the policy with the initial default settings that are applied when the first domain controller in the domain is brought online. Keeping this in mind, only make changes to the security settings that are applied to either of these two policies and make sure the settings are documented. After running `dcgpofix.exe`, the settings that define the corporate security standards can then be reset.

If you were to add settings to the Default Domain Policy, and then run `dcgpofix.exe`, the settings would be lost and you would have to re-create them. However, if you were to create a new Group Policy and add the settings to it instead, when the Default Domain Policy is re-created, the new Group Policy would not be affected. The same rule holds true for the Default Domain Controllers Policy. Because some settings should be applied to domain controllers to ensure their security, do not edit the settings on this Group Policy. The `dcgpofix.exe` utility can be used to regenerate this policy as well.

NOTE *For more information on* `dcgpofix.exe` *and how to regenerate the Default Domain Policy and Default Domain Controllers Policy, look within the Windows Server 2003 Help files.*

As a general rule of thumb, when you plan where the policies should be linked, if the policy applies to a large number of users, link it at the parent OU. If the policy applies to a discreet subset of users, link the policy at the child OU. This should alleviate the need to have elaborate filtering and blocking schemes that will affect the natural inheritance of GPOs.

Creating the OU Structure

When creating the OU structure, you need to base it primarily on administrative needs. Although we keep hitting on that point, it cannot be stressed enough. You should build the OU structure to make the administration of the domain as easy and efficient as possible. You can create GPOs to take advantage of the administrative structure of the OUs, and you can create additional OUs if the Group Policy requirements dictate it, but do so sparingly.

Two containers exist within Active Directory: the Users container and the Computers container. If a user or computer account is created and an OU membership is not specified, then the user account is created in the Users container and the computer account is created in the Computers container. GPOs cannot be set on these containers. The only GPOs that will apply to these users are the settings applied at the site or domain level. If you are following the recommendation that GPOs be applied at the OU level as much as possible, these users and computers will not be under the jurisdiction of GPOs that would otherwise control what the accounts can do.

To avoid this scenario, Microsoft has included two utilities with Windows Server 2003: `redirusr.exe` and `redircmp.exe`. As you can probably tell from their names, these utilities redirect the accounts to OUs that you specify instead of the default containers. However, there is one caveat to using these utilities: the domain has to be at the Windows 2003 functional level. Unfortunately, not many organizations are ready to move to this functional level. Those that have had the good fortune to change their domain functional level to Window 2003 will find that they can take advantage of creating new OUs for controlling those new user and computer accounts.

NOTE   *For more information about the* `redirusr.exe` *and* `redircmp.exe` *commands, see TechNet article 324949, Redirecting the Users and Computers Containers in Windows Server 2003 Domains.*

IDENTIFYING OU STRUCTURAL REQUIREMENTS

After redirecting new accounts to the new OUs, you can identify the rest of the OU structure needs. Most of the OU structure should already be designed because it is based on the administrative structure of the organization. In the first part of this chapter, I discussed creating the top-level OUs based on a static aspect of the organization. This still holds true for Group Policy design. If the top-level OUs are based on either locations or functions, the structure is resistant to change. The child OUs can then reflect the administrative requirements. This allows for the administrative staff to have efficient control of those objects they need to manage.

GPOs will use this structure, but other OUs may need to be created to further enhance the Group Policy requirements. Do be careful when you create additional OUs to implement Group Policy. The more layers in the hierarchy, the harder it is to manage the objects within. Remember, the key to the OU structure is to make administrative tasks easier. Investigate all of the possible options when you are determining how to apply GPOs.

New OUs should be added to the OU structure only if they enhance the application of GPOs and make the assignment of settings and restrictions to a group of users or computers easier than if they were linked at an existing OU. Use the Group Policy Modeling Wizard within the GPMC to determine if the application of policies is going to work as you expect it to. Experiment with the linkage of GPOs at those OUs that you already have defined. View the results and see which accounts are adversely affected before determining that an additional OU is required. You may find that filtering the GPO to a new group that you create allows you to assign settings to those users within that group while keeping the users within the OU instead of creating a new OU to host them.

Those users who need to create and link the OUs will need the appropriate rights delegated to them. You will also need to identify how you are going to maintain the GPOs and monitor how the GPOs are administered. Once the OU structure has been identified for applying Group Policy, the staff who will be responsible for the creation and maintenance of the GPOs will need rights delegated to them and training provided. If you are delegating the ability to perform specific functions to those users who are working with GPOs, you can give them the ability to create GPOs, edit GPOs, and link GPOS. One user could have the ability to perform all three functions, or you could separate the functions so that only certain users can perform an individual task. The following section will describe how you can design your GPO management for delegated administration.

IDENTIFYING ADMINISTRATIVE REQUIREMENTS

In smaller organizations, the same administrator who creates user accounts will maintain the servers and work with the GPOs. Such an administrator, sometimes known as the Jack-of-All-Trades administrator, does it all. For this type of administration, identifying who is going to perform the tasks is simple. That administrator has to make sure that they are trained to perform the tasks at hand. In larger environments, however, one administrator cannot do it all. Usually specific tasks are assigned to users, and they are responsible for their own little piece of the organization. In this case, the users who are delegated the tasks of maintaining GPOs have to be trained on the proper methods of maintaining the Group Policy infrastructure.

Training Users

Different users can be assigned to create GPOs than those who are allowed to link the GPOs. In larger organizations where specialized job functions are assigned to employees, or in organizations that use the hybrid administrative model, users who are in charge of corporate standards can be allowed to create unlinked GPOS and modify GPOs with the settings determined by the corporate administration. The domain and OU owners are then responsible for linking the appropriate GPOs to their OUs or domains.

When you delegate the permission to perform actions on GPOs to users other than administrators who already have that ability, you need to make sure that you are giving the user permission to do so only for the portion of Active Directory for which they are responsible. Within the GPMC, you can delegate the ability to link GPOs at the site, domain, or OU level. By changing permissions within the discretionary access control list for the GPO, you can control who is able to edit the GPO. By granting someone the Read and Write permissions, that user could modify setting within the GPO. Figure 5.17 shows the Delegation tab within the GPMC for an OU.

FIGURE 5.17

Delegation tab for an OU

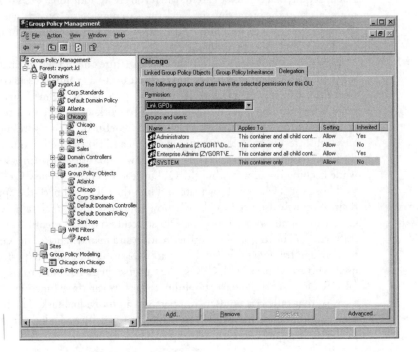

A special group exists to make the task of delegating the creation of GPOs easier: the Group Policy Creator Owners group. When a user is added to this group, they will be able to modify any GPO that they create but they will not be able to link the GPO anywhere within Active Directory unless they have been delegated the right to do so at a site, domain, or OU.

When employees are granted the ability to create, modify, and/or link GPOs, they should be trained on the proper methods of handling their responsibilities. Guidelines for the functions that can be performed should be explained to the OU owners, domain owners, and forest owners. Without a basic set of guidelines, users could inadvertently make changes or create GPOs that will not function properly within your environment. Document the guidelines that you want to use and make sure everyone involved understands them.

The Group Policy administration training methodology should include best practices for the following topics:

- Creating GPOs
- Importing settings
- Editing settings
- Linking GPOs
- Setting exceptions for inheritance
- Filtering accounts
- Using the Group Policy Modeling Wizard
- Using the Group Policy Results Wizard
- Backing up and restoring GPOs
- Learning which settings apply to specific operating systems
- Using WMI filters
- Handling security templates

If users understand how each of these work, they will have a better understanding of why GPOs should be implemented the way they are, and as a result, the troubleshooting required to determine problems should ease. The more training and understanding that goes on before the users are allowed to create and maintain GPOs, the less time will be spent troubleshooting later in the life cycle of Active Directory.

Identifying Required Permissions

For the most part, GPOs should be linked at the OU level. This allows you to use the most versatile method of controlling how the settings are applied. Sometimes you will find that the best method of applying policies is performed if the policy is linked at the site or domain level. As mentioned previously, the account policies are always set at the domain level. You may also find a reason to link them at the site level, such as when all computers at the site need to have an IPSec policy applied to them.

In order for a GPO to be linked at the site level, the administrator who is performing the linking has to have enterprise-level permissions or have the permission to link to the site delegated to them. Adding an account to the Domain Admins global group or Administrators domain local group at the root domain or Enterprise Admins universal group is not a recommended practice unless that administrative account is the forest owner.

Administrative staff responsible for linking at the domain level will need to be members of the Domain Admins global group, or they will need to have the Manage Group Policy Links permission delegated to them. Members of the Domain Admins global group will also be able to use the GPMC and edit any GPOs for their domain. To have access to GPOs for any other domain, they will need permissions delegated to them for the objects within the other domains, or they will need to be members of the Enterprise Admins universal group.

Policies linked at the OU level require the administrative staff to be members of the Domain Admins global group for the domain or have the proper permissions delegated to them to work with GPOs.

Best Practices for Organizational Design

An OU design can take on many different styles depending upon the nature of the business and the goals of the organization. In order to make sure that the design you want to use meets the requirements for your organization, you should follow a few guidelines.

- Create the OU structure to support the administrative needs of the company.

- Delegate permissions to groups of users at the OU level in order to reduce the membership of accounts in high-power built-in groups.

- Delegate permissions as high in the Active Directory hierarchy as possible, and take advantage of inheritance.

- Build on the administrative design to support Group Policy.

- In a Windows Server 2003 domain, use the Group Policy Management Console (GPMC).

- Use Group Policy Modeling within the GPMC to determine how GPOs will affect users and computers.

- Use GPOs to help alleviate administrative costs.

- Minimize the number of GPOs that are applied to a user or computer to allow more efficient logons.

- In a Windows Server 2003 domain, use WMI filters so that you can more efficiently control the GPOs that will apply to Windows XP and Windows Server 2003 computers.

- Use block inheritance, enforced, loopback, and filtering options sparingly in order to ease troubleshooting.

- In a Windows Server 2003 functional-level forest, redirect the users and computers to OUs instead of the default containers.

Next Up

Up to this point, we have concentrated on a pristine Active Directory environment, but as most people know, adding Exchange Server modifies Active Directory in several ways. Additional attributes added to the Schema and object classes are changed to support Exchange, and you may have to make changes to the network infrastructure to support the services that Exchange requires. In the next chapter, we will take a look at placement of the domain controllers, global catalog servers, and DNS servers so that they will support Exchange.

chapter 6

Exchange Design Considerations

IF YOU ARE PLANNING to use Microsoft's e-mail server, Exchange 2000, or Exchange Server 2003, within your organization, you will need to implement Active Directory. You will also need to understand the requirements for Exchange and the changes that will go into effect when you introduce Exchange into Active Directory. In this chapter, we are going to look at the changes that Exchange will cause and the additional support that will be needed to have a functional e-mail system.

Understanding the Changes

Active Directory is never the same once Exchange gets its hands on it. Thousands of modifications occur just to allow an Exchange-based mail system to work with Active Directory. To keep the size of the Active Directory database as small as possible, the Exchange-specific attributes are not included in a standard install of Active Directory. Instead, the Exchange setup program searches for the Schema Master and attempts to add the necessary attributes and then changes objects within the Configuration and Domain partitions.

In a small organization where the Active Directory administrative staff and the Exchange administrative staff work tightly together or are combined into one group, installing the first Exchange server and having it modify Active Directory at the same time may be acceptable. However, in larger organizations, the administrative responsibilities are usually divided amongst several groups. Those administrators who are responsible for Exchange usually do not have the ability to modify Active Directory, and vice versa. Microsoft realized this when they were designing applications that relied on extending the Active Directory schema. The Exchange setup program has two special switches (ForestPrep and DomainPrep) you can use to allow the appropriate administrators to perform their individual tasks so that the Exchange administrators do not wield too much power.

NOTE *Although this chapter is devoted to enhancements made to Active Directory when an Exchange server is introduced into a network, it is not meant to cover all aspects of Exchange administration and maintenance. This book simply does not have enough pages to do that justice. Instead, for more information concerning Exchange, grab a copy of Jim McBee's* Microsoft Exchange Server 2003 24seven *(Sybex, 2004) or his* Exchange 2000 Server 24seven *(Sybex, 2001).*

Prepping the Forest

Running the Exchange setup program using the ForestPrep switch will modify Active Directory with the attributes and object changes that are necessary for Exchange to work. To perform this step, which is also the first step in the setup of Exchange if you do not use the switch, you must be a member of the Enterprise Admins and Schema Admins groups. If you are not a member of these groups, the install will fail due to the administrator not having the appropriate permissions.

As administrators who are responsible for Active Directory and not Exchange, you will need to interface with the Exchange team in order to gain a good understanding of the changes that will occur to your directory service. You will need to understand the changes that the directory service is going to go through, and you will also require the proper information to enter during ForestPrep.

Once you have the proper information for the Exchange organization, insert the Exchange CD into the CD tray of the domain controller holding the Schema Master role. Alternatively, you could run the Exchange setup program from a network share. No matter which of the options you choose, you should make sure you are running ForestPrep from the Schema Master. If you attempt to run ForestPrep from another system on the network, the Schema Master will still have to be contacted because the changes to Active Directory can be made only on the Schema Master. The network traffic that will occur as ForestPrep is executing on one system and updating the Schema Master could be considerable.

NOTE *If you are not sure which system is the Schema Master, you can use any number of utilities that will tell you. Active Directory Schema snap-in will show you the Schema Master for the forest as will other utilities. See Chapter 17, "Troubleshooting Flexible Single Master Operations Roles," for more information.*

When running ForestPrep for an Exchange 2000 installation, you will need to enter the name of the Exchange organization. While this sounds like an innocuous bit of information, you should be aware that the organization name cannot be changed without uninstalling every Exchange server in the organization. Of course, you can make the change before any Exchange server is installed, but that will require you to run ForestPrep again. Make things easy on yourself, find out the correct information and enter it the first time.

If you want to extend the schema for the Exchange 2000 installation but you do not want to perform any of the other configuration changes or specify the organization name, you can import the schema attributes by following these steps:

1. From the Exchange 2000 Server CD, copy the `schema*.ldf` files from the `Setup\I386\Exchange` directory to a folder on a local drive.

2. Open a command prompt and change directory to the folder where you copied the `ldf` files, and run the command `copy *.ldf exschema.ldf`.

3. Open `exschema.ldf` in a word processor.

4. Replace all instances of `<SchemaContainerDN>` with the full path to your schema naming context. For example, if you were using `zygort.lcl` for your root domain name, you would replace `<SchemaContainerDN>` with `CN=Schema,CN=Configuration,DC=zygort,DC=lcl`.

5. Make sure you are a member of the Schema Admins group and the schema is configured to allow updates. Run the following command from a command prompt: `ldifde -i -f exschema.ldf -s yourservername`. Replace *yourservername* with the name of your domain controller that holds the Schema Master role.

This allows you to replicate the schema changes throughout the forest early in your Active Directory deployment while not having to commit to a specific organization name. This is essentially how Exchange Server 2003 performs when you run ForestPrep. Later, as you need to install Exchange, if you are installing Exchange 2000 Server, you can run ForestPrep to create the organization name. You will not have to go through the trouble of extending all of the schema attributes again. Exchange 2003 Server does not ask for the organization name until the first Exchange server is installed.

TIP *To see the attributes that are added when ForestPrep is run, you can either use ADSI Edit or the Active Directory Schema snap-in and look for attributes that begin with ms-Exch, or you can view each of the* `schema*.ldf` *files on the Exchange CD.*

There are a couple of ways to run ForestPrep. If you are planning to install Exchange 2000 or Exchange Server 2003, you can start ForestPrep using the `/forestprep` switch with the setup program from the CD or the network share from which you are installing. The command used is *<drive>*:`\setup\i386\setup.exe /forestprep`. Exchange Server 2003 has a new program, Exdeploy, that you can run, and it will start ForestPrep with a click of the mouse. Figure 6.1 shows the Forest-Prep option when using Exdeploy.

Once setup starts with the ForestPrep switch, you will have the opportunity to choose the partition where files will be copied. Notice that the option for ForestPrep, as seen in Figure 6.2, shows up as the action you are performing. If that does not appear, you either haven't specified the ForestPrep switch or you mistyped the command.

FIGURE 6.1

Exchange Server 2003 Exdeploy Wizard used to start ForestPrep

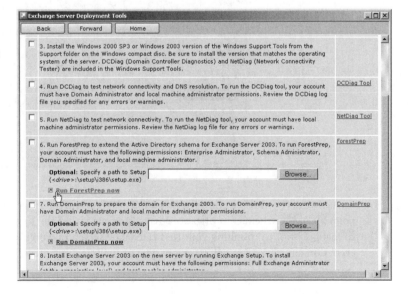

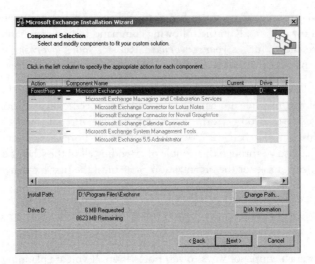

Once you start ForestPrep, you will see a progress screen like the one in Figure 6.3. Notice the
warning "This may take several minutes." Depending on the speed of the system, and whether or not
you are running ForestPrep on the Schema Master, ForestPrep could indeed take a very long time.

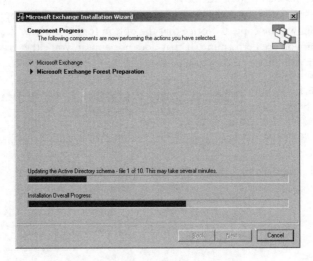

As soon as ForestPrep completes, you will see a completion page like the one in Figure 6.4. At this
point all of the schema modifications have been made and the forest is almost ready to take on
Exchange. Prior to installing your first Exchange server, however, you should run DomainPrep in
every domain where you will have any type of mail-enabled accounts. Before running DomainPrep,

allow the schema changes a chance to replicate to all of the domain controllers throughout the forest so that DomainPrep will run without failing.

NOTE *See Chapter 13, "Troubleshooting Active Directory Replication," for information about how to verify that replication has completed on all domain controllers.*

FIGURE 6.4

ForestPrep
summary page

Prepping the Domains

This next step, DomainPrep, is required so that every domain has the appropriate groups to allow Exchange the ability to interact correctly with Active Directory. When you run DomainPrep, you will not have to wait nearly as long as you did for ForestPrep. Where ForestPrep needs to validate all of the changes made to the schema, DomainPrep merely creates a couple of new groups and assigns permissions to them.

Just as you did with ForestPrep, you can run the setup program using the `/domainprep` switch. However, you must be a member of the Domain Admins group to perform a DomainPrep. If you are installing the first Exchange server into the domain and you are a member of the Domain Admins group, you do not have to run DomainPrep by itself. However, if the staff members responsible for installing and maintaining Exchange are different than the Active Directory staff, you will need to have a domain administrator run DomainPrep.

Once you run DomainPrep, you will have the opportunity to choose the partition where the changes will occur. Notice that the option for DomainPrep, as seen in Figure 6.5, shows up as the action you are performing. If that does not appear, either you haven't specified the DomainPrep switch or you mistyped the command.

After you specify the options that you want to use, you will briefly see the progress page, as seen in Figure 6.6, and then the summary page will appear. That is it; nothing else needs to be performed in order to allow the accounts within the domain to be included in the Exchange system.

FIGURE 6.5
DomainPrep option
screen

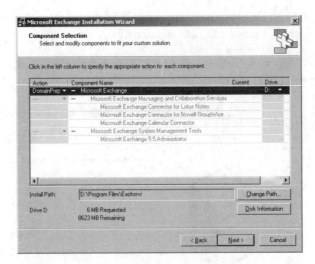

FIGURE 6.6
Progress screen for
DomainPrep

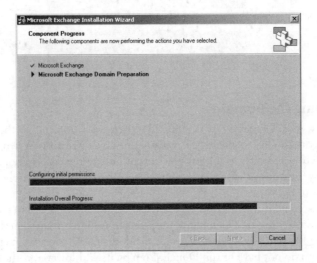

Although DomainPrep appears to have performed its job very quickly, it configures some very important updates. A noticeable update is the inclusion of two new groups to the domain: a global security group, Exchange Domain Servers, and a domain local security group, Exchange Enterprise Servers. As soon as these two groups are created, the Exchange Domain Servers global security group is added to the Exchange Enterprise Servers domain local security group. Later, as the Recipient Update Service (RUS) runs, the Exchange Domain Servers global groups from the other domains in the forest will automatically be added to the Exchange Enterprise Servers group and the Exchange Domain Servers global group from this domain will be added to the Exchange Enterprise Servers groups in all of the other domains.

Another function of DomainPrep is to assign the appropriate permissions and rights to the Exchange Enterprise Servers domain local group. The Manage Auditing And Security Log right is assigned, and full read and right permissions are granted to the AdminSDHolder Active Directory system object. Finally, the Microsoft Exchange System Objects container is created at the root of the domain's domain naming context.

While this sounds like it is a lot of work to go through just to allow the Exchange server to interoperate within the Exchange organization, you should know that for security purposes, each Exchange server uses a local system account instead of a service account. In order for all of the Exchange servers to interoperate, the Exchange Domain Servers and Exchange Enterprise Servers groups are used to allow them to authenticate properly to one another.

NOTE   *You will need to run DomainPrep in every domain where you have users, contacts, or groups that will use an Exchange server for e-mail, even if the Exchange server is located in another domain.*

Creating Administrative Groups

Once you have prepped the forest and each domain, you will have the ability to configure some of the Exchange properties prior to adding an Exchange server to the infrastructure. Having this ability comes in very handy when you are designing how the Exchange servers will be administered. Each Exchange server will have to become a member of an administrative group within the Exchange organization. Once added to an administrative group, the only way for an Exchange server to move into another administrative group is to uninstall Exchange from the computer and reinstall.

Fortunately, the ability to create an administrative group for your Exchange servers exists as soon as the schema has been extended to include the Exchange attributes. You can install only the Exchange management tools to a Windows XP Professional workstation with SP1 or later installed, any Windows 2000 Server with SP3 or later installed, or any Windows Server 2003 server. Once installed, you can use the Exchange System snap-in to create the appropriate administrative groups to host the Exchange Servers.

Automatic Display Name Generation

This is a topic that comes into play for Exchange administration and is also something you should consider for any Active Directory installation. When a user account is created, the display name for the user that appears in all of the utilities is automatically generated from the combination of the First and Last name fields of the user's account. The default display name is generated in the form *Firstname Lastname.* If you are like most administrators that I have met, you will not like searching for names that show up with the first name first. Instead, most of us are familiar with looking up names like we do in a telephone book, *Lastname, Firstname.* This will make finding users easier within the administrative tools, and users will not be as disgruntled when they search for names in address lists.

The utility that you will have to become familiar within in order to make the change is ADSI Edit. You will need to load the support tools onto the system in order to have access to this utility. Windows 2000 Server has a utility within the Support Tools menu for ADSI Edit, Windows Server 2003 includes it as an MMC snap-in.

NOTE   If your language locale is English, you are going to use the code 409. If not, you will need to determine what your language code is.

No matter which version you are using, you need to open ADSI Edit and connect to the Configuration container. Once there, you will need to locate `cn=DisplaySpecifiers,cn=409,cn=User-Display` and open its properties. With the properties open, click on the dialog box for Select A Property To View and choose CreateDialog, as seen in Figure 6.7. In the Edit Attribute box, type **%<sn>, %<givenName>** and then click OK. Do note that the entry you make here is case sensitive.

FIGURE 6.7
ADSI Edit used to change user's display name

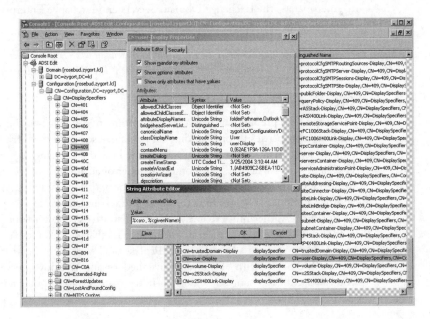

You can follow the same steps to change how the display names for contacts are generated. The only thing you will need to change is the attribute within ADSI Edit to `cn=DisplaySpecifiers,cn=409,cn=Contact-Display`. Again, if your language is not English, change the 409 code to your language code.

Names already entered within Active Directory will not be changed when you apply this fix. You will need to either change them manually to reflect the new naming standard or use a script to change them. If you want to see a script that will perform the task for you, check out this web page: `http://www.somorita.com/Exchange2000/ChangingDisplayNamesinActiveDirectory.doc`.

Extended Attributes

Once you have extended the schema to support Exchange, there will be 15 new attributes that you can use to populate with information that doesn't fit within any other attribute field. The best part is, you will not have to add your own attributes to Active Directory in order to have a special field that wasn't covered by Microsoft's development staff.

The problem is, these attributes don't have very pretty names. They are named extensionAttribute1 through extensionAttribute15. Luckily, you can use ADSI Edit to change the display name to something a little more meaningful to your organization. To make the change to the display name, you will need to be a member of the Schema Admins group. Just follow these steps:

1. Connect to the Schema container with ADSI Edit.

2. Find the CN=ms-Exch-Extension-Attribute-# attribute, and open the properties of the attribute. (Replace # with the attribute number you are changing.)

3. In the Select Which Properties To View dropdown list, select Both, as seen in Figure 6.8.

4. In the Select A Property To View dropdown list, select LDAPDisplayName.

5. Enter the new display name in the Edit Attribute text box.

FIGURE 6.8
ADSI Edit used to change a custom attribute display name

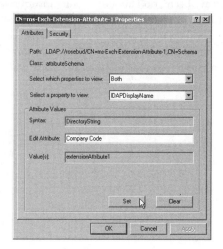

Once changed, the attribute's new display name will replicate to all of the domain controllers within the forest and can be easily identified for all who have the permission to see it.

Best Practices for Design

Exchange Server has found its way into many organizations due to the robust nature of this e-mail server. In order to use is effectively, you should plan for the roll-out of the servers, and you should also anticipate the affect it will have on your Active Directory. The following is a brief run-down of the best practices you should take into consideration when introducing Exchange in to your Active Directory infrastructure.

◆ Run ForestPrep and DomainPrep early in the Active Directory deployment.

◆ Run ForestPrep on the domain controller holding the Schema Master role.

- Use the `ldifde` command line tool to add the schema attributes to Active Directory in a Windows 2000–based domain so that you will not have to identify the organization name.

- Allow the new attributes to replicate before running ForestPrep or trying to install the first Exchange server in a domain.

- Change the automatic display name generation early in the Active Directory deployment so that accounts are created with a display name in the *Lastname, Firstname* format.

- Change the 15 custom attributes so that they have an easily identifiable display name.

Next Up

We are going to move on to hardware sizing recommendations for domain controllers and Global Catalogs. Microsoft has always been good about releasing information regarding the minimum system requirements needed to install their operating systems and software, but the minimums are just enough to get them installed and do not guarantee that the software will run efficiently. Lately, they have also been handing out hardware recommendations to support their operating systems and software. We will take a look at those recommendations and what you should do to see just what your hardware should be.

chapter 7

Hardware Sizing and Placement

WELCOME TO THE TOPIC that causes more consternation than nearly any other. Any instructor will tell you that their first reaction is to cringe when they are approached with the question "How big should my server be?" Server size is not a simple concept to nail down. Every company is different, and no matter how hard Microsoft tries to clump companies into specific categories, you must perform some testing against hardware to determine what you will need for your environment.

Throughout this chapter, we are going to look at the sizing recommendations that Microsoft has set forth; however, the majority of the chapter will be spent discussing the placement options you will have when deploying your domain controllers and Global Catalog servers. Your design will also need to include the placement of the Master Operations roles for the forest and each domain. For your Active Directory infrastructure to perform optimally, you should know where to place each of these roles.

Determining Domain Controller Specifications and Placement

Domain controllers are probably the single most important server type within your organization. Without them, you would not have a nice unified database that holds the objects used for authentication, stores application information, and provides centralized security control.

To have this functionality available to users, you need to determine where you will place domain controllers within your environment. This includes the domain controllers you will use primarily for authentication purposes, those designated as Global Catalog servers, and those that hold the Master Operations roles. You can start choosing the hardware you will use for a domain controller and then base the number of domain controllers required for each site on the hardware, or you can determine how many domain controllers and Global Catalog servers you would like to locate at each site and determine the hardware you will need to support the design.

Determining Domain Controller Specifications

Although it is best to test the hardware you would like to use as domain controllers to determine how they perform when they are supporting users, some general guidelines (see Table 7.1) can give you an idea of how many domain controllers you will need to support your infrastructure. The values you find on the following pages are according to Microsoft's calculations. I included them for a reference because many companies continue to use their existing hardware instead of purchasing new systems. As a rule of thumb, always test your hardware before implementing a system. Newer processors, bus speeds, memory speeds, and drive subsystems work more efficiently than the older technologies. As with anything, your mileage may vary.

TABLE 7.1: PROCESSOR AND MEMORY SPECIFICATIONS FOR DOMAIN CONTROLLERS

NUMBER OF USERS	PROCESSOR(S)	MEMORY
1–499	Single 866Mhz or faster	512MB
500–1,499	Dual 899Mhz or faster	1GB
1,500+	Quad 899Mhz or faster	2GB

If you use Table 7.1 to determine how many domain controllers are required to support a campus of 11,200 users and the hardware the company wants to purchase for domain controllers has dual 2000MHz processors with 1GB of RAM each, then you would need to have at least eight domain controllers. With the faster processors that you have included within the system, you will probably be able to exceed the recommendations in Table 7.1, but the memory or network subsystems may be your bottleneck. Again, your best bet is to test the hardware that you plan on using to see what type of performance you can get out of it.

As far as the amount of drive space you will need to support your domain controller goes, there are also guidelines you can follow. For every 1,000 users, you will need 0.4GB of disk space. For 11,200 users, you will need approximately 4.5GB of disk space.

As a rule of thumb, if the domain controller is also used as a Global Catalog server, you will need to have enough drive space to support half of the drive space requirements from each of the other domains. In a scenario where a company may have three domains—DomainA with 10,000 users, DomainB with 18,000 users, and DomainC with 4,000 users—the space requirements for each of the domains would work out as shown in Table 7.2.

TABLE 7.2: GLOBAL CATALOG DRIVE SPACE REQUIREMENTS

DOMAIN	DOMAIN REQUIREMENTS (# USERS/1,000 * .4)	TOTAL SPACE REQUIRED (DOMAIN + (TOTAL OF OTHER DOMAINS /2))
DomainA	4GB	8.4GB
DomainB	7.2GB	10GB
DomainC	1.6GB	7.2GB

You will need additional drive space for the transaction logs that are generated as the domain controller performs its functions. All transactions that occur on the domain controller are performed in memory. These transactions are written sequentially to the transaction logs so that the data is safeguarded in case the domain controller fails before the transaction is committed to the database.

Once you have determined what the server specifications for your domain controllers should be, you need to determine where they will be located. In the following section, you will find the reasons for locating domain controllers in sites and what happens when a domain controller is not located in a user's site.

Choosing Domain Controller Placement

Choosing where domain controllers will be placed can be difficult. You should take several things into consideration before deciding to place a domain controller at a location. Security, replication traffic, and user authentication should all be taken into account. When determining the placement at the design phase, some questions will help you determine in which site the domain controller should be placed.

Will the domain controller be physically secure at the location?   If the domain controller will not be locked away, the computer could be physically attacked and the drives containing the database could be compromised. In some small organizations, this consideration may not be as important as in large companies, but it should be considered nonetheless.

Can the domain controller be administered by local staff?   If the staff members from the location do not have the ability to manage the domain controller, will you be able to provide remote access capabilities to the domain controller? Built-in tools allow an administrator to manage the domain controller remotely, and you need to determine if having those tools loaded is worth the trade-off of having the domain controller located at another location where it can be managed by local administrators. Make sure that your network infrastructure will allow you to connect to the remote servers because firewalls and connectivity issues could limit your access to the domain controllers.

Is the WAN link reliable?   If the link is not reliable enough, you need to determine if you can get by without a domain controller for the site. I recommend that you do not allow a site to be left without a domain controller if the WAN link is unreliable. However, if security concerns are greater than the users' ability to authenticate for a short period of time, or if the user base is small enough that you cannot justify the cost of a domain controller, you may choose to have them authenticate to a domain controller in another site away from the users.

If you are allowing authentication across the WAN link, is the logon performance acceptable?
If it is, you should be able to host a site without a dedicated domain controller. However, if users complain about logon times, consider moving the domain controller to their site so that they can authenticate more efficiently. You may have to consider a trade-off between local authentication and replication traffic. Replication traffic in large domains or domains that have many Active Directory updates could consume too much of the available bandwidth. If the logon traffic is less than the replication traffic, it may make more sense to locate the domain controller so that it is not within the site.

You may encounter cases when domain controllers from the forest root will be placed within a site even though users from the forest root will not be authenticating within that site. If resources are located in another domain, having a domain controller from the forest root in the same site as the users will alleviate some of the WAN traffic caused by the Kerberos ticket passing that occurs. Of course, creating a shortcut trust between the domains that are affected may be a more efficient solution in a small environment, but locating a forest root domain controller within the site will alleviate traffic and the need for multiple shortcut trusts if the users are accessing several domains.

After determining where the domain controllers should be placed, you should determine where Global Catalog servers are needed. The following section details the reasons for having a Global Catalog in a site.

Choosing Global Catalog Placement

Global Catalog servers provide functionality to users as well as applications within the domain. Global Catalog servers are responsible for collecting information about the objects that exist in the domain partition of other domains in the forest. Although this is just a subset of the attributes for the objects, this could still be a considerable amount of information. Once a domain controller is specified as a Global Catalog server, additional replication will occur so that information from the other domains will populate the database. You need to determine if this additional replication is going to affect the performance of the network links.

When determining if you should have a Global Catalog server placed within a site, you should consider how much the Global Catalog server will be used and whether applications within the site need to use a Global Catalog server. The following questions should be asked to determine whether or not a Global Catalog should be placed within a site.

Are any applications, such as Exchange 2000 Server or Exchange Server 2003, located within the site? If this is the case, you will want to locate a Global Catalog server within the same site as the application because the LDAP queries being posted to the Global Catalog server will probably consume more bandwidth than replication. Test the network requirements to determine which will consume more bandwidth. If the WAN link is not 100 percent reliable, you should always have the Global Catalog server local, otherwise the application will not function properly when the link goes down.

Do you have more than 100 users located within the site? If you have more than 100 users within a site, you will need to determine if stranding them without having the ability to access a Global Catalog server if the WAN link goes down is an acceptable option. You will also need to determine if the query latency is worth the cost savings of keeping the Global Catalog server at another location and not dedicating hardware for the site in question.

Is the WAN link 100 percent available? If you do need application support and the user base is less than 100 users, you could have those users access a Global Catalog server in the remote site if the WAN link is reliable. Although no WAN link will ever be 100 percent available, the higher the reliability of the link, the better your chances of being able to support the user base from a remote site. If the WAN link is not always available and no other applications rely on the Global Catalog server, you could implement universal group membership cacheing to alleviate some of the problems associated with user authentication.

Are there many roaming users who will be visiting the site?   If many roaming users will be logging on at the site, you will want to locate a Global Catalog server within the site. Whenever a user logs on, the user's universal group membership is retrieved from the Global Catalog server. However, if the user population at the site is relatively static, you may be able to implement universal group membership cacheing on a domain controller.

One of the new features of Windows Server 2003 is universal group membership cacheing. This feature is available only when the domain is in the Windows 2000 Native Mode or a higher functional level, and only Windows Server 2003 domain controllers provide this functionality. The benefit of using universal group membership cacheing is that a domain controller does not have to be made a Global Catalog server in order to provide the user with their universal group membership, which is required to log on. As users authenticate, the domain controller contacts a Global Catalog server from another site to retrieve the required information. The group membership is then cached on the domain controller ready to be used the next time the user logs on. Because the domain controller does not have to provide Global Catalog services, replication across the WAN link is reduced.

You can control whether or not universal group membership cacheing is used on a site-by-site basis. You do not have to turn it on for every site within the domain or forest. Universal group membership cacheing is not meant for sites with large user populations, nor is it meant to be used where applications such as Exchange need to access a Global Catalog server. A maximum of 500 users is supported using this cacheing method. Also, each domain controller within a site that is configured to use universal group membership cacheing will only update its cached data once every 8 hours. If you are planning on performing group membership changes on a regular basis, your users may not receive those changes in a timely manner. You can reduce the timeframe for updating the cache, but in doing so you will be creating more replication traffic on your WAN link. Make sure you weigh the trade-offs before you decide where you will place a Global Catalog server.

Sizing and Placement Made Simple

Microsoft has made available a sizing and placement tool that will aid you when trying to determine how many domain controllers you will need and the placement of each domain controller. If you don't want to use any of the calculations that I have provided up to this point, you can download the Active Directory Sizer utility and use it instead. I didn't mention it earlier in the chapter because I wanted you to understand how server sizing and placement options are selected. Using the Active Directory Sizer, you will be able to determine how many domain controllers you will need, along with which of those domain controllers will be Global Catalog servers and bridgehead servers for sites. It will not, however, tell you where you need to place your Master Operations roles. I will discuss where you should place them in the next section.

To access the Active Directory Sizer, you simply download it from the Microsoft website (`http://www.microsoft.com/windows2000/techinfo/planning/activedirectory/adsizer.asp`). The download consists of a file called `setup.exe`. Rename it to something more descriptive, such as `adsizer.exe`, so that you will know what it is later on when you are going through your files.

The first time you run the Active Directory Sizer after you have installed it, you will be presented with the splash screen in Figure 7.1. To enter information about your Active Directory infrastructure, choose New from the File menu and start inputting data into the wizard. You may be unsure of some criteria as you enter the data. "Guestimates" are allowed, but make sure you base every estimate on valid criteria. For instance, you will be asked the average logon rate per second during peak hours. If you are unsure of this number, you can use the legitimate Estimate Logon Rates check box, as seen in Figure 7.2.

FIGURE 7.1
Active Directory
Sizer

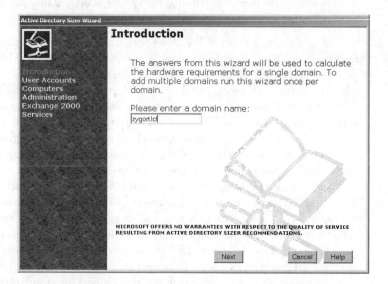

FIGURE 7.2
Estimating
Logon Rates

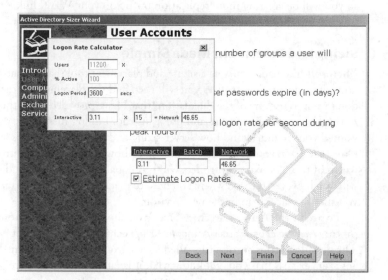

Once you have entered all of the information into the Active Directory Sizer, you will be presented with recommendations as to how many domain controllers, what type of domain controller they should be, and a list of locations for each. While using the wizard, you were probably not able to enter all of the information you have concerning sites and domains within your infrastructure. Never fear, you have the ability to modify those items now.

Chances are you will have additional sites that you want to add. To do so, right-click on Site Configuration and choose Add Site. Specify the site name and optionally the IP address. Once the site is added, right-click on the site and choose Distribute Users. From here, you can select the site from which you want to move users and then select the site to which you are going to move the users. Enter the number of users to move, as seen in Figure 7.3, and then click OK.

FIGURE 7.3

Distributing Users

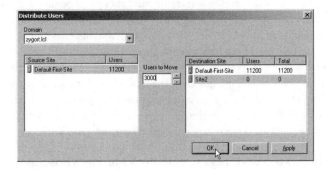

Once you have added all of the sites and distributed the users accordingly, you will be presented with the recommendations for your domain controllers. Note that some sites will show only a bridgehead server, while other sites may show domain controllers, Global Catalog servers, and bridgehead servers. Because all of the servers shown in the Active Directory Sizer are domain controllers, only those with the special roles are listed as not simply domain controllers. Global Catalog servers are domain controllers that have been identified as Global Catalog servers. Bridgehead servers perform the functions of a Global Catalog server and bridgehead server for the site.

A drawback to this tool is that it was created with Windows 2000 in mind and has not been updated for Windows Server 2003. Due to this lack of updating, you will find that the server hardware sizing options are limited to older processor types. If you took issue with the sizing recommendations that I presented earlier, you may find that you are generating your data using the same criteria when using this tool.

Manufacturers of server equipment sometimes provide their own server sizing utilities. When you are preparing to purchase new hardware, consult the sales representative or the company's website to determine whether they provide a sizing solution for their hardware. You might find that they have kept their recommendations more up-to-date than Microsoft has.

Another Active Directory technology whose location needs to be determined is the Master Operations roles. Because only specific servers support the Master Operations functions, you should know the criteria for their placement.

Choosing Master Operations Placement

Due to the importance of the master operations, you should carefully choose where the domain controllers holding each of these roles are placed. The following sections discuss what guidelines you should take into consideration.

OPERATIONS MASTERS IN A SINGLE DOMAIN FOREST

Within a single domain forest, the Infrastructure Master does not play a very important role. As a matter of fact, its services are not used at all. Because you will not have any remote domains for the Infrastructure Master to compare domain information to, it will not matter if the domain controller is a Global Catalog server or not. In fact, in a single domain environment, all domain controllers could be enabled as Global Catalog servers because there will be no additional replication costs.

By default, the first domain controller within the domain will hold all of the Master Operations roles and will also be a Global Catalog server. You should also designate another domain controller as a standby server. You do not have to configure anything special on this domain controller. Just make sure that all administrative personnel are aware of your preference to use a specific server as the standby in case the first fails. Then, if a failure of the first server does occur, you can quickly seize the master operations on the second server. Make sure that the two systems are located close to one another and connected via a high-speed connection. You could even create connection objects between the two systems so that they replicate directly to one another, ensuring that their directories are as identical as possible.

OPERATIONS MASTERS SITE PLACEMENT IN A MULTIPLE DOMAIN FOREST

The five Master Operations roles will have to be placed on domain controllers where they will be the most effective. You should take certain criteria into consideration when you are deciding on which site these domain controllers will be placed.

Schema Master

The Schema Master role, of which there is only one per forest, is not one that is used very often. Typically, the only time the Schema Master needs to be online after the initial installation of Active Directory is when you are making changes to the schema. When you are planning the placement of the Schema Master, place it in a site where the schema administrators have easy access to it. Also take into consideration the replication that will be incurred when a change is made. For this reason alone you may want to place the Schema Master within a site that has the most domain controllers within the forest.

Domain Naming Master

As with the Schema Master, the Domain Naming Master is not used very often, and it is also a forest-wide role. Its role is to guarantee the uniqueness of domain names within the forest. It is also used when removing domains from the forest. For the Domain Naming Master to perform its function, you should locate it on a Global Catalog server, although with Windows Server 2003 this is not a requirement as it was in Windows 2000.

The Domain Naming Master and the Schema Master can be located on the same domain controller because neither of the roles will impact the way the domain controllers function. As with the Schema Master, the Domain Naming Master should be located where the administrative staff can access it.

Relative Identifier (RID) Master

The RID Master is responsible for generating and maintaining the RIDs used by the security principles within the domain. Each domain controller will contact the RID Master to obtain a group of RIDs to be used as the accounts are created. If your domain is in native mode or higher, you should place the RID Master in a site that has domain controllers where administrators are creating a majority of the accounts for its domain. This will allow the RID master to efficiently hand out allocations of RIDs to the domain controllers. If your domain is in mixed mode, consider placing the RID Master on the same server as the PDC emulator from its domain. The PDC emulator is the only domain controller that can create accounts within the domain when the domain is in mixed mode.

Infrastructure Master

The Infrastructure Master holds a very important role within a multiple domain forest. If users from one domain are added to the membership of groups from a second domain, the Infrastructure Master is then responsible for maintaining any updates when changes occur within the remote domain.

For instance, if a user from DomainA is added to a group in DomainB, and the user's name changes because she gets married, the user account name in DomainA does not match the entry within the group membership of DomainB. The Infrastructure Master is responsible for reviewing the information from Domain A and checking for discrepancies. If it finds that a change has been made, the Infrastructure Master updates the information in DomainB so that the new name information within the group can be replicated to all of the domain controllers.

If the infrastructure master is located on a Global Catalog server, it will check for differences between DomainA and DomainB, but it will not notice any discrepancies because the Global Catalog server hosts information from DomainA. Other servers that are not Global Catalog servers in DomainB will not have the correct information for the group, and the infrastructure master will not update the other domain controllers. So, in a multiple domain forest, move the Infrastructure Master to a domain controller that is not a Global Catalog server. Of course, if you make every domain controller a Global Catalog server, you will not have to worry about the Infrastructure Master placement because every domain controller will host information from every domain and replicate changes whenever they are made.

When you are choosing the placement of the Infrastructure Master, place it within a site that also contains domain controllers from the other domains. This ensures that the queries and updates performed are local.

Primary Domain Controller (PDC) Emulator

The other Master Operations role that you need take into consideration is the Primary Domain Controller (PDC) emulator. Whenever Windows NT 4 Backup Domain Controllers (BDCs) exist within the domain, the PDC emulator is responsible for keeping the Windows NT 4 BDCs and all other Windows 2000 Server or Windows Server 2003 domain controllers updated. The PDC emulator is also responsible for accepting password change requests from pre–Active Directory clients. If the domain is placed in Windows 2000 Native Mode or the Windows Server 2003 functional level, the PDC emulator becomes the clearinghouse for password changes within the domain. Any time another domain controller receives a password change from a client, the PDC emulator is passed the change so that the other domain controllers can be notified of the change. If a user has entered a bad password, the PDC emulator is passed the authentication request to validate that the user's password was not changed on another domain controller prior to the authentication request.

Another important function of the PDC emulator is time synchronization. All members of the domain, whether they are running Windows 2000, Windows XP, or Windows Server 2003 as their operating system will synchronize their clocks according to time on the PDC emulator and use the timestamp to authenticate clients. This timestamp is then used with the Kerberos service to authenticate clients.

When deciding the most appropriate site for the PDC emulator role, choose a site that is close to the majority of users within the domain. Also, make sure that domain controllers placed in other sites have reliable links and available bandwidth to support the traffic that will be used by the PDC emulator.

Best Practices for Hardware Sizing and Placement

Using servers that have resources that can support the requirements of the services in use, and have room to grow, will make your network appear to work efficiently, which should keep the users happy. Judicious placement of the domain controllers and the services that they provide will also help maintain an efficient network and allow you to manage your systems with ease. The following best practices should be followed in order to make sure your domain controllers are as efficient as possible:

- Use the Active Directory Sizer for initial design options, and then modify the topology based on your hardware.

- Be generous with your estimation of how many domain controllers you will need when designing the domain controller topology. It is usually cheaper to add additional resources to a system when you purchase it than to add the resources later.

- Do not underestimate the importance of physical security. Even if no one is trying to break into a computer, a user could accidentally unplug the domain controller.

- Allow users to authenticate across a WAN link only if there are very few users in the remote site.

- Use universal group membership cacheing when you have a small user population at the remote site and do not have applications that rely on a Global Catalog server.

- Understand the ramifications of placing the Master Operations roles within a site.

Next Up

As we leave the Design section, we'll move on to troubleshooting Active Directory and the services that support it. Whereas design topics are necessary at the outset of your Active Directory rollout, troubleshooting is an ongoing function. Understanding some of the tools you have to assist you in troubleshooting issues will greatly reduce the amount of time required to get a system up and going again.

Deployment and Migration

part2

In this part:

chapter 8

Deployment

A SOLID DEPLOYMENT PLAN will reduce many of the problems you will encounter during the deployment phase of your Active Directory infrastructure. Understanding the deployment methods and the options you have available to you will help you make the correct decisions for each phase of your deployment plan. This chapter will cover deployment and give you the knowledge to make informed decisions.

As we work through the following chapters, you will find deployment options that are specific to the different upgrade methods that you may be taking on. This chapter is going to focus on the options that are common amongst all of the deployment scenarios. Within this section, you will find naming options and decisions you can make when deciding how your forest root will be created. Then we will discuss the deployment methods that are available to you in the section that follows.

Defining Domain Names

In Chapter 3, "Domain Name System Design," we discussed the name resolution requirements for the Active Directory and network infrastructure design. During the design phase, we need to identify what the domain name will be for each domain in the forest. The Active Directory namespace will follow the DNS namespace. Although Active Directory and the Windows DNS allow for the full Unicode character set, if you require interoperability with other DNS servers, you should make sure you follow the DNS naming standards, which allow only the following characters:

◆ A–Z

◆ a–z

◆ 0–9

◆ hyphen (-)

If the name that is going to be used will be used for an Internet presence, the name will have to be registered. Registering the name with a registrar, such as Network Solutions or any other registrar, guarantees that the name is reserved for that organization; no one else can use the name on the Internet.

If the name is going to be a *local-only name,* meaning that it will be used internally within your organization and not on the Internet, then registration is not required. However, if you think you might eventually need the name for use on the Internet, register it before it is too late.

If you require an Internet presence, you need to choose how you will implement the domain names for internal and external use. Three options exist:

- A domain name that is used for internal and external resources and those resources reside in the same infrastructure

- A domain name that is used for internal resources that is the same as the external resources in different infrastructures

- A domain name that is used for internal resources that is different than the name used for external resources

Of the three, the last option is the easiest to administer. Separating the domain names from the internal and external resources allows you to have internal users accessing resources in both infrastructures without having to perform additional administration. It also allows you to protect internal resources from external users. If the first option is employed, there is a risk that the internal resources could become compromised because they are part of the same domain infrastructure as the external resources. With the second option, additional administrative overhead will occur because the replication of data between the two infrastructures will be necessary for users to access all resources.

The root domain provides the initial Active Directory domain name. This is also the root of the first tree within the forest. Most companies want this tree to define the corporate presence. All of the child domains within this tree off the root share the same namespace as the root domain. With this in mind, you will want to make sure that the name reflects the corporate image. Names should be easy for users to understand and type. Long names are not accepted very easily. Short names are easier to work with and allow you to add additional domains without making an unwieldy namespace.

Identifying the Forest Root Domain

The *forest root domain* is the most important domain within the Active Directory design. Several critical services exist within the forest root. By default, the two forest-wide single master operations exist in this domain: the Schema Master and the Domain Naming Master. The two high-level groups reside here as well: Enterprise Admins and Schema Admins. You must carefully plan the membership of the root domain administrative accounts. Any account that becomes a member of the Domain Admins account in the forest root domain can add other accounts into the Enterprise Admins or Schema Admins groups, thereby giving them ultimate control over the forest.

If a single domain is used for the design, the domain will be the forest root. All of the resources will be organized within this domain and a single domain name is all that is required. It is still imperative that the name is a meaningful name and that the domain be registered in case an Internet presence may be required using that domain name. Internal namespaces that are not seen on the Internet do not have to be registered, however, so you can create a different internal namespace to increase security. When an organization takes advantage of the single domain forest design, the forest owners are the service administrators. In this situation, monitoring of the administrative groups will be a necessity because any domain administrator can modify the membership of the forest-wide service group, Enterprise Admins.

It is possible to build a forest to allow for isolation or autonomy of services or data between organizations or divisions within an organization within the single forest design. Creating domains for each of the units of the organization allows the administrators from each business unit to control their own resources and access to those resources. The forest still needs to have a forest root, and that root contains the service accounts that have control throughout the forest. The decision then becomes, "Who has control over the forest root?" Many companies will create a dedicated forest root, sometimes referred to as a *headless forest root* or an *empty root,* that does not contain any resources or accounts for any of the business units.

This dedicated forest root domain contains only the high-level service accounts and the forest-wide master operations. Using this scenario, the Enterprise Admins and Schema Admins groups will not fall under the control of any organizational domain administrators. Of course, trusted administration staff members still need to have access to the forest root, and those administrators have control over the entire forest. Carefully plan who you will allow to have control over the dedicated forest root domain.

Another benefit to this design is that by its nature, the forest will be immune to organizational changes. Acquisitions and mergers will not drastically alter the forest design. New organizational domains can be added to the forest and will not affect the existing domains. Because all of the domains can interoperate, resource access can be allowed to any account within the forest where necessary.

Deployment Methods

Domain controllers can be deployed in much the same manner as any of your servers within your environment. There are advantages and disadvantages to the methods we are going to look at, and it will be up to you to determine which method will work best within your organization. For small organizations, you may want to stay with the manual setup, described in the next section, whereas administrators of large enterprises will benefit from the speed and efficiency of using an automated setup method.

Manual Setup

Performing a manual setup is the more time-consuming method of installing the operating system for your domain controller. You also run into the "human error" issue; if you enter the wrong information, the domain controller will probably need to be rebuilt. However, with all that being said, in smaller companies, you will find that most of the domain controller builds are performed through a manual install.

To perform the manual install, all you need to do is boot to the Windows 2000 or Windows Server 2003 CD and run the `winnt` command from the `i386` directory. If you are installing the operating system from a network share point, you will need to have a network boot disk available so that you can connect to the distribution share to run the `winnt` command.

TIP   *You can create network boot disks in several different ways, but one of the most efficient is to use Bart's Network Boot Disk creator found at* `http://www.nu2.nu/bootdisk/network/`*.*

The `winnt` command will start with the text mode portion of setup and ask you questions pertaining to the installation location, as well as give you a chance to read the End User License Agreement (EULA). After you have provided the information for your system, files will be copied to your local drive and the system will reboot to start the second part of setup.

TIP *Whether you are performing a CD installation or network installation, make sure that you have* `smartdrive` *loaded from your startup media. This will considerably reduce the time needed to perform the file copy.*

The second phase of setup is the graphical phase. Make sure that you enter all of the networking information correctly at this point. Plus make sure you name the computer correctly. During domain controller promotion, you will need to be able to access a DNS server that has the appropriate records for other domain controllers. If this is going to be the first domain controller, you will need a DNS server in order to register the appropriate SRV records for the domain controller.

Automatic Setup

In larger organizations, administrators will usually opt to install operating systems using another method, one of the automated setup methods. Using an automated method of installing the operating system allows the administrator to work on other issues instead of babysitting a system as it is built. They are usually faster than manual install also.

The three methods of performing an automatic setup include using answer files, Remote Installation Services (RIS), and cloned images. Each has its strong points, and the administrator will decide which will work best in their environment. The following sections describe each one.

ANSWER FILES

An answer file can be used to provide the information that is required during setup. Using an answer file, the administrator can have all of the required parameters saved within the file and will not have to worry about human error when the setup program is running.

To create an answer file, you can use Setup Manager, which is part of the deployment tools that you can find on the Windows 2000 or Windows Server 2003 CD. In order to use Setup Manager, you will need to extract it from the *cd_drive:*`\Support\Tools\deploy.cab` file. When you run this utility, you will be able to create an answer file that will contain all of the required information for setup. Make sure you test it so that you know you have the right settings specified, and then you can use it by issuing one of the following commands:

```
cd_drive:\i386\winnt /s:\cd_drive\i386 /u:filepath\answerfilename.txt
```

or

```
\\network_path\i386\winnt /s:\network_path\i386 /u:filepath\answerfilename.txt
```

For example, if you were to run Setup Manager and save the resulting answer file as `unattend.txt` to a floppy disk for use with a CD-based install, and your CD drive was the E: drive, you would type:

```
E:\i386\winnt /s:E:\i386 /u:A:\unattend.txt
```

If you were starting the setup from a network distribution point and the file is saved within the same distribution point, and you mapped the distribution point as the X: drive, you would type:

```
X:\i386\winnt /s:X:\i386 /u:X:\unattend.txt
```

You can also use Setup Manager to create a file used for a CD setup. If you choose this option, Setup Manager will create a file named winnt.sif and save it to a floppy disk. When the system is booted to the Windows 2000 or Windows Server 2003 CD, the first thing the setup program will attempt is to find the `winnt.sif` file on the floppy disk. If it is there, it will use the information provided to start the setup program. If all of the data is provided, the user performing the install will not have to answer any prompts.

TIP   Make sure that when you are using the winnt.sif file, the system you are installing the operating system on is configured to boot from the CD before the floppy disk. Otherwise, you will receive an error because the floppy disk will not be a bootable disk.

REMOTE INSTALLATION SERVICES (RIS)

Remote Installation Services (RIS) is used to install an operating system from a RIS server without having to use any type of boot disk, either CD or floppy. Instead, a Preboot Execution Environment (PXE)–enabled network card is used to connect directly to the RIS server and initiate the setup.

In order to use RIS, you need to make sure you have a DHCP server and a RIS server authorized within Active Directory. During the installation of the RIS service, you are required to create a Windows 2000 Professional CD-based image on the server. Once that is created, other images can be placed on the RIS server, and answer files can be associated to the images.

NOTE   Unless you are using RIPprep, Microsoft's disk imaging tool that only works with RIS, the "images" that you are creating are actually the setup files for the operating system and the answer files are used to instruct the computer how the operating system will be installed.

CLONED IMAGES

There are several third-party utilities that will create a binary image of a system's hard drive. The image can then be used to build another system that will require the same settings. Domain controllers will typically be built using the same options because they are usually configured to work only as domain controllers.

Before you create the image, you need to make sure that the identifying information from the initial system has been removed. Microsoft includes a utility, `sysprep`, that will remove the computer name and the Security ID (SID) of the computer. When the image is then placed on another system, a new SID is generated and the person starting the computer is requested to provide a new computer name.

WARNING   When imaging the computer, do not promote it to a domain controller. If the computer is promoted, the directory service will be populated. The image of the domain controller will then contain objects that exist at that point in time. While this initially may not seem like a bad thing, some of these objects may be removed over time. If the image is used to build a new domain controller, the objects within the directory service database may have been deleted; however, if the tombstone lifetime has passed, the object will be reintroduced into your domain. At the same time, the replication that occurs when you promote the domain controller may flood your WAN link if another local domain controller is not available.

First Domain Controller

The first domain controller for the forest or for a domain is usually promoted by running through the promotion process manually. The options you choose during promotion of this domain controller will be different than the replica domain controllers for the domain. Once the first domain controller is in place, the rest of the domain controllers will use the same options and can be installed by using an answer file.

NOTE *If you are creating the forest root domain, you will need to have an account with administrator privileges on the computer where you are running Dcpromo.*

The following series of screen shots show the Active Directory Installation Wizard, dcpromo.exe, running and the options you would choose when creating a child domain within the forest zygort.lcl. During the creation of the child domain, the user who is running Dcpromo will need to have an account that is a member of the Enterprise Admins within the forest, or an Enterprise Admin will need to delegate the ability to create child domains to the user. Figure 8.1 shows the domain controller options. To create the child domain, select Domain Controller For A New Domain.

WARNING *Make sure you can connect to the domain controller holding the Domain Naming Master role. If you cannot, promotion of your domain controller will fail because you cannot create a child domain without the consent of the Domain Naming Master.*

TIP *Knowledge Base article Q254185 has more information about "precreating" the CrossRef objects needed to delegate child domain creation to an account that is not a member of the Enterprise Admins group.*

FIGURE 8.1

Choosing to create a domain controller for a child domain

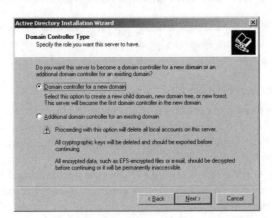

After clicking Next, choose Child Domain In An Existing Domain Tree, as seen in Figure 8.2.

The user who is promoting the domain controller will need to supply credentials in order to add the domain to the domain tree. Figure 8.3 displays this screen. The account that is used at this point will need to either be a member of the Enterprise Admin group or have the appropriate permissions delegated to them.

The parent domain name will need to be entered at this point, as well as the name of the child domain. (See Figure 8.4.)

FIGURE 8.2
Choosing the child domain option

FIGURE 8.3
Providing credentials to add the domain

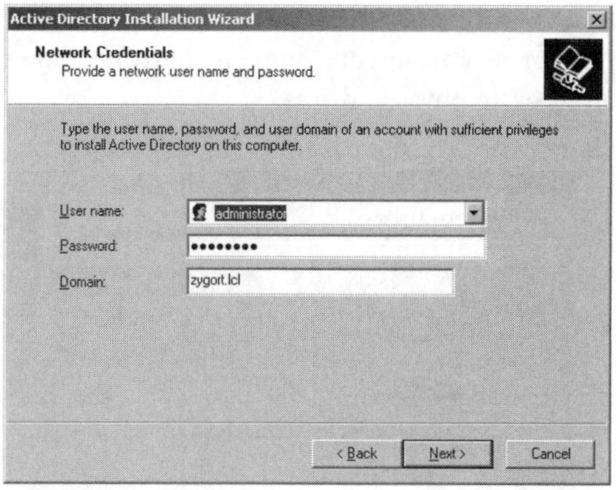

FIGURE 8.4
Providing the domain names

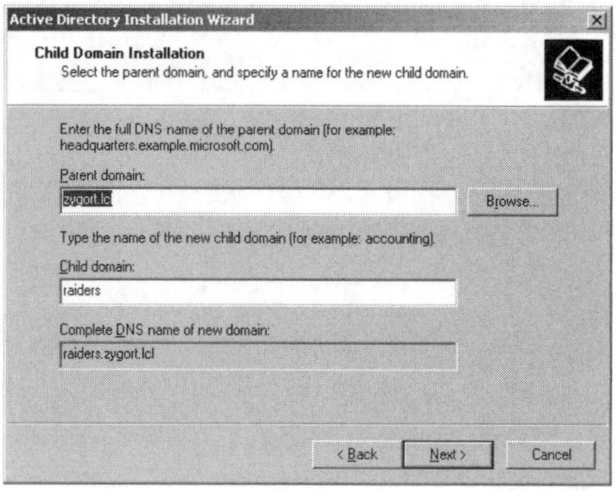

You will also be required to add the NetBIOS name of the domain so that downlevel clients will be able to authenticate to the domain controllers for the new domain. (See Figure 8.5.)

FIGURE 8.5
NetBIOS name

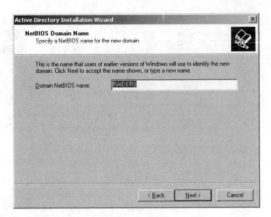

The next screen (see Figure 8.6) allows you to enter the database and log file locations. For best results and better performance from your domain controller, you should consider placing the database and log files on separate physical drives.

FIGURE 8.6
Database and log file locations

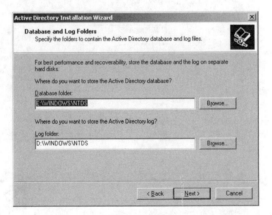

The Sysvol folder holds the group policy templates. A partition formatted with NTFS is required for this folder. (See Figure 8.7.)

FIGURE 8.7
Sysvol folder
location

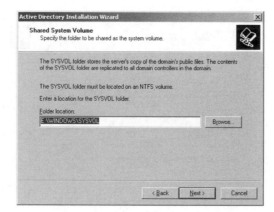

At this point, DNS is checked to make sure that the zone information is valid and dynamic registrations are allowed. If the test completes successfully, you will receive a message similar to Figure 8.8.

FIGURE 8.8
DNS validation

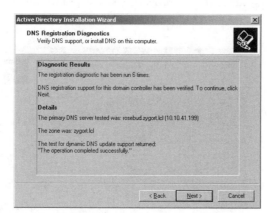

If you have any applications running on your servers that were not written for Windows 2000 or Windows Server 2003, and the application needs to view group membership or have access to resources with elevated privileges that Windows 2000 or Windows Server 2003 do not provide, you may have to select the first option in Figure 8.9. If your applications are certified for either of these operating systems, you can select the second option.

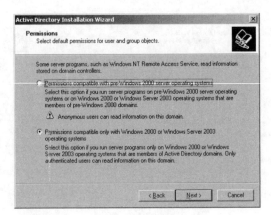

When the directory service needs to be restored, the domain controller will need to be rebooted into Directory Services Restore Mode (DSRM). The directory service is not accessible once you start up in this mode, so a local administrator account is used to safeguard the local directory service database from becoming attacked. You provide the password for this account in the screen found in Figure 8.10.

FIGURE 8.10
Directory Services
Restore Mode
password

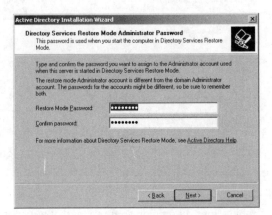

Finally, the summary screen is displayed as seen in Figure 8.11. Review the options you chose, and if everything appears correct, click Next to install Active Directory.

Once the first domain controller is in place, the domain is available and awaiting replica domain controllers, as well as a client to connect to it. In the next section, we will discuss how to create the replica domain controllers.

FIGURE 8.11

Summary screen
for Dcpromo

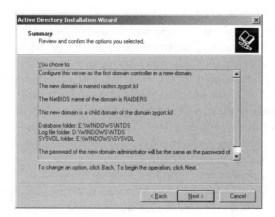

Replica Domain Controllers

You should never have a domain that contains only a single domain controller. To do so would be a suicide move if your domain controller failed and you were unable to restore from backup media. Always have at least two domain controllers, with a preference of having more to reduce the load from the initial two. In a small environment where you are running a single domain, you can probably get by with having two domain controllers. However, in larger domains, you will probably need more than one domain controller to support the larger number of users who will be logging on, and you will probably need to have domain controllers placed in branch offices.

Populating the directory service on a new domain controller needs to be performed as soon as the domain controller comes online if it is to service user requests. The following sections discuss the various methods of populating the directory service.

INITIAL POPULATION

Each of the replica domain controllers within the domain will need to populate the database so that they can perform their functions. Because all of the domain controllers act as peers within the domain, they all need to have the same database information. For the most part, the incremental database updates that occur due to replication are just a small part of the total database. The initial replication of the database to a new domain controller could include a large amount of data. This initial population could strain your network, especially if you are trying to promote a domain controller across a WAN link.

In order to make sure that you do not cause problems on the network when you promote your domain controllers, you need to determine how you will initially populate the directory service database. You have two options: use the network to populate the database or use the System State of an existing domain controller. The following sections will describe these options in better detail.

REPLICATING ACROSS THE NETWORK

This is the only option you have if you are using Windows 2000–based domain controllers. Due to this limitation, you need to determine how you will promote the domain controllers and populate the directory service. Most WAN links will not support the amount of traffic that is incurred when the first domain controller for a site is promoted. Instead of promoting the first domain controller at the site where it will provide its services, you should promote the domain controller in a site with an existing domain controller and then deliver the new domain controller to the site where it will function. This will reduce the amount of WAN traffic you will incur during promotion

The remainder of the domain controllers for the site in question will replicate from domain controllers that exist within the site. This does introduce a few issues that you need to address. When the first domain controller is promoted, the IP address for the domain controller will reflect the site where it is promoted. Once replication has completed, you will need to move the domain controller to the location where it is going to reside. To do so, you need to change the IP address and also make sure that you move the domain controller's computer account to the correct site within Active Directory Sites and Services. Failure to do so will result in an incorrect replication topology. Once you change the location of the domain controller's computer account, the Knowledge Consistency Checker will build the correct connection objects.

USING SYSTEM STATE

If you do not want to inundate your WAN links with replication traffic, or the WAN link does not have enough available bandwidth to support the replication traffic and the current network traffic, you have another option for promoting your Windows Server 2003 domain controllers. Running Dcpromo in advanced mode by using the /adv switch will allow you to use the system state data from another domain controller for the initial population of the directory service database.

In this scenario, you can back up the System State of a domain controller and then deliver the backup media to the remote location where it can be used for the domain controller promotion.

NOTE The System State should be as recent as possible so that you minimize the replication that occurs due to object changes after the System State was backed up. Older copies of the System State may require more replication to bring your new domain controller up-to-date and cause your WAN links to become saturated.

WARNING If your System State is older than the tombstone lifetime, the System State cannot be used.

Prior to using the System State during promotion, you will have to restore the files to the server you are promoting. Figures 8.12 through 8.16 show the screens that appear if you are using the advanced mode of Dcpromo. These are the screens that are different than those we looked at in the previous section. You will find that many of the screens are the same.

You will need to provide the path to the restored files, and this path must be on a local drive.

If you back up the System State from a domain controller that is configured as a Global Catalog server, you will be prompted as to whether you want the new domain controller to also be a Global Catalog server. If not, you can simply deselect the option. Otherwise, all the objects and attributes from the other domains within your forest will be copied to this domain controller also.

If you are copying the Global Catalog data to the server, it is even more imperative that the System State backup is as current as possible. Make sure that all of the replication to the Global Catalog has completed, and then back up the System State.

FIGURE 8.12
Choosing option for replica domain controller

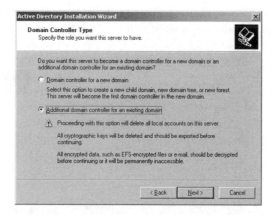

FIGURE 8.13
Entering System State location

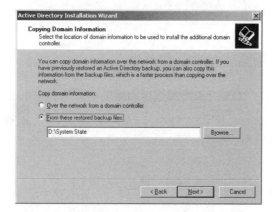

FIGURE 8.14
Specifying the Global Catalog option

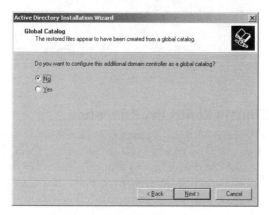

The credentials you provide here will need to be an account that is a domain administrator or that has the appropriate permissions granted to it.

FIGURE 8.15
Providing domain credentials

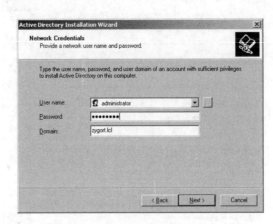

The summary information should now show the options you selected.

FIGURE 8.16
Summary information

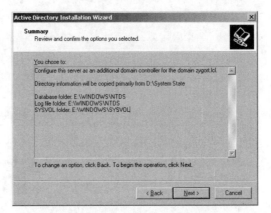

Automating Domain Controller Promotion

After your first domain controller is promoted, the remaining domain controllers for the domain will probably use the same settings when you are promoting them. To make things easy, an answer file can be created so that you do not have to manually enter all of the information into the Dcpromo Wizard for each and every domain controller you build. If you are using an answer file to automate the installation of the operating system, you can include a section within the operating system answer file that will force the system to run Dcpromo with an answer file as soon as the operating system completes its install.

If you like allowing the computer to do all of the work, promoting the domain controller automatically while the computer installation is completing is a wonderful thing. The first thing you need to do is verify that the operating system unattended installation file is working correctly. Then you need to add a new section to the answer file that will allow the domain controller to be automatically promoted, and add another that will automatically log on the administrator so that the promotion can occur.

The first section you need to add is the [DCInstall] section. This section will contain the keys and values that will be used to create an answer file for the promotion. For instance, if you are promoting a domain controller that will be a member of the zygort.lcl domain and you already have other domain controllers in place, you would add the following lines to the answer file:

```
[DCInstall]
UserName=administrator
Passwordpassword
UserDomainzygort
DatabasePath=c:\windows\system32\ntds
LogPath= c:\windows\system32\ntds
SYSVOLPath= c:\windows\system32sysvol
SafeModeAdminPassword=DSRM_password
ReplicaOrNewDomain=Replica
ReplicaDomainDNSName=zygort.lcl
ReplicationSourceDC=rosebud
RebootOnSuccess=yes
```

The entries within this file assume that the administrator name is still administrator, the administrator password is password, and the Directory Services Restore Mode password is DSRM_password.

When the operating system answer file is parsed, the keys and values that are contained within the [DCInstall] section are written to a file $winnt$.inf within the %systemroot%\system32 folder. Although the file is created, it is not used until an administrator account logs on to the server. To make sure that an administrator is the first user to log on, you should configure the automatic administrator logon option. To do so, you can add the [GUIRunOnce] section into the answer file. Two lines will need to be added so that you can allow the Administrator account to automatically log on as soon as the system is rebooted, and also guarantee that this automatic logon will occur only one time.

The entries that need to be added to the answer file will look like the following:

```
[GUInattended]
Autologon = yes
AutoLogoncount = 1
```

When the setup program finishes and the system is rebooted so that the operating system can start, the administrator account is automatically logged on and Dcpromo is started using the options you entered into the answer file. After the information from the $winnt$.inf file is read, the administrator password is removed so that is does not constitute a security risk. However, the answer file will have the administrator password, so you should delete it as soon as possible.

Best Practices for Deployment

A strategic deployment plan will alleviate many of the problems associated with rolling out an Active Directory infrastructure. Don't just rush forward and promote a domain controller without making sure you understand the ramifications of your actions. Some practices you should follow are:

◆ Make sure you follow the naming guidelines for your domains, especially if you have third-party clients or DNS within your environment.

◆ Choose the deployment method that will make the least impact on your network.

◆ When you have several domain controllers to roll out, create an answer file to streamline and automate the process.

◆ Make sure you remove all answer files that contain an administrative password included in them.

◆ Do not use a disk imaging utility to create an image of a domain controller. Make a disk image of the system installation prior to promotion.

Next Up

After taking a look at the deployment options to install the operating system and promote the system to a domain controller, you should have a good feel for how you will perform your domain controller creation. Not every business is created equal, so you should weigh the options that you have and choose the one that will fit your style of administration.

In the next chapter, we are going to take on domain migration and consolidation. While most people consider domain consolidation to be a function of moving from Windows NT to Windows 2000 or Windows Server 2003, it can also be very useful in a move from Windows 2000 to Windows Server 2003.

chapter 9

Domain Migration and Consolidation

MOST ADMINISTRATORS THINK OF migrating from Windows NT 4 domains to Active Directory when domain consolidation is brought up in conversation; however, domain consolidation can also pertain to Windows 2000 and Windows Server 2003 Active Directory domains.

At this point, within the lifetime of Windows NT 4, the support that Microsoft provides is waning. Quite a few companies use Windows NT 4 and several of them are looking at upgrading their infrastructure to use Active Directory. Their existing infrastructure is probably not optimized for administration; it is probably optimized for Windows NT 4 support. If you are planning a migration, you and your administrative staff will need to decide how you will migrate all of your domains into the Active Directory structure. At the same time, you will need to make sure that you are not overloading the domain controllers as they are upgraded. This chapter will address these concerns. In this chapter, we are going to look at the Active Directory Migration Tool (ADMT), which is the primary tool that administrators use when they perform a domain migration or migrate accounts into another domain. You can use other tools, including some from third-party companies; however, Microsoft released a very good utility with the 2.0 version of ADMT.

Keeping Connected

One of the primary concerns when migrating accounts from one domain to another is the ability to access resources using the account once it is in the new domain. This concern stems from the fact that the account will not retain its original SID as it would if the domain were upgraded. As the account migration occurs, a new account is created in the target domain and a new SID is generated for the account. This could give your administrative staff severe headaches as you try to figure out how you will rework access to all of the resources to which the account originally had access.

To alleviate this problem, the ADMT will not only migrate the account, it will copy the account's original SID into the new account's SIDHistory attribute. Active Directory will use the account's new SID and the entries within the SIDHistory attribute when building the access token for the account. However, for the SIDHistory attribute to be available, the target domain for the account must be in

Windows 2000 Native Mode or a higher functional level. If the domain does not meet this requirement, your administrative staff will need to manually grant the account access to the resources.

NOTE *Each SID can exist in the forest as either an entry within an account's primary SID or within the SIDHistory for the account. The same SID cannot exist within two accounts within the same forest.*

Migration Options

When restructuring domains, you will find that you have to migrate more than just the user accounts. Several other components will need to migrate along with the accounts. Service accounts for applications and services, group accounts, user profiles, computer accounts, and trusts will usually migrate as well. The ADMT will allow you to migrate all of these components. As you decide how your new domain structure will be built, you will need to run the ADMT to migrate each of the components to the correct location within the target domain or domains.

Remember that the migration of accounts from domain to domain does not necessarily mean that you are only going to be moving accounts from a Windows NT 4 domain; you could have accounts within other Active Directory domains that you want to move. The primary differences are that when you are migrating from Windows NT 4, the accounts are created within the target domain and the original Windows NT 4 accounts will remain within the source domain—the Active Directory accounts do not. When an account is migrated from one Active Directory domain to another, the account is removed from the source domain; only the migrated account within the target domain will exist.

You will find that there are two types of domains within the Windows NT 4 infrastructure that you will need to migrate. The first is the Account Domain; the other is the Resource Domain. Each of the domains will contain accounts that are used to support the organization, but they will need to be migrated differently, due to the account types and the uses for the domains. Account domains typically are the repositories of user and group accounts. Administrators who are responsible for these domains control the accounts that have access to the resources within the organization.

Resource domains on the other hand host the resources that the users need in order to perform their daily functions. These domains will typically contain very few user and group accounts. Instead, they host the computer accounts and some group accounts that are necessary to give users access to resources and administrators an efficient means of maintaining the resources.

With the previous information in mind, note that you will migrate the two domain types differently. When you are migrating account domains, you will need to migrate service accounts, user accounts, global groups, computer accounts, user profiles, and trust relationships. Resource domains, on the other hand, have fewer components to migrate, and you will probably only need to migrate the computer accounts and shared local groups.

ADMT Interface

At the time this book was published, the latest version Microsoft had released was ADMT Version 2.0. This version was a great improvement over the initial release that was available for Windows 2000. Version 2.0 addresses some of the limitations of the original version, and allows an administrator to migrate nearly every aspect of one domain to another.

To install the ADMT, you can either access it from the i386\ADMT directory on the Windows Server 2003 CD or a network share that hosts the installation files, or you can download it from the Microsoft website. The program is contained within an MSI file called `ADMIGRATION.MSI`. ADMT can be added to any Windows 2000, Windows Server 2003, Windows XP, or Windows NT 4 system.

As you can see in Figure 9.1, the ADMT console is a very unassuming tool. However, as you can also see from the menu that is shown, there are several wizards that you can start. Each wizard will allow you to perform a distinct part of your migration. As you learned in the previous section, you need to migrate specific objects for the account domains and you need to migrate other objects from the resource domains.

FIGURE 9.1
ADMT console

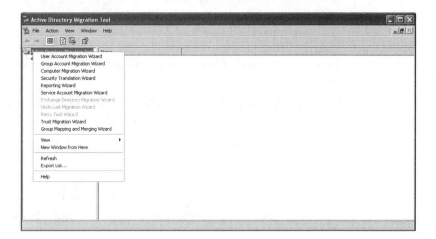

One of the most useful features of the ADMT is the ability to perform a trial migration to determine the impact that it may have on the accounts. From any of the wizards, you can select the Test Migration Settings And Migrate Later option. If everything appears as though it is going to work as you had expected after you perform a trial migration, you can perform a live migration. If the live migration does not go as expected, you can perform a rollback of the migration using the Undo Last Migration Wizard. For each step of your migration, you will want to choose the appropriate wizard. They are summarized here:

User Account Migration Wizard   This wizard migrates the user accounts from the source domain to the target domain. When you are running the wizard, if the target domain is in Windows 2000 Native Mode or higher, the accounts SID from the source domain is added to the SIDHistory of the new account within the target domain

Group Account Migration Wizard   This wizard migrates the group accounts from the source domain to the target domain. As with the User Account Migration Wizard, if the source domain is in Windows 2000 Native Mode or higher, the SIDHistory attribute is populated.

Computer Migration Wizard   This wizard migrates the computer accounts from the source domain to the target domain. Using this wizard will not affect the computer's local SAM database, but it will change the domain membership of the targeted systems. Once the computer is rebooted, it will belong to the new domain and have all the same rights and privileges as any other member of the domain. This wizard will work for member servers and workstations alike.

Security Translation Wizard   This wizard will translate the rights that accounts have on a member server so that the accounts used within the target domain will have the same rights that were assigned within the source domain. This is typically used to allow service accounts to have the same rights to perform system functions.

Reporting Wizard   This wizard will create reports that will help you plan the migration.

Service Account Migration Wizard   This wizard will identify the services that are not using the Local System account so that you will be able to determine which accounts need to be migrated to the target domain. This wizard does not actually migrate the service accounts that are identified; it merely determines the service accounts that need to be migrated. You will be required to migrate the accounts using the User Account Migration Wizard in order to migrate the accounts to the target domain.

Exchange Directory Migration Wizard   This wizard will migrate the Exchange mailboxes from the source domain to the target domain.

Trust Migration Wizard   This wizard will identify the trust relationships that are in place between the domains, and it will allow you to copy the trust if it is still needed after migrating users.

Group Mapping and Merging Wizard   This wizard allows you to merge groups into a single group when you are migrating several domains to a single domain.

Preparing for Migration

You should make sure you have a good migration/consolidation plan before you attempt to migrate objects between domains. This chapter covers migrating Windows NT domains to Active Directory as well as Windows 2000 to Windows Server 2003–based Active Directory domain migration/reconstruction. As we move through the chapter, I will present information specific to the migration type you are attempting, but first we need to cover information that is common to both scenarios.

ADMT Prerequisites

One of the first things you need to determine is which system you will install the ADMT on and run it from. You can install the ADMT on any Window 2000 Professional, Windows XP Professional, Windows 2000 Server, or Windows Server 2003–based system; however, you will want to make sure that you run the utility from the same system each time so that the reports that are generated are consistent. The database that is used during the migration, `protar.mdb`, is not replicated between systems even though it is the database used to generate the reports; therefore, you may not receive a full accounting of the migration if you run AMDT from different systems.

No matter which system you decide to run ADMT from, you will need to make sure that it has good RPC connectivity to all of the domain controllers you are using for the migration. To check RPC connectivity, you can use the RPCPing utility. This is a two-part utility, the server side resides on the system to which you are attempting to connect, and the client side is installed on the system from where you are running the utility. RPCPing will help you determine if RPC communication is working correctly between the two systems.

Trust relationships will need to be created between the source and target domains. Each of the domains will need to trust the other so that the identifying information and object data can be read and processed. The source domain will verify the account that is performing the migration, and the target domain will need to validate the account that is used on the source domain so that it can audit the migration correctly.

As for the user account that is performing the migration, you will need to make sure that it has the correct group memberships. After the trust relationships have been created, you will need to add the migration account to the source domain's Administrators group, as well as make sure that it is a member of a group that has Administrator rights on any computer that is migrated or security is migrated. For the target domain, the migration account needs to be a member of the Domain Admins group.

The domain controller within the target domain that you identify as the target domain controller must have the administrative shares present. Although nearly every domain member will have these available, they can be disabled, so make sure the administrative shares have not been altered.

You will need to make an alteration to the PDC within the source domain to allow for RPC over TCP/IP while preserving the domain controllers security. This can be performed by adding the TcpipClientSupport Registry entry to `HKEY_LOCAL_MACHINE\System\CurrentControlSet\Control\Lsa` on the PDC and giving it a value of **1**.

Both domains are required to audit the migration. To do so, you will need to enable the success and failure auditing of group management on the source domain and the success and failure of account management on the target domain. A special group named *source_domain*$$$ will need to be created so that the auditing of SIDHistory attributes can be performed. For example, if we were migrating accounts from the Windows NT 4–based domain `BLOOMCO` to the Active Directory domain `zygort.lcl`, the group would be named `zygort$$$`.

WARNING *Do not add any accounts to the source_domain$$$. Doing so will cause SIDHistory migration to fail.*

If you are using an account with the appropriate permissions within both domains and on all servers, and you have not correctly configured all of the settings, ADMT will give you an error when you run ADMT for the first time. You might not need to stop, however. If you did not create the *source_domain*$$$ group, did not set the TcpipClientSupport Registry entry, or did not enable auditing in either of the domains, ADMT will do it for you. ADMT will not create the trust relationships between the domains, nor will it add your account into the appropriate groups so that you have the correct level of permissions—but it will do the "little things" for you.

The Rollback Plan

The rollback plan is a must for any organization that wants to make sure they have a means of recovering their original domain in case the migration or consolidation fails miserably. The best way to ensure that you have a way to return to the original directory service is to take a BDC offline and lock it away. Doing so will give you a system that is configured with the settings and account information that existed prior to any migration attempts.

At the same time you should make sure that you have valid backups of all of your important systems. During a migration you will be able to access any of your systems as if you were still within the original domain configuration. However, if a catastrophe strikes, you will want to make sure you can return to your original domain structure. This is easier said than done if you are in week 5 of your consolidation, but having a backup plan at the start of your migration or consolidation will ease your worries some.

Profile Migration

This is a topic that is the subject for much debate. If you are using roaming profiles, you will have a much easier time with user profiles than if you are using local profiles. Roaming profiles reside on servers within your organization. As you migrate users from one domain to another, as long as you are taking advantage of the SIDHistory, the users' profiles will be available to them the next time they log on. This is due to the fact that SIDHistory will reflect the appropriate SID to allow a user access to his or her profile.

Local profiles can be problematic, however. You will need to determine if you are going to migrate the users' profiles or if you will use a new profile next time they log on. System policies under Windows NT 4 did not have a lot of flexibility or options to control the user's environment. Using Group Policies within an Active Directory domain, the administrator can control nearly every aspect of the user's environment. You need to make a decision on whether you need to keep the user's original profile or you are going to control it using GPOs. Sometimes, it does not make sense to attempt a migration of profiles if you are going to lock down the profile.

Migration Order

Sit down at a table and look at your existing domain structure and ask yourself, "Where do I begin?" Look at your organization's needs to determine where you may need to start. Applications that require Windows 2000 or Windows Server 2003 or that require Active Directory to function may force you to upgrade those domains first. If your company has decided that Exchange Server 2000 or 2003 is the direction the message system is going, you will have to implement Active Directory. Decide whether you will upgrade a domain to support the application or build a new Active Directory forest and migrate users.

Another option is to upgrade the domain with the most users and then migrate users from the other source domains into the newly upgraded target domain. Upgrading a domain will allow you to retain the original accounts without having to use a utility such as ADMT in order to retain the SID of the accounts. The remainder of the domains that you are planning to migrate should be determined by the application access needs the accounts have and the priority you determine for the accounts. You will probably have several meetings to determine the migration order, so make sure that everyone involved understands the ramifications of using any of the migration tools.

NOTE   *For information about migration order of account and resource domains, see the section "Migrating from Windows NT 4" later in this chapter.*

Prior to migrating any accounts, you should create a test account to use for a test migration. Add the account to a group that has access to resources within one of the source domains and then attempt the migration. Once the migration of the test account is complete, log in with the test account and verify that the migration worked as anticipated. If the migration did not complete as you had planned, check out the reports to determine the problem. This will save you the embarrassment of having everything ready to go and the migration failing.

Maintaining Unique Accounts

If you have several domains that you are consolidating into a single domain, you may find that you have duplicate account names. This could be especially problematic if you have acquired or merged companies and there are identically named user accounts. Group accounts could also pose this same problem for you. As you plan out your migration strategy, determine how you will handle duplicate names. For groups, you can rename the group with a prefix or suffix. User accounts can be more difficult to work with though. Users have grown accustomed to their user accounts and don't take kindly to using a new account name after the migration. If you do have to rename user accounts when you migrate, make sure that you mitigate the problems by training the users and preparing them for the changes.

Verifying Account Status

One of the most common problems within an organization's directory service is having accounts that are no longer used, yet they still exist within the directory. These accounts take up space within the directory service database and the backup tapes. Before you extend the same problems to Active Directory, you should identify the accounts that are no longer needed and delete them, or at the very least make sure they are not included within the set of objects that you are migrating to the target domain.

After you have migrated a service account, make sure that the original account is disabled within the source domain. Service accounts will typically have broad permissions to the resources that the service needs access to, and allowing the service account to remain active grants an attacker another account to exploit.

Scripting ADMT

Of the features that were made available with the latest version of ADMT, the ability to script all of the functions it provides is a welcome addition. With the inclusion of scripting, administrators can provide a script that will automate the functionality of ADMT and allow them to provide a text file with the accounts they want to migrate.

The ADMT command allows you to identify an option file that specifies the accounts that you want to migrate. If you have several computers that you want to migrate, you can include all of the computer names into a file, one computer name per line. The following command line assumes that you are migrating users from the Windows NT 4 domain BLOOMCO to the OU bloomusers within the Windows Server 2003 Active Directory domain zygort.lcl using the option file users.txt:

```
Admt user /F  C:\optionfiles\users.txt /SD:BLOOMCO /TD:zygort.lcl /TO:bloomusers
```

The command-line version of ADMT will allow you to migrate many of the accounts and objects that the GUI version allows. You can use the User, Group, Computers, Security, Server and Report options to control exactly what you want to migrate. These options work just as their GUI counterparts do, so you can create a set of scripts that provide the means to migrate the objects from one domain to another and then identify the objects within the option file.

When would you want to use the command-line version of ADMT instead of the GUI? If you want to use an option file for a specific set of objects, and you know the options you want to use, you can enter the command at the command line. The GUI version comes in very handy if you are performing trial migrations and you want to get a good feel for the objects and how they will migrate. Creating scripts to perform the migration allows you to control the objects that you will migrate, while pulling the object information from option files or databases. Scripting will also allow you to test the migration and roll it back if the migration does not go exactly as you envisioned.

Password Migration

In order to allow the user's passwords to remain associated with their accounts when a migration is performed, a utility called pwdmig.exe is included with ADMT. Of course, this utility alone is not sufficient to allow the migration of passwords. You still need to perform a few other steps. These steps are listed here for your convenience:

WARNING *These steps assume that all of the prerequisites for running ADMT, such as the group* source_domain$$$ *and the TcpipClientSupport Registry entry, are in place.*

1. Log on to a domain controller from the target domain that has the ADMT installed.

2. Open a command prompt, and change to the directory where ADMT is installed.

3. Place a blank floppy disk in the floppy drive.

4. Enter the following command at the command prompt:

    ADMT KEY *Source_Domain floppy_drive_letter* *

5. Open regedit.

6. Navigate to the Registry key HKEY_LOCAL_MACHINE\System\CurrentControlSet\Control\LSA.

7. Change the RestrictAnonymous Registry entry to **0**.

8. Add the Everyone group to the Pre–Windows 2000 Compatible Access group.

NOTE *If you are migrating to a Windows 2000–based Active Directory domain, you can add the Everyone group to the Pre–Windows 2000 Compatible Access group by entering the command:* **net localgroup "pre-windows 2000 compatible access" everyone /add**. *The same task can be performed for a Windows Server 2003–based domain by issuing the command:* **net localgroup "pre-windows 2000 compatible access" "anonymous logon" /add**.

If you are attempting to create a shared key that will allow you to migrate passwords from the BLOOMCO domain to the zygort.lcl domain, and you want to store the key on the A: floppy drive, you would enter the command:

    ADMT KEY bloomco A: *

The asterisk will prompt you for a password, but the password will not display on the screen. If you enter the password as you type the command, the password will be displayed until you clear the screen.

NOTE *If the domain controller does not have a floppy drive, you can use any location to store the shared key. Place it on a network share and then move it to a floppy disk.*

Once you have stored the shared key on a floppy disk, you will need to configure the domain controller in the source domain that is going to act as the Password Export Server (PES). Before you can perform any password migrations, you will need to make sure that you have the 128-bit High Encryption pack installed on the Windows NT 4 domain controller that you are using as the PES. Once you have installed the encryption pack, you can follow these steps to enable password migration from the domain controller:

1. Insert the floppy disk into the PES.

2. From the Windows Server 2003 CD, navigate to the `I386\ADMT\PWDMIG` directory and run `pwdmig.exe`.

3. Enter the password to gain access to the shared key.

4. Reboot the domain controller.

5. Open `regedit`.

6. Navigate the Registry to the `HKEY_LOCAL_MACHINE\System\CurrentControlSet\Control\LSA` key.

7. Change the value of the `AllowPasswordExport` to `1`.

WARNING *For security purposes, do not change the `AllowPasswordExport` Registry entry to* **1** *until you are ready to migrate accounts.*

WARNING *You must run ADMT from the domain controller in the target domain where you created the shared key. The key is created specifically for that domain controller and will not work with any other domain controller within the domain.*

Migrating from Windows NT 4

Before you attempt any type of migration, you need to determine if the existing hardware will support Windows 2000 or Windows Server 2003. Windows 2000 and Windows Server 2003 have a minimum requirement of 133MHz Pentium Processor with 128MB of RAM. However, running a domain controller with this configuration is not going to work well at all. The recommended configuration should be 550MHz Pentium processor with 256MB of RAM for Windows 2000 and 733MHz Pentium processor with 256MB of RAM for Windows Server 2003. Of course, the more resources you can throw at your server, the more efficiently it will perform.

When upgrading the first Windows NT 4 domain controller, you will need to upgrade a system that is acting as the Primary Domain Controller (PDC). The preferred method of upgrading is to put a new system in place that has the resources to support the new operating system, but install it as a Backup Domain Controller (BDC). Once installed, it should be promoted to the PDC and the original PDC, which is now a BDC, should be taken offline.

The new PDC should then be upgraded to the new operating system, which will make it an Active Directory domain controller. All of the accounts will now be members of Active Directory and still have their original security IDs (SIDs). The remainder of the domain controllers can then be upgraded or decommissioned, depending on how the organization wants to work the migration.

Migration Strategies

Windows NT 4's directory service was not very efficient. The model used did not scale well for large environments, and as such, multiple domains were usually created to organize resources. *Master User Domains (MUDs)* were created to host the user accounts for the domain. MUDs were created in a Windows NT 4 environment so that the user accounts for an organization could be organized neatly. Administrators responsible for account control were made administrators of these domains so that they could modify the account requirements. In very large environments with thousands to hundreds of thousands of users, several domains would be created. Resource domains would be created to hold the resources, such as member servers. Collapsing these domains into one Active Directory domain so that the resources are arranged logically within the simplest domain model possible will help reduce the administrative overhead.

The following sections present the options available for migrating the accounts from the MUDs and resource domains into the new design.

Incorporating the Master User Domains

When updating the MUD to Active Directory, you want to retain the account SIDs. Performing an in-place upgrade of the MUDs keeps all of the properties for the accounts intact. In fact, the account is still the same account as it had been under Windows NT, but it has been enhanced with additional functionality due to the new features available with Active Directory.

There is a major drawback to the in-place upgrade, however. The domain structure remains the same as the Windows NT 4 domain structure. If you have a single MUD and three resource domains, you will end up with the same domains in Active Directory. Figure 9.2 shows the original Windows NT 4 domain structure and the Active Directory structure after the upgrade.

Upgrading a Windows NT 4 domain structure that uses multiple MUDs poses another problem. The first domain that you upgrade becomes the forest root. As the rest of the domains are upgraded, they usually take on the roles of child domains in the first tree of the forest. However, in the case of multiple MUDs, the administrators of the MUDs usually have autonomy over the accounts for which they are responsible. If one of the MUDs becomes the forest root, they will have the ability to affect the accounts from the other MUDs. Because this is usually not acceptable when you are trying to retain the same level of control, the best design option is to create an empty forest root and then upgrade the domains to be child domains within the tree.

FIGURE 9.2

Comparison of the Windows NT 4 domains and the upgraded Active Directory structure

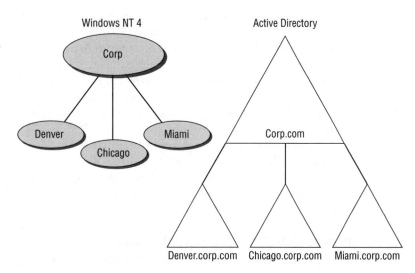

Figure 9.3 shows an example of a tree with an empty forest root and upgraded MUDs. Because the domains are controlled by different administrative groups that should not be administering objects from the other's domains, the empty forest root was created and the MUDs were upgraded as separate domains beneath the root.

The forest root will contain the service administrator accounts for the forest, but only the forest owner will have the ability modify the membership of these accounts. The domain owners of the upgraded MUDs will still retain their autonomy over their accounts and will be able to control and maintain those accounts as they were able to under Windows NT 4.

FIGURE 9.3

Empty forest root and upgraded MUDs

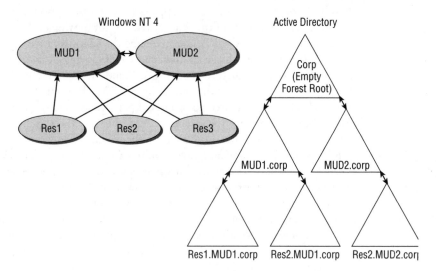

To avoid having the same domain structure, the domains can be consolidated within a single domain structure or within a simpler multiple domain structure if necessary. Tools such as the ADMT exist to make the migration of accounts to Active Directory an easy proposition.

Because many companies were tied to the account restrictions within Windows NT 4, they created multiple MUDs, but the same administrative staff supported all of them. Collapsing the MUDs into a single domain makes administration far easier than before and reduces administrative overhead. Accounts will no longer have to be added to groups in multiple domains so that they will have the proper rights to perform their duties.

The trust relationships that are automatically created within an Active Directory forest are transitive and will allow the accounts to have access to the same resources as they had before. Due to the transitive nature of the trusts, far fewer trust relationships are required, and access to the resources is more efficient. Once the resource domains are upgraded, the users will have the same resource access as before.

Incorporating the Resource Domains

Resource domains under the Windows NT 4 model were created to delegate control to data administrators or they were required due to the account limitations of the Windows NT 4 directory service. Most organizations will want to collapse the domain structure so that the accounts and resources reside within the same domain. Unless the resources must be isolated, the domain consolidation can incorporate them into OUs that will mimic the resource domain structure. If the resources must be isolated, a resource domain can remain, giving the administrators of the resource domain autonomous control over the resource. If true isolation is required, the design requirements may dictate that a resource forest be created. Upgrading the resource domain retains the domain structure. Performing an upgrade of the domain does not allow you to restructure or collapse the domains into a smaller, more manageable design. This is the easiest of the upgrade methods, but you do not gain any administrative benefits. The domains have to be controlled separately as they were under Windows NT 4.

When looking at this migration approach, review the reasons for maintaining the same design as was previously used. One of the primary reasons for moving to Active Directory is the reduced total cost of ownership (TCO). Without reducing the administrative overhead associated with multiple domains, you will not achieve the maximum TCO savings. Figure 9.4 shows an example of a Windows NT 4 domain structure upgraded to Windows 2003 Active Directory. All of the existing domains are retained within the new design. The MUD, Corp, has been upgraded to become the forest root. Each of the resource domains are upgraded as child domains so that the current administrative staff can still manage the resources. Also note that the administrative staff from Corp.com will now be able to control the objects within the resource domains.

Restructuring the domains allows you to take advantage of the new features of Active Directory. If data administrators decide that they need autonomy over the resources they control, an OU can be identified in which the resources can be migrated. Delegating the appropriate rights to the OU allows the administrators to control their resources without having to worry about other administrators having rights over the resources. This does not include the service administrators, however. Remember, service administrators within the forest or domain can still access resources anywhere in the container where they have service rights. Figure 9.5 shows an example of a Windows NT 4 domain restructure under Windows Server 2003 Active Directory.

FIGURE 9.4
Upgrading Windows NT 4 to Windows 2003 Active Directory

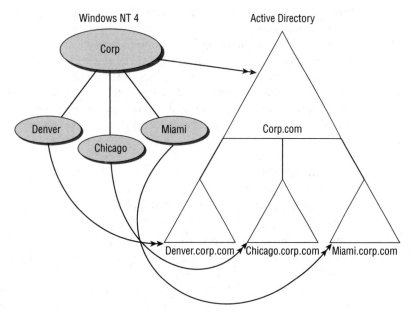

FIGURE 9.5
Windows NT 4 restructure

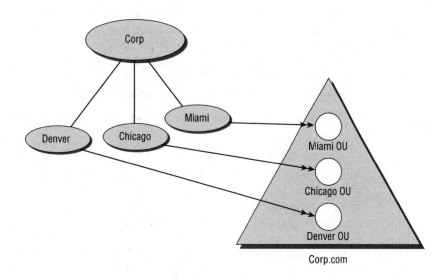

Controlling Domain Controller Overrun

As you start the migration from Windows NT 4 to Windows 2000 or Windows Server 2003, clients that can connect to and use Active Directory services will start using Active Directory domain controllers instead of Windows NT 4 BDCs. This is actually the preferred nature of Windows 2000

Professional and Windows XP Professional workstations and Windows 2000 and Windows Server 2003 member servers. In a site where you have very few of these computers in place, you could promote your first domain controller within the site and let the clients connect and work normally. The Windows NT 4 and earlier clients will still be able to utilize the Windows NT 4 BDCs.

The problems start when you have several Active Directory–capable clients and you drop your first Active Directory domain controller into the site. Suddenly you find that all of your Windows 2000 Professional and Windows XP Professional workstations are ignoring the Windows NT 4 BDCs and your Active Directory domain controller is overloaded as clients log on and perform searches.

Emulating a BDC

If you are upgrading a domain controller from Windows NT 4 to Windows 2000 or Windows Server 2003, you should add the NT4Emulator Registry key prior to performing Dcpromo. Doing so will guarantee that the clients will not lock onto the Active Directory domain controller. Once an Active Directory–capable client sees the Active Directory domain controller, it will no longer attempt to connect to any Windows NT 4 domain controllers unless you remove them from the domain and add them back.

If you already ran Dcpromo before you added this Registry key, and you now have all of your Active Directory–capable clients connecting to your Active Directory domain controller, the only way to force them to work with the BDCs is to remove them from the domain and add them back. Once added back, they will revert to finding any domain controller. It does not matter if it is running Active Directory or not. If the NT4Emulator Registry key is added to the Active Directory domain controller, it will appear to the clients as just another BDC.

The preferred method of keeping the domain controller from being overrun by clients is to add the key to the Windows NT 4 domain controller prior to running Dcpromo. To do so, you will need to use the Registry editing tool `regedt32.exe`. Traverse the Registry to the following key:

```
HKEY_LOCAL_MACHINE/System/CurrentControlSet/Services/Netlogon/Parameters
```

Because the NT4Emulator value does not exist, you will need to add it. To do so, open the Edit menu and click Add Value. In the Value Name field enter **NT4Emulator**. In the Data Type field, pull down and select `REG_DWORD`. In the Value Data field, enter **0x1**. Once you exit Regedt32, you should apply the latest Windows NT 4 service pack and reboot the system. If you are upgrading to Windows 2000, you will need to make sure you apply the latest Windows 2000 service pack before promoting the domain controller. The NT4Emulator Registry key is not supported on domain controllers unless Service Pack 2 or later is installed.

After you have applied the latest service pack, rebooted the server, and logged back in, you will be able to run Dcpromo. When the domain controller comes online, all of the clients will behave as if the domain controller is actually a Windows NT 4 BDC. At the same time, using the NT4Emulator key can cause other problems, such as administering Active Directory and promoting successive domain controllers.

Neutralizing the Emulator

If you attempt to promote another domain controller within a site where the only Active Directory domain controller is functioning with the NT4Emulator key turned on, Dcpromo will not be able to locate the existing domain controller. It will simply see all Windows NT 4 BDCs within the domain.

The same thing will occur if you attempt to manage Active Directory using any of the Active Directory tools from another computer besides the domain controller. The existing domain controller will hide behind the NT4Emulator key and not let any other system know that it is really an Active Directory domain controller.

If you want a Windows 2000 Professional, Windows XP Professional, Windows 2000, or Windows Server 2003 member server or the Dcpromo utility to see behind the façade that the domain controller is putting up, you can create the NeutralizeNT4Emulator key on the client system. To do so, you need to run `regedt32.exe` and create the value within the following Registry location:

```
HKEY_LOCAL_MACHINE/System/CurrentControlSet/Services/Netlogon/Parameters
```

From the Edit menu, select Add Value and enter **NeutralizeNT4Emulator** in the Value Name field. Make sure the value is of type REG_DWORD and give it a value of **0x1**.

Once completed, you will be able to promote the domain controller or run the Active Directory tools from your client system. Of course, if you are promoting another domain controller and you still don't think you will have enough domain controllers to handle the client load, make sure you add the NT4Emulator value to the domain controller you are promoting.

There is one other instance when you may have to enter the NeutralizeNT4Emulator Registry entry: when you want to test Group Policy application on systems within the site. Because the client systems will not see that the domain controller is running Active Directory, the Group Policies will not be processed. Add this Registry entry to the clients you want to affect so that you can test the Group Policy application.

NOTE   *Knowledge Base article 289713 contains more information on NT4Emulator and NeutralizeNT4Emulator.*

Migrating from Windows 2000

Before you start any domain controller upgrade, you need to make sure that the hardware and software you are currently using are supported by Windows Server 2003. For the most part, all of the hardware used with Windows 2000 is supported, and the minimum requirements are nearly identical. Where you may run into problems, however, is the software that is running on your domain controllers. Most administrators will tell you that you should not run applications on your domain controller. They should only be allowed to support Active Directory requests from clients and replicate changes. However, you may have monitoring software and support software, such as antivirus software, running on them. Make sure that all of the current software is supported under Windows Server 2003.

Double-check the event logs to make sure that you have rectified all problems that may exist. Errors and warnings that appear in the logs should be fixed prior to upgrading the domain controller. Problems that exist within Windows 2000 could be exacerbated within Windows Server 2003.

How good is your disaster recovery plan? Have you tested it? If the domain upgrade fails and leaves Active Directory in an unusable state, you may be forced to recover your original infrastructure. Make sure you have backups of your domain controllers, especially the Master Operations role owners. If your backup tapes are not good, you may lose everything.

Windows 2000 Server Active Directory migration to Windows Server 2003 Active Directory can be a straightforward process. Because Windows Server 2003 Active Directory is based on the same technology as Windows 2000 Server Active Directory, the upgrade process is very straightforward. The two platforms have several differences (most of them in the form of feature enhancements) that have piqued the interest of administrators who have large Active Directory environments.

Prior to promoting a Windows Server 2003 member server to a domain controller or upgrading an existing Windows 2000 domain controller to Windows Server 2003, you need to extend the schema to support the new object classes and attributes. The utility that you will use to extend the schema is Adprep. Two switches, `forestprep` and `domainprep`, are used to prepare Active Directory for all of the new features that are provided by Windows Server 2003. They are described in the following sections.

The minimum service pack level that your Windows 2000 domain controllers should be at before extending the schema with Adprep is Service Pack 3. If your domain controllers are not patched to SP3, you could consider applying the service pack; otherwise, you will need to apply hotfixes to your domain controllers prior to Adprep. (For a complete list of hotfixes that are required before running `forestprep`, see Knowledge Base Article 331161.)

WARNING   *Service Pack 3 may cause a few problems with your environment, so you will need to apply the service pack in a test environment before you put it into your production environment. Microsoft recommends updating your systems to the latest Service Pack. However, we stress, you should always test them before putting them into production.*

Prepping the Forest

The first step is to prepare the forest for the added functionality by running `adprep /forestprep`. Doing so will extend the schema by adding additional attributes and classes that are necessary to allow the new features within Windows Server 2003 Active Directory. Make sure you are running `forestprep` on the domain controller that is holding the Schema Master role. All of the changes occur on this system and if you are not running `forestprep` on the Schema Master, the changes will have to be sent across the network, which will increase the network traffic and cause the process to take considerably longer.

Because there are changes that are made to the schema, the person running `forestprep` needs to be a member of both the Schema Admins and Enterprise Admins groups. If your account is not a member of these accounts, `forestprep` will fail and you will be required to start again from an account with the appropriate permissions.

As `forestprep` processes, it keeps track of its progress within the ForestUpdates container within Active Directory. This way, if the process fails, you can restart it and it will pick up where it left off. This can save time instead of having the entire process run again. In fact, if you want to see if `Forestprep` has completed, you can open the ForestUpdates container within ADSI Edit and view the two subcontainers, Operations and Windows2003Update. If the Windows2003Update container exists, that means that `forestprep` completed successfully. If it is not there, you can look at the objects within the ForestUpdates container. When `forestprep` completes, there will be 36 objects. If you are having problems trying to get **forestprep** to complete, you can contact Microsoft Product Support Services and they can troubleshoot your problem based on the objects that do exist within that container.

Figure 9.6 shows the Operations container and the objects that are created during **forestprep**. If you would like to see when **forestprep** completed, you can look at the timestamp of the Windows2003Update container as seen in Figure 9.7.

FIGURE 9.6

Objects added to the Operations container during **forestprep**

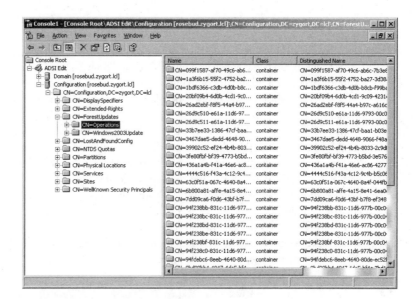

FIGURE 9.7

Timestamp on the Windows2003 Update container denoting the time **forestprep** completed

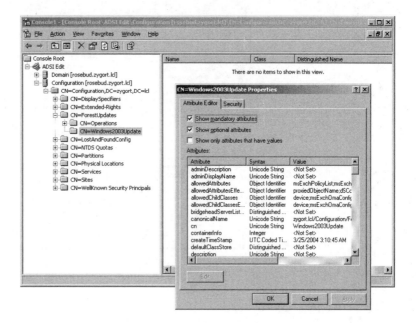

Prepping the Domain

After you have injected the new attributes and classes into the forest using forestprep, you will need to run Adprep again using the /domainprep switch, once in every domain within your forest. Before you do so, however, make sure that replication has completed. You can use Replication Monitor to check the status of replication.

NOTE *For more information about Replication Monitor, see Chapter 13, "Troubleshooting Active Directory Replication."*

In order to run domainprep you must be logged on with an account that is a member of the Domain Admins group. The domain controller on which you are running domainprep should be holding the Infrastructure Master role. If not, you will incur additional network traffic while updating the domain.

Just as forestprep kept track of all of the objects that were updated, so does domainprep. If you use ADSI Edit to view the domain partition, you will find the DomainUpdates container beneath the System container. As the updates are performed, entries are added into the Operations container. As with forestprep, you will be able to keep track of all of the updates—52 in all. Once domainprep completes, the Windows2003Updates container is created. If you do not see this container, domainprep has not completed successfully.

Figure 9.8 shows the Operations container and the objects that are created during forestprep. If you would like to see when forestprep completed, you can look at the timestamp of the Windows-2003Update container as seen in Figure 9.9

FIGURE 9.8

Objects added to the Operations container during domainprep

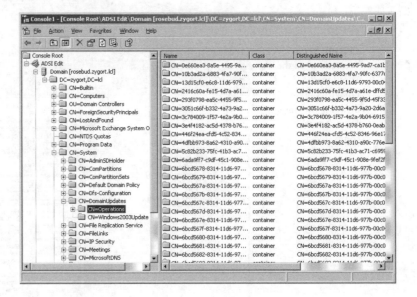

FIGURE 9.9

Timestamp on the Windows2003 Update container denoting the time domainprep completed

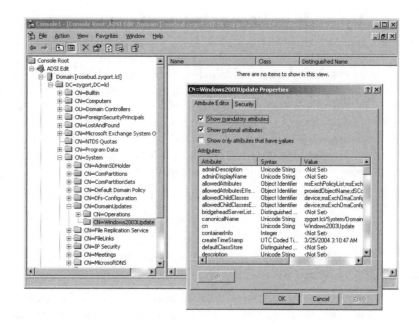

NOTE *For a list of all of the changes that occur during* forestprep *or* domainprep, *see Knowledge Base article 309628.*

Application Issues

If an application uses an incorrect naming convention for attributes or classes, it could cause issues when the forest is updated using adprep /forestprep. Exchange 2000 causes problems due to incorrectly named display names. When you run Adprep, duplicate objects are created. In order to correct this, you will need to perform a quick fix that Microsoft has issued.

First, you need to locate the inetorgpersonfix.ldf file on the Windows Server 2003 CD. It is located within the \support\tools\support.cab file. Copy this file to the hard drive of the domain controller that holds the Schema Master role. You then need to import the inetorgpersonfix.ldf file using the LDIFDE utility. For example, if you want to import the file to correct the error in the zygort.lcl domain, you should issue the following command:

```
Ldifde /i /f inetorgpersonfix.ldf /c "DC=X" "DC=zygort, DC=lcl"
```

The /i switch denotes the import function, /f specifies the file to input, and the /c will replace the "DC=X" within the ldf file with the name of your forest root, "DC=zygort, DC=lcl".

Service for Unix 2 will also cause problems for administrators who want to upgrade Active Directory. If you are currently running this program, check out Knowledge Base article 293783. You will probably need to contact Microsoft Product Support Services to obtain the required hotfix.

Upgrade or Reconstruction

Because Active Directory is based on the same technology for both Windows 2000 and Windows Server 2003, most companies can perform an upgrade of their existing infrastructure. This allows them to add the new features of Windows Server 2003 while maintaining their existing directory service design. This is the easiest and most straightforward approach to moving to Windows Server 2003.

After the required service packs and hotfixes are applied and Adprep has run for the forest and all of the domains, the domain controllers can be upgraded to Windows Server 2003. All this can be performed without having to modify the Active Directory design in any way.

However, not every company has a directory service design that fits their needs. Companies may want to change their designs for many reasons, including:

◆ The initial designers did not fully understand the ramifications of their decisions.

◆ Initially, the Windows NT 4 domain design was preserved and now the company wants to consolidate.

◆ New features within Windows Server 2003 will allow the company to work more efficiently, such as using the new forest trusts.

Whatever the reason, a reorganization of your Active Directory design may allow your organization to perform more efficiently—and sometimes more securely. The primary tool that you can use to perform the reconstruction of your design is going to be the Active Directory Migration Tool (ADMT). There are other utilities that you can purchase from third-party vendors, but remember that Microsoft provides this one for free and the version supplied with Windows Server 2003 provides nearly all of the functionality you will need.

Other Migration Utilities

Unfortunately, Microsoft does not provide a comprehensive utility that will show you everything you need, nor do they have a utility that will provide you with all of the migration options you may need. Several utilities are part of the Support Tools, or you can download them from Microsoft's website. These utilities provide migration options that may not be available within the ADMT, or they provide an easier way to perform a single function.

ClonePrinciple   ClonePrinciple is actually a set of scripts that will allow you to copy user and group accounts from one domain to another and keep the original object within the originating domain. This utility can come in very handy if you want to script the migration of accounts by using VBScript or if you are migrating accounts from one Active Directory forest to another and want to keep the original accounts in the source domain.

NetDom   NetDom is a command-line utility that will allow you to create, delete, and verify trusts, along with managing computer accounts within a domain. This utility will allow you to verify the trust relationships between domains as you are migrating and consolidating.

MoveTree   MoveTree is a useful utility that will allow you to move parts of your forest to new locations within the forest. You can use this utility to move an OU structure to another OU tree or another domain. You can also move domains to become child domains of another domain. This utility comes in handy when you want to restructure large portions of your Active Directory structure.

Best Practices for Domain Migration and Consolidation

Windows Server 2003 has added in so many new features for medium to large Active Directory infrastructures, administrative teams are now looking at how they will move to the new platform. The following are some tips that you should consider as you are migrating or consolidating your directory service.

- Always have a rollback plan in case the upgrade fails and you need to recover your original configuration.

- Test your migration before you actually migrate users so that you can be assured that the migration will complete as you have planned.

- If you are consolidating multiple domains using the same settings, script ADMT so that the migration is easier.

- Verify that the accounts within the source domain will be used within the target domain. Do not migrate unnecessary accounts, as they will only clutter your shiny new directory service.

- Design Active Directory to take advantage of its administrative capabilities so that you can consolidate domains into the fewest Active Directory domains as possible.

- Do not change the AllowPasswordExport Registry entry to allow passwords to be exported until you are ready to migrate accounts.

Next Up

This chapter allowed us to focus on the utilities needed for domain consolidation, namely the Active Directory Migration Tool. Once you understand how ADMT works and what it requires, you are ready to make the transition to a more efficient directory service.

In the next chapter, we are going to review the steps necessary for a proper migration from Novell's NetWare to Active Directory. The process itself is not difficult, but if not completed correctly, could cause more headaches than you need. If completed correctly, the migration should allow your users to access all of the resources that they normally work with, and you will be the hero of the day.

chapter 10

NetWare Migration

SEVERAL IMPLEMENTATIONS OF NOVELL'S NetWare are still in existence. For many years, NetWare was the premier network operating system before Microsoft started throwing its weight around. As more and more companies adopt Active Directory as the de facto directory service, you could need to migrate from NetWare. To do so seamlessly is nearly impossible. Although some companies with small implementations might be able to perform a quick cutover to the new system, just as many will need to maintain both directory services for a period of time.

This chapter is an overview of the steps and options that are available to you when you perform your migration. This book does not have enough space to give a complete step-by-step, blow-by-blow description of everything you will need to migrate. Instead, we will take a look at what you need to have in place and some of the utilities that are available for an easy, smooth transition. Microsoft has introduced tools to make migration easier, but you will find that they are limited in their scope. Third-party utilities exist that fill in the gaps; but as you may have already figured out, you will have to purchase them.

NOTE   *In this chapter, the generic term* NetWare *refers to both bindery-based and NDS-based Novell environments when the references can be used in either case.*

Preparing for Migration

Nothing is as easy as it seems. Migrating from one operating system to another is troublesome enough—but when you are migrating your entire directory service infrastructure from one network operating system to another, you are faced with several challenges. In previous chapters, we discussed some of the methods to migrate from earlier Windows operating systems to Windows Server 2003. The process of migrating from NetWare begins the same way it begins with the Microsoft operating systems—with planning.

The more comprehensive your plan, the better the migration will proceed. You need to sit down with a layout of the NDS structure and determine how it will map out to Active Directory. Be forewarned that there are structures within NDS that do not have corresponding Active Directory objects and that do not function completely the same way in both directory services.

For instance, organizational units (OUs) within Active Directory are not used to assign permissions to other objects. In Active Directory, only groups are used for this purpose. If you are using OUs to organize user accounts so that you can assign them access to resources, you will have to map them to Active Directory groups.

While you are investigating the structure of NDS, try to determine how you will migrate the objects so that they can be administered efficiently within Active Directory. Typically, you will find that the structure used by NDS is not conducive to an efficient Active Directory infrastructure. If the organization built NDS to take advantage of geographic segmentation, and this is the administrative structure you are planning for Active Directory, you might have an easier time migrating the accounts. If you are planning to configure the upper-level OUs in Active Directory using a geographic layout so that you can minimize the effects of reorganizations, direct migrations may not be out of the question.

After looking at the NDS layout, also take the network infrastructure into consideration. If the NDS servers are centrally located, migrating the objects from one directory service to another might be easy; however, anytime you have WAN links in the way, the migration could be more difficult. NetWare creates partitions within NDS to segment the directory service so that it performs efficiently. Active Directory, on the other hand, works well in a WAN environment due to sites and the compression of replicated data passing through the site links.

You also need to consider the servers and workstations you have in your environment. Servers running NetWare do not typically have the same hardware requirements as those running Windows 2000 or Windows Server 2003. You may find yourself in a position where you will need to purchase hardware to support your new Active Directory environment. Perform an inventory of the servers that you are currently using to determine which will work as domain controllers, which will be decommissioned, and which will be reentered into your domain as member servers.

If your workstations are configured with only the NetWare client, you will need to determine how you will roll out the Microsoft client. Walking around to each and every system and changing the client might not seem like a fun proposition, but it may be your only alternative. Of course, the Microsoft client is a default option on Windows operating systems, and unless someone has removed it, you may be able to roll the clients into an Active Directory environment pretty easily. Just remember, you will probably want to remove the NetWare client when the system no longer needs to access the NetWare servers, so you will still need to go around and touch each one.

A Bird's Eye View of Migration

Microsoft created an excellent guide for anyone who is interested in migrating from NetWare, and you can find it on Microsoft's website at `http://www.microsoft.com/windowsserver2003/techinfo/overview/sfnmig.mspx`. You are not reading this text so that you can read a brief synopsis of Microsoft's document, so I will not rehash the information that they have included. Instead, this section will concentrate on some of the topics that will help you make the move as painless as possible. The steps to perform migrations using Microsoft Directory Synchronization Services (MSDSS) are briefly described at the end of this chapter, however.

Application Compatibility

Applications that are supported under both NetWare and Windows are few and far between. Some applications are supported and will run—but for the most part, you will need to purchase a version of the application that is specific to the operating system. Inventory all of the applications that are supported within your environment and contact the vendors. Many will have a Windows-based version and will be very happy to take your money so that you can continue to use their product.

Migration could also be a good time to cut over to another product that performs the same functions as one of your current applications, but that has more features. After Novell announced that they were moving to provide their eDirectory service on every platform imaginable and step away from the NetWare OS, many vendors stopped supporting applications for a NetWare environment. While NetWare still exists, nearly every program that uses NDS, or eDirectory as it is now known, is supported on other operating systems—the most popular of which is the Windows platform.

NOTE *From here on, I will use the term NDS to reference both NDS and eDirectory.*

Data Migration

Migrating the data from NetWare to Windows 2000 or Windows Server 2003 can be handled very efficiently with MSDSS. As you plan your migration, you can choose to migrate the data from the NetWare platform, and MSDSS will migrate the folders and files with the permissions intact. This is especially helpful when it comes to user's home directories. You are not required to reestablish all of the correct permissions on the files after they are copied from one server to another, and the users can have immediate access to their data when they log on.

WARNING *When migrating data that has the Novell permission Modify assigned to it, the default permission within a Windows environment is Read. You can change the permission as you are migrating—but if you forget, the users will not have the same level of access to their data as they had under NetWare.*

One thing to note, however, is that Novell has a very efficient and widely used compression algorithm that administrators take advantage of when they store data on their servers. When you migrate data from NetWare to Windows, you need to be prepared for the full amount of data that is going to populate your drives. Make sure you take a full inventory of the actual data size, and prepare the correct amount of space on the Windows partitions. Otherwise, you might find yourself moving the data again when you run out of drive space allocated.

Mail Migration

Moving users from GroupWise to Exchange can be problematic. Although GroupWise allows users to connect to their mail system through an Outlook client, most GroupWise installations take advantage of the GroupWise client. Training users on the differences between the mail systems can be a nightmare, especially for those users who are not happy with having to change in the first place. If users are familiar with Outlook, the transition will not be nearly as painful because they will still use the same interface that they were accustomed to using.

During the migration from GroupWise to Exchange by using the Migration Wizard, the mailboxes are moved from one server to the next; however, Microsoft does not provide a method of migrating the archives. Due to differences in how the two mail systems provide address lists and distribution lists, transitioning from one to the other could be difficult. Third-party suppliers such as Wingra (`http://www.wingra.com`) provide utilities that make the move from GroupWise to Exchange a much easier proposition. Research your options to determine how much your time is worth as you are going through the migration.

Mapped Devices

The one thing that more administrators complain about than any other is that Microsoft does not give you an easy way to map devices based on the user's account information. NetWare allows you to control the mapping of drives and printers based on the user's account, group membership, and NDS OU scripts. When a user logs on, the logon script evaluates the user's group and OU membership and will map the devices that the user will need. This can be extremely handy so that you do not have to instruct a user to map a drive when their job role changes or disconnect a drive due to their new role.

Utilities such as KIXtart and ScriptLogic allow you to perform the same type of conditional mapping that NetWare uses. These tools can make an administrator's life easier because a single logon script created by one of these utilities can map all of the required devices as users starts their day.

Test, Test, Test

I cannot stress enough that you should test every detail of your migration. If at all possible, try to build a test environment that is a miniature version of your production environment, and test all of the migration options that you are planning. This will give you a chance to review whether the steps you are taking will work the way you hope. If not, you can rethink your migration plan before you introduce a problem into your production environment.

Users do not like to change, but they will really take exception to a new system if they have problems from the start. The more seamless the changeover is to them, the quicker they will accept it. Choose a pilot group, and have them work with your test-bed. Let them see what you are planning, and give them a chance to beat on the system. Users will find problems far faster than you will because they try things that you may not even think of trying.

If you are migrating users in phases, migrate the pilot group first because they should already be trained on the system. They may be a little more forgiving if something goes wrong because they have already seen what the system is supposed to do and will have a slightly vested interest in the new system. Some may even feel partially responsible if a problem occurs in the new environment that did not rear its ugly head in the test environment, because they did not bring it to your attention then.

Train Users

One of the best methods of getting users to begin accepting a new system is to train them as the migration occurs. Not every company can do this, but I have found that if users can attend a training session as you are making the cutover to a new system, they will arrive at their desk with fresh knowledge about the system and can start taking advantage of it immediately.

This assumes that you have enough time to take your systems "offline" long enough to transition the users and efficiently migrate the systems simultaneously. Some companies will have to migrate in phases instead of a single cutover, but the same scenario can work for them. During the planning phase, determine which groups of users can migrate at the same time so that you will have the least amount of impact on the current operations. Migrate them in phases while you perform your "just-in-time" training.

You will find that users will take to the new system and remember more about it if you take this approach. They will have new logon methods, new mapped drives, and new e-mail. If you train them too far in advance, they will naturally forget some of what you taught them simply because they will not be using the new tools. You might need to refresh their memories. Just-in-time training allows them to step away from the training environment and use the new skills immediately.

TIP   Warn users that their passwords will not be the same once they are moved to the new system because MSDSS cannot copy user passwords to Active Directory.

Due to Active Directory naming conventions, you may have to change users' logon names so that they are unique. NetWare allows a user logon name to be the same as another user so long as the container where the account is located is different. Active Directory requires the user logon name to be unique within the domain. Users will need to be notified of these changes. You might want to implement the new name on the original system so that the affected users can become familiar with their new logon names.

WARNING   If you do not manually change a user's logon name, MSDSS will append a number to the end of the logon name if it encounters a duplicate within the domain.

Working with Microsoft Directory Synchronization Services

When you use MSDSS, you have the ability to make a one-time cutover to Active Directory, or you can perform a phased migration. The ideal case is to perform the one-time move, but not all organizations have that luxury. When you are forced to use a phased migration, you can use MSDSS to keep the directory services synchronized. Your options for keeping the accounts and data in synch are listed here.

WARNING   Using MSDSS to migrate from NetWare to Active Directory requires that you extend the Active Directory schema. If you are migrating from NDS and want to perform two-way synchronization, the NDS schema must also be extended. See the MSDSS documentation for more information.

One-Way Synchronization   One-way synchronization allows you to manage the objects in both directory services from the Active Directory tools. As you make changes to the objects in Active Directory, MSDSS updates the objects in the NetWare environment.

Two-Way Synchronization   Two-way synchronization allows you to manage objects from either directory service. This allows the administrators who are responsible for NetWare to continue managing the system as they have in the past, while allowing the administrators to become familiar with the Active Directory tools.

WARNING   Make sure you create any OUs within Active Directory before you begin your initial synchronization. The wizard does not give you an option to create OUs.

Best Practices for NetWare Migration

Migration from one operating system to another is never a fun proposition. When you are moving from one Microsoft operating system to another, at least the clients will be somewhat familiar with the operations. Moving from a Novell environment to a Microsoft environment can be very frustrating for them. Follow these tips to help make the transition easier.

◆ Test everything before you implement your plan.

◆ Train your users in a just-in-time fashion so they don't forget how to use the new system before they actually get to use it.

◆ Use Microsoft's migration utilities, but also research third-party options that will make your migration easier.

◆ Although Windows allows users to maintain their mapped drives and printers within their profiles, if you like the flexibility that NetWare has for mapping devices to accounts, you can use a third-party tool to leverage that functionality.

Next Up

Deployment can be one of the most stressful times for any administrator. Most organizations already use a network-based infrastructure, and moving users to a new environment can cause many sleepless nights. Once the deployment and migration of the systems has completed, it will be time to sit back and relax. Okay, I was only kidding about that. You still have a lot of work to do. Once deployed, it will be up to you to make sure the systems are working as efficiently as possible, monitor systems for problems, and troubleshoot issues as they arise. In the next section, we are going to look at some of the practices you can use to make sure that your Active Directory infrastructure works efficiently and allows you to go home early.

Maintenance and Administration

part3

In this part:

chapter 11

Backup and Disaster Recovery

WELCOME TO THE TROUBLESHOOTING part of this book. Unlike the previous parts of the book, which dealt with designing your Active Directory infrastructure and deploying your domain controllers, this part discusses problems that you will probably be troubleshooting frequently. In this part, we will take a hard look at some of the issues you will encounter as you manage your Active Directory infrastructure. Starting with this chapter, we will work with backing up and restoring Active Directory and its associated files, and then we will turn our attention to troubleshooting the Active Directory infrastructure.

Reactive versus Proactive

Are you constantly running around your organization putting out fires, or are you one of the lucky ones who are able to watch over their systems and detect problems before they become serious? That is the difference between reactive and proactive administration. If you are in a reactive mode, you probably don't have time to monitor your systems. Your time is consumed by fixing problems that arise on a daily, sometimes hourly basis. Many administrators find themselves in this position, and it is a very difficult position to get out of. If your company's upper echelon does not understand the cost savings associated with proactive management (or they are of the mindset "You're here anyway, so I should be paying you to take care of this"), you will probably be stuck in this rut for a long time.

Companies that have discovered the cost savings associated with proactive management are usually glad that they made the move from reactive to proactive. Now, don't get me wrong: no amount of proactive management will completely free you from putting out fires, but at least you will reduce many of the problems you could be facing.

There are two camps within the proactive management ranks: those that use monitoring tools and those that work manually. Smaller organizations that take a proactive stance will usually opt for the manual method because they do not have as many resources to monitor. Manual monitoring can be a time-consuming proposition, however, and it incurs its own level of administrative costs. These administrative costs are usually outweighed by the dividend of having the services available for longer periods of time, thereby not incurring user downtime.

Organizations that use monitoring tools have to pay the cost of the monitoring solution and the training to employ it. They gain the ability to monitor many services at the same time—many more than human administrators can manually oversee. Monitoring tools usually have intelligence written into them that will watch for common problems and can monitor multiple machines for the same problem. They offer the advantage of possibly catching an attack as it is being executed.

Domain Controller Backup

As with every server in your organization, you need to make sure that you have the data safeguarded in case you need to restore your domain controllers. If you have taken precautions and built multiple domain controllers, you probably feel safe. If one domain controller were to fail, the others could still perform their duties for your users. However, always remember that the first word of disaster recovery is "disaster." Backing up your data is the front line of defense in your disaster recovery plan. If a disaster, such as a tornado, earthquake, fire, or flood, should strike and effectively render all of your systems useless, you will need to make sure you have a method of returning that data back to a useful state.

So let's cover some of the backup and restore needs of the typical organization. In the following section, you will find some tips to follow when planning your disaster recovery plan as well as the steps to perform for each of the special cases for restoring a domain controller back to a useful state.

System State Backup

When you back up the Active Directory database, you also need the corresponding files that help maintain it. Without these files, you would simply have a database file without a function. The database and associated files on a domain controller are known collectively as the *System State*. The System State files are listed here:

◆ Active Directory Database

◆ Active Directory Database Log Files

◆ Boot Files

◆ COM+ Class Registration Database

◆ Registry

◆ Sysvol

NOTE *If your domain controller is also acting as a certificate authority, the certificate database is backed up as part of the System State.*

Performing a System State Backup

The System State backup is easy to perform, even with the built-in Backup utility. As you start the Backup utility, you can either use the Backup Wizard, which will prompt you for what you want to back up, or you can choose to manually select the backup options. Either way, the System State is an option you can make. Figure 11.1 shows the System State option if you are manually selecting the files you are going to back up.

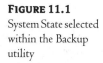

Figure 11.1

System State selected within the Backup utility

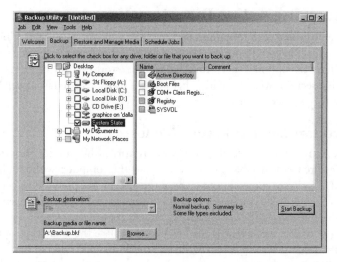

Once stored on backup media, the System State can be stored in a safe location until you need to restore it to your domain controller. Make sure that you store the media in a very safe location, because anyone with access to the media could hack the database and discover information about your domain, which could include the passwords for your user accounts.

Limitations of Windows Backup

As with quite a few of the Microsoft utilities that are included with the base operating system, the built-in backup program, Windows Backup, is not a feature-rich utility. It does provide enough functionality for a small company to effectively perform backup and restore procedures; however, a larger organization may find that it lacks some advanced features that they need for their enterprise-level disaster recovery.

One limitation is its inability to back up the System State remotely. If you want to perform remote backups, you will need to tweak the backups or use a third-party backup utility. If your organization is small and you want to use the free Backup utility that Microsoft has provided, you can still centrally back up the System State on all of your domain controllers. To do so, schedule your System State backup, and specify a network location to save the backed-up files. You can then back up all of the files from all of the domain controllers to a single backup set.

NOTE Enterprise-level backup solutions that provide complete disaster recovery capabilities for your organization are available from third-party vendors. Covering them is out of the scope of this book, however. If you are concerned about the limitations of the built-in backup solution, you should investigate these solutions to see which one best fits your needs and budget.

Another Windows Backup limitation is its inability to manage an enterprise-level backup library. It has a logging feature that allows you to manage your backups and locate the files you want to restore, but it does not allow you to work with large databases of information that the third-party utilities support.

Restoring Active Directory

When working with Windows Server 2003, you will have three options when performing a restore of Active Directory: primary restore, normal restore, and authoritative restore. Windows 2000 does not have the option to perform the primary restore, but the other two options are available. The following sections will shed a little light on the methods you have available to you when restoring your directory service database.

Directory Services Restore Mode

The Active Directory database cannot be restored while it is functioning. In order to perform any type of restore to the database, you need to start the computer without allowing the database files to be used. To do so, you will need to boot the system and press F8 to get to the Startup Options menu. Of all the options you have to choose from, you will need to concentrate on the Directory Services Restore Mode (DSRM) option. When you choose this option, the operating system will start in a version of safe mode that will allow you to replace the database from backup media.

Because the system is starting in safe mode and you will not have access to Active Directory, you will have to authenticate against the local security authority. During the promotion to a domain controller, the person who promoted the domain controller was prompted to enter a password for the DSRM administrator. You will need to provide that password to log onto the system and restore the database.

Once you have authenticated to the local system, you will have the ability to start the Backup utility and restore the System State. Remember that the data you are placing back onto the system will only be as up-to-date as the data that resides on the backup media. In most cases, this will not be an issue; once the domain controller comes back online, it will receive up-to-date information through replication. Of course, there may be instances where you will not want to replicate the existing data to the restore domain controller. We will look at those reasons in the next few sections. But first, you need to know how you can control the DSRM administrator password.

DSRM Password

Windows Server 2003-based domain controllers have an additional command that you can run from the NTDSUTIL utility that will allow you to reset the DSRM administrator password. To do so, you do not need to know the current password. Simply open a command prompt, start NTDSUTIL and follow these steps:

1. From the `ntdsutil:` prompt, type **set DSRM password**.

2. At the `Reset DSRM Administrator Password:` prompt type **reset password on server server**.

NOTE *If you are changing the password on the local domain controller, you can type **NULL** instead of the server name.*

3. Type **quit** to return to the `ntdsutil:` prompt, and then type **quit** again to exit NTDSUTIL.

Of course, if you do know what the password is, you can restart your domain controller, enter Directory Services Restore Mode, and change the password just as you can with every other local account. However, you would have to take the domain controller offline long enough to perform the password change. This may not be a preferable option.

Having the ability to change the password from the NTDSUTIL utility garners another problem you need to address. Anyone who has the ability to log onto the domain controller with an account that has the credentials to run NTDSUTIL will have the ability to change the DSRM password and possibly enter Directory Services Restore Mode, start a restore, and inject objects into your domain. While this may seem far-fetched, you should still consider the possibility.

On a Windows 2000-based domain controller, if you cannot remember the DSRM administrator password, you will either need to rebuild the server (usually not an option), or use a third-party utility such as ERD Commander from SysInternals (`http://www.sysinternals.com`). You should note, however, that you will need to reboot the system into Directory Services Restore Mode in order to change the account.

Primary Restore

A primary restore is used when all of the domain controllers have failed and you need to bring a domain controller online. This domain controller will effectively become the first domain controller within the domain. It will contain only the objects that were backed up, and you will not be able to recover any changes that were made between the last backup and the complete failure.

You should not attempt a primary restore if there are any functional domain controllers for your domain. If you do have a functional domain controller, you will want to run the normal restore as discussed in the following section.

To perform a primary restore, select the System State option from the restore option within the backup program. As you are advancing through the wizard, choose the option to make each naming context the primary version. Figure 11.2 shows the option as seen when you are stepping through the Restore Wizard, and Figure 11.3 shows the option when choosing Advanced settings from the manual file selection.

FIGURE 11.2

Choosing a primary restore from the Restore Wizard

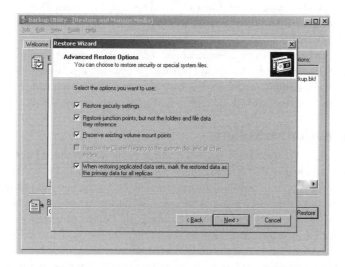

FIGURE 11.3
Manually choosing a primary restore option

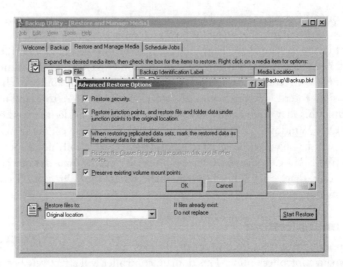

Once the restore is complete, each of the directory service naming contexts will be set as the primary version, and any additional domain controller that you bring online will receive the data contained on this server. The beauty of the primary restore method is that the domain controller becomes the holder of each of the Master Operations roles. On a Windows 2000-based server, you do not have the option to perform a primary restore; therefore, you must seize the roles if the domain controller you are restoring did not originally hold any of the roles.

Normal Restore

In most cases, when you have hardware that fails and you have to restore the directory service to a rebuilt system, you will perform a normal restore. The normal restore replaces all of the files from the backup media, and then Active Directory replication replicates any changes that had occurred after the backup was taken.

In order to perform the normal restore, you must restart the affected domain controller in Directory Services Restore Mode and restore the System State. Once you have restored the System State, reboot the domain controller and any objects that have been added, deleted, or updated since the last System State backup will be replicated to the domain controller.

Authoritative Restore

Have you ever mistakenly deleted a file or folder and realized later on that it was still needed? You check and realize that it is no longer in any Recycle Bin and you do not have a copy anywhere on the network. If your backup solution is working correctly, you can restore the file so that you can use it once again. In this scenario, restoring the file back to its original location is a straightforward process. But what happens when you have an object that needs to be restored to several systems and they all think that the object should not exist so they are instructed to delete it?

This is the reason for the authoritative restore. When an object is deleted from Active Directory, the object is stripped of most of its attributes and deposited within the deleted items container. All of the other domain controllers within the domain are notified of the deletion and perform the same action on their copy of the object. The authoritative restore tells the domain controllers to rethink their position on this object and allow it to exist within the domain once again.

Before you perform an authoritative restore, you must restore Active Directory as if you were performing a normal restore. However, before rebooting the system, open a command prompt and start NTDSUTIL. The following steps will show you what you need to do in order to restore an Organization Unit named Sales within the zygort.lcl domain.

1. From the `ntdsutil:` prompt, type **authoritative restore**.

2. From the `authoritative restore:` prompt, **type restore subtree ou=Sales,dc=zygort,dc=lcl**.

3. Type **quit** to return to the `ntdsutil:` prompt, and then type **quit** again to exit NTDSUTIL.

NOTE *If you want to make the entire database authoritative, you can use the* `restore database` *command. If you want to restore a single object, you can use* `restore object object-FQDN`.

If the authoritative restore includes Group Policy objects, you will also need to restore the Group Policy template within the `Sysvol` container so that the version ID that is reflected in the Group Policy container object in Active Directory refers to the Group Policy template within the `Sysvol`.

In order to do this, you will need to make sure that after you have restored the System State, you restore another instance of the System State to an alternate location. After you have performed the authoritative restore of the Active Directory objects, restart the domain controller and allow replication to occur. After all replication has brought your domain controller to a consistent state, copy the contents of the `Sysvol` folder in the alternate location to the existing `Sysvol` folder. This will return any Group Policy templates that you need to replace due to the replacement of the older Group Policy objects.

When restoring objects that have been deleted from Active Directory, you should take care in making sure that the restored objects have their original group memberships returned to them. Under most circumstances, when an account is deleted, the account's SID is removed from the groups where the account was a member. When the account is restored, the link between the account and groups it was a member are severed. In order to recover the group membership, you can manually add the account back into the groups it was originally a member, you can restore all of the user and groups to a previous state, or you can use the groupadd.vbs utility to generate the group membership of the account and then import the group membership links by using the resulting LDIF file. This can be a lengthy process. For more information and a step-by-step description of the recovery process, see TechNet article 840001.

The Tombstone

Remember all of those horror movies where the antagonist seems to return to haunt the good guys? Just when you thought it was safe to open your eyes because the bad guy had been done in, all of a sudden he bolted upright and another fight was on. Or worse yet, some Hollywood hack writer came up with a way to write a resurrection sequel so that you would pay to see how he was done in again and again and again.

Active Directory objects can work the same way. When you delete an object, it is gone. Or is it? As you probably already know, an object is "marked" for deletion. Like our horror movie baddie, you think that you are safe from the offending object, but it could come back to haunt you.

When an object is "deleted," most of the attributes of the object are removed and a new attribute, the tombstone time is added, and then it is moved to the Deleted Items container. The tombstone lifetime is, by default, 60 days. Any time within the 60-day period, you can perform a restore of the database and any objects that are marked for deletion are herded right back into the Deleted Items container to await their impending demise.

Problems arise when you try to restore objects past the tombstone lifetime. Microsoft's Backup utility will not allow you to use backup media that is older than the tombstone lifetime. To do so would be like having your horror-movie antagonist return to haunt you all over again. If the object were to be reintroduced after the tombstone lifetime had expired, Active Directory would not be aware of the objects deleted status and would reintroduce it into your forest. Suddenly, you would have objects that are no longer valid, thereby compromising your directory service.

We mentioned that the Backup utility will not allow you to restore from media that is older than the tombstone lifetime. But what if you are following the lead of many companies and using a system imaging utility to restore your systems? These imaging utilities are becoming increasingly popular. You can use them to configure a system, and when you have it built just the way you want it to perform, you can use the imaging utility to create a binary image of the system's hard drive and store it on the network, a CD, or DVD. When the system fails, it can be repaired and the imaging utility can be used to restore the operating system back to its initial state.

Imaging utilities are not concerned about the tombstone lifetime of Active Directory objects. Hence, if you restore a domain controller from an image, you will have all of the original objects that existed when the domain controller had been imaged. If any of those objects have been deleted and the tombstone lifetime has come and gone, you will be facing the ghosts of the objects you thought you had purged. It will be time for you to start exorcising your own Active Directory demons!

Automated System Recovery

The Windows Server 2003's Automated System Recovery (ASR) is new to the Windows family of server operating systems. This tool addresses a limitation within previous server operating systems when trying to restore your system after a disaster has struck. In previous operating systems, an Emergency Repair Disk (ERD) was used. As operating systems grew larger and larger, the ERD became an obsolete option because the files that it backed up were usually too large to fit on a single floppy disk. An ERD contained only the configuration information about the operating system and drive system, and it did not have a mechanism to store the important operating system files. The ASR solves some of those limitations.

Other disaster recovery solutions provided by third-party vendors provide the same functionality as ASR, but this is the first built-in solution that Microsoft has offered. The ASR process includes a backup portion and a restore portion. To access the backup portion, you need to start the Backup utility and select the Automated System Recovery option, as seen in Figure 11.4. This will start a wizard that will step you through the process of creating the ASR disk and saving the files.

FIGURE 11.4

Automated System
Recovery option in
the Backup utility

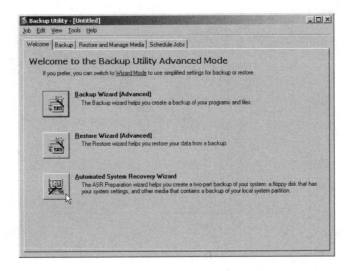

The files that are saved during this process include the following:

◆ System State

◆ System services

◆ Volumes that contain boot and system files

The ASR Backup

During the backup procedure, you will be prompted for a backup location. It can be any backup media or file location. Wherever you save these files, make sure that you can get to them while you are performing the ASR restore procedure. You will also be prompted to provide a floppy disk. This is the drawback to this procedure; it requires a floppy disk. If you do not have a floppy disk drive on your system, you will have to find a way to attach a floppy drive, or you will have to use another method.

TIP   There is a way to use the RIS service for ASR instead of a floppy drive. Microsoft Knowledge Base article 824184 has all the steps you need for a successful RIS ASR

The floppy disk will contain two files, `Asr.sif` and `Asrpnp.sif`. These files are used when starting the ASR restore so that the system will know where the files are located and how the drives should be configured. If you lose this floppy, do not fret. You can retrieve these files from the backup media. To do so, start Backup and choose to restore. From the ASR backup set, expand the Automated System Recovery Backup Set, expand the second instance of the drive letter that contains your system files, and expand the *systemroot*/repair folder as seen in Figure 11.5. The two files that you need to copy to the floppy disk are kept there.

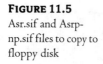

FIGURE 11.5
Asr.sif and Asrp-np.sif files to copy to floppy disk

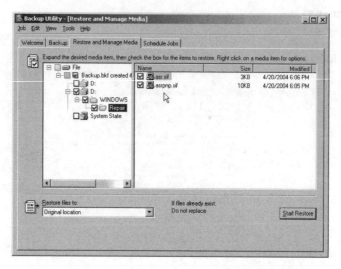

The ASR backup will not make a complete backup of your entire server. Only the volumes on which the system and boot files are located, referred to as the critical drives, will be backed up. At the same time, this is a manual process. You cannot automate the procedure using the Task Scheduler. If you think these are two limiting factors that you cannot live with, you should check out other third-party solutions.

The ASR Restore

The ASR restore procedure is not part of the Backup utility. As a matter of fact, it is not available from the operating system. You need to boot your system from the Windows Server 2003 CD. You should make sure that you have enough drives with the appropriate capacity to hold the data that will be restored to the critical drives.

Note that the partition on which the operating system files are placed will be reformatted prior to the files being restored. You should also make sure that the system to which you are restoring the data has identical hardware—with the exception of the hard drives, video, and network subsystems.

As the CD boot is starting, you will be prompted to press the F2 key to start ASR. Once you supply the floppy disk, you will be prompted to provide the backup media if it is stored on tape. Finally, you will be prompted for a destination for the operating system files. Provide the path and then watch as the recovery process completes. If you had completely lost your original system, after the ASR process is complete, you can restore the data drives to bring the system back to a completely functional level.

Best Practices for Disaster Recovery

Creating a disaster recovery process is considered by many administrators as one of the most boring tasks they have to perform. Furthermore, updating the process as changes occur within your environment are not a welcome addition to the daily routine. However, when a disaster does strike, having the ability to recover your systems, especially your directory service, back to an operational state is a blessing, considering the alternative.

- Make sure your domain controllers are physically secured so that an attacker cannot gain access to the system itself.

- If a domain controller is not physically secured, turn it into a "headless system" by removing the monitor, keyboard, and mouse. Use remote administration tools to work with it.

- Perform a System State backup regularly. You should back up the System State at least twice during the tombstone lifetime.

- Do not perform an authoritative restore on the entire domain naming context unless you know the ramifications of your actions. Understand exactly what will happen to all of the objects and the version to which they will revert.

- Verify that you need to return to an older version of a configuration naming context object prior to performing an authoritative restore on it.

- Do not store other data on the system and boot partitions. When you have to run ASR, you could lose data when these partitions are reformatted.

- Make sure you have enough drives to support ASR, and make sure they have enough capacity to hold the system data from the ASR backup set.

Next Up

We have gone through the necessary backup and restore options that you have when working with Active Directory. In the next chapter, we are going to look at some of the utilities and methods used to troubleshoot and maintain your directory service database. These utilities are very useful when you need to make repairs to a failed database or when you need to perform actions against your database in order to keep it running efficiently.

chapter 12

Optimizing the Active Directory Database

To MAKE ACTIVE DIRECTORY work efficiently, the database needs to remain in good working order. Problems with the database can cause issues with users trying to authenticate and search for resources and domain controllers replicating to one another. This chapter will introduce a way to increase the logging level that the directory service uses, and it will also introduce two tools to maintain the database, ADSI Edit and NTDSUTIL.

Configuring Diagnostic Logging

As most administrators will tell you, the Event Viewer is always the best place to start troubleshooting. The only problem is the events that are logged are either too few or too vague. The nice thing about the Active Directory directory service is that you can increase the logging levels on the server. By default, only critical events and error events are recorded to the Directory Services log of the Event Viewer. For the most part, this will be sufficient. However, there are times when you may want to perform more troubleshooting and gather additional information concerning the directory service. The drawback to increasing the amount of logging that you are performing is that you will also increase the overhead on the domain controller and fill up the logs at a faster rate.

You will not find a nice, quick-and-easy GUI tool to increase the logging level. You will be required to edit the Registry in order to change the amount of logging you require. Although Microsoft will always warn you about the dangers of editing the Registry, you shouldn't have any problems if you follow the steps correctly. However, at the same time, there is that chance that you could irreparably damage your system if you do not understand the ramifications of a change.

With that said, you will need to open the Registry Editor and navigate to the `HKEY_LOCAL_MACHINE\SYSTEM\CurrentControlSet\Services\NTDS\Diagnostics` key, as seen in Figure 12.1.

FIGURE 12.1
Registry key to change the diagnostics level for the directory service

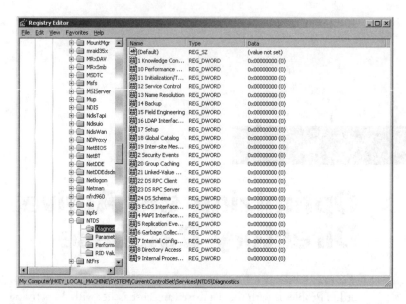

Notice that there are several values within this key. Each one represents a separate event type that will write to the Directory Service event log. Looking at the values shown in Figure 12.1, values 1 through 19 are available for both Windows 2000– and Windows Server 2003–based domain controllers. Values 20 through 24 are available only on Windows Server 2003 domain controllers.

The diagnostic level on all of the values is set to 0 by default. At this level, only the critical events or error events are delivered to the Event Viewer logs. To increase the amount of logging that you are performing, you will need to change the logging level to one of the levels seen in Table 12.1.

TABLE 12.1: DIAGNOSTIC LOGGING LEVELS

LOGGING LEVEL	LOGGING PERFORMED
1	Minimal
2	Basic
3	Extensive
4	Verbose
5	Internal

As you start troubleshooting, you should incrementally increase the logging level to determine where the problem may lie. Increasing the logging level to 3 or 5 will consume far more resources than you may want to allocate to logging and will inject so many events into the event logs that you may have to increase the size of your Directory Service log.

As you determine the service or category with which you are having issues, you can increase the logging level temporarily. Set the level to 3 once you have ascertained the service or group of categories that might have problems. Doing so will give you more information in order to narrow your search. Once you have narrowed the search to a specific category, reduce the logging level on the unaffected categories and increase the affected category to 5 for a short period of time. Once you move the logging level to 5, everything that affects that category will be logged—and I mean *everything*. You will probably receive more information than you will have time to parse through. Remember to always reduce the logging levels as soon as possible.

Using ADSI Edit to View Directory Service Partitions

ADSI Edit is a utility that is part of the support tools. Once you add the support tools, ADSI Edit is available from Start Menu➤ Programs➤ Support Tools. The Windows Server 2003 version is an MMC snap-in. With either version, you can connect to domain controllers and view the Directory Service partitions.

Figure 12.2 shows the dialog box that appears when you use the Connect To option from the ADSI Edit context menu. From here, you can name the connection you are making to anything that will help you identify the naming context you are accessing. Within the Connection Point text options, either you can enter the fully qualified name of the naming context to which you are connecting, or you can choose one of the four well-known naming contexts. If you are connecting to one of the new Application Partitions, you will need to identify it by its fully qualified name.

FIGURE 12.2
ADSI Edit connections dialog

In the Computer section, you can choose a domain controller to connect to, or you can default to the domain controller you are logged onto if you are running ADSI Edit from a domain controller.

Once you choose the naming contexts to which you are connecting and the server to which you are connecting, you will see them reflected within the ADSI Edit window, as shown in Figure 12.3. You can now expand the appropriate naming context to locate the objects you need to manipulate. Later in this chapter, and in other chapters in the book, we will show you how to use ADSI Edit to perform some of your administrative troubleshooting.

FIGURE 12.3
ADSI Edit with naming contexts added

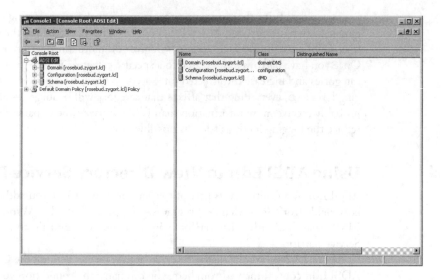

Using NTDSUTIL for Active Directory Database Troubleshooting and Repair

The Active Directory database is the same type of database that is used within Exchange servers. If you are familiar with the utilities used with an Exchange server, you should be familiar with some of the utilities used with Active Directory. A benefit of using NTDSUTIL is that the cryptic commands that were needed to manage the Exchange databases are encapsulated into easier-to-understand commands.

Upcoming chapters will introduce some of the other utilities such as DSASTAT and DCDIAG; however, for now we will concentrate on the tool that is used to manage the consistency of the Active Directory database, NTDSUTIL. Using this tool, you will be able to perform the following actions:

- ◆ Checking database integrity
- ◆ Recovering the database
- ◆ Compacting the database
- ◆ Moving the database
- ◆ Moving the log files
- ◆ Removing orphaned objects
- ◆ Maintaining security accounts

In the following sections, I will detail the steps that are required to perform each of these actions. Although you may rarely have to perform most of these actions, you should understand when and how to use NTDSUTIL to perform each one.

The NTDSUTIL utility is included on Windows 2000 and Windows Server 2003 domain controllers. There are very few differences between the two versions, so most of what is presented within this chapter applies to any of your domain controllers. I will point out the differences as we go along.

Committing Transactions to the Database

Due to the nature of the ESE database, all of the transactions are processed in memory and written to log files before they are committed to the database on the hard drive. If the server were to fail, the transaction logs would still contain all of the information necessary to bring the database back to a consistent state.

Prior to performing most of the actions that follow, you should commit the transactions to the database, which is also known as performing a *recovery procedure.* Just follow these steps:

1. When starting the computer, press F8 to enter the Startup Selection screen.

2. Select Directory Services Restore Mode.

3. Once you log on with the Directory Services Restore Mode administrator account, open a command prompt.

4. From the command prompt, type **ntdsutil** and press the Enter key.

5. From the ntdsutil: prompt, type **Files** and press the Enter key.

6. From the file maintenance: prompt, type **Recover** and press the Enter key.

As shown in Figure 12.4, the screen will display information regarding what is taking place as the recovery is running. After the recovery is complete, the database will be consistent and you will be able to run other utilities as necessary.

FIGURE 12.4
NTDSUTIL used to commit the transactions

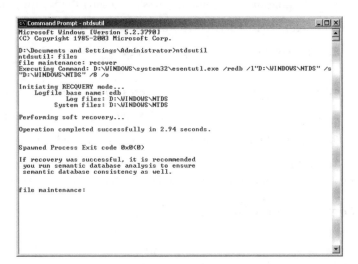

If errors crop up while running the recovery on a Windows 2000–based domain controller, and the recovery option does not repair them, you may need to repair the database. Exercise caution before you run this against your database because you could lose data in the process.

Make sure you have a good backup of your domain controller. You might want to contact Microsoft Product Support Services to make sure that you have covered all your bases. They may have another option for you to try before you run a repair.

Once you are committed to running the repair process, follow these steps:

1. When starting the computer, press F8 to enter the Startup Selection screen.

2. Select Directory Services Restore Mode.

3. Once you log on with the Directory Services Restore Mode administrator account, open a command prompt.

4. From the command prompt, type **ntdsutil** and press the Enter key.

5. From the ntdsutil: prompt, type **Files** and press the Enter key.

6. From the file maintenance: prompt, type **Repair** and press the Enter key.

Checking Database Integrity

When you are checking the integrity of the database, every single byte of data within the database is analyzed for corruption. This procedure can take a great deal of time if you database is large. This is not something you should run just because you feel like you want to see what happens. Prior to starting an integrity check, make sure you have performed the recovery option as detailed in the previous sections. The steps to perform an integrity check are as follows:

1. When starting the computer, press F8 to enter the Startup Selection screen.

2. Select Directory Services Restore Mode.

3. Once you log on with the Directory Services Restore Mode administrator account, open a command prompt.

4. From the command prompt, type **ntdsutil** and press the Enter key.

5. From the ntdsutil: prompt, type **Files** and press the Enter key.

6. From the file maintenance: prompt, type **integrity** and press the Enter key.

As you can see in Figure 12.5, the utility will perform the check against the database. If any errors are reported, you should contact Microsoft Product Support Services to determine how you should proceed.

Compacting the Database

During normal operations, the Active Directory database will not need to be compacted. Every domain controller will perform its own garbage collection every 12 hours by default. During this garbage collection, the database will be defragmented, but the database size will not be reduced. This usually does not present a problem, because databases tend to grow over time to take up the additional free space.

FIGURE 12.5
NTDSUTIL integrity check

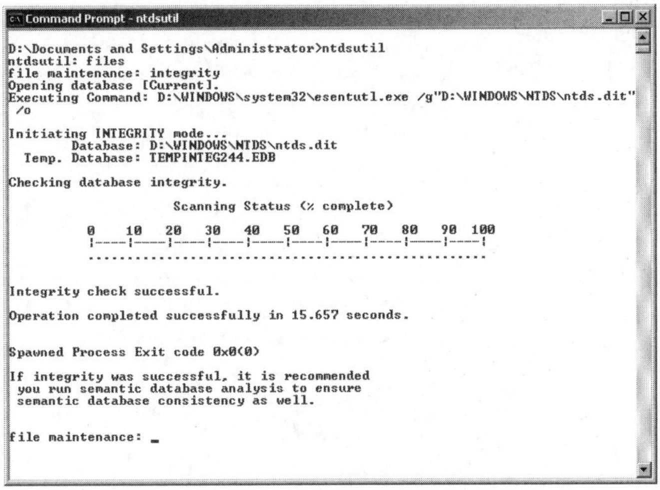

With that being said, there are times when you may want to recover disk space with an offline defragmentation and compaction. If you have just deleted a large number of objects from Active Directory, have removed the Global Catalog role from a domain controller, or you have just moved several accounts to another domain, you may want to reduce the size of your database.

TIP *To log an event to the Directory Services event log that will tell you the amount of space that you can free up during an offline defragmentation, you can change the Registry entry at* HKEY_LOCAL_MACHINE\SYSTEM\CurrentControlSet\ Services\NTDS\Diagnostics\6 Garbage Collection *to a value of* **1***.*

To compact your database, follow these steps:

1. When starting the computer, press F8 to enter the Startup Selection screen.

2. Select Directory Services Restore Mode.

3. Once you log on with the Directory Services Restore Mode administrator account, create an empty directory to store the new compacted database.

4. Open a command prompt.

5. From the command prompt, type **ntdsutil** and press the Enter key.

6. From the ntdsutil: prompt, type **Files** and press the Enter key.

7. From the file maintenance: prompt, type **compact** and press the Enter key.

After the compact command finishes, you should copy the new compacted database file, ntds.dit, to the location of the original database file. The utility will let you know where to copy the database if you are unsure, as seen in Figure 12.6.

FIGURE 12.6
NTDSUTIL after
moving the database

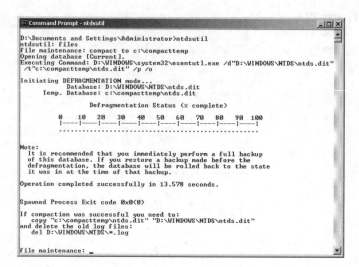

You should also delete the old log files that were associated with the original bloated database file. Again, if you are unsure of the location of the log files, the Compact utility will let you know where they are located.

Moving the Database

As databases age, they have a tendency to grow. Even with our best intentions and attempts to create partitions and volumes large enough to hold databases, there are times when they grow too large. There are also times when you may want to take a database off of a spindle that may be showing signs of having problems. Being proactive and moving the database to another drive may save you headaches later on.

To move the database, follow these steps:

1. When starting the computer, press F8 to enter the Startup Selection screen.

2. Select Directory Services Restore Mode.

3. Once you log on with the Directory Services Restore Mode administrator account, open a command prompt.

4. From the command prompt, type **ntdsutil** and press the Enter key.

5. From the ntdsutil: prompt, type **Files** and press the Enter key.

6. From the file maintenance: prompt, type **move DB to *\<directory\>*** and press the Enter key.

The *\<directory\>* can be any location on a partition or volume that has enough space to hold the database, and preferably have room to continue growing. If the directory to which you are moving the database does not already exist, the utility will create it for you.

The utility will also configure the system to use the new location so that you do not have to perform any other steps to tell the operating system where to locate the database. However, you should perform a backup of the domain controller after moving the database so that your backup files reflect the new location of the database.

Moving the Log Files

The same issues hold true for the transaction log files that affect the database. You may not have enough room on a partition or volume to hold the logs, but more than likely you will either have a failing drive or you will simply want to separate the transaction log files and the database. As a matter of fact, I recommend that you move the transaction logs off of the same physical disk as the database files. Place them on their own physical disk so that they do not have to compete for disk time with any other service. Once you do so, the system will actually perform better.

The steps to move the transaction logs are basically the same as moving the database:

1. When starting the computer, press F8 to enter the Startup Selection screen.

2. Select Directory Services Restore Mode.

3. Once you log on with the Directory Services Restore Mode administrator account, open a command prompt.

4. From the command prompt, type **ntdsutil** and press the Enter key.

5. From the ntdsutil: prompt, type **Files** and press the Enter key.

6. From the file maintenance: prompt, type **move logs to *<directory>*** and press the Enter key.

Again, the *<directory>* does not have to previously exist; the system will create the directory for you. You should back up the system after performing the move so that the files can be restored if necessary.

Removing Orphaned Objects

Typically, when you decommission a domain controller, the entries for the domain controller are removed from the database. The same holds true when you remove the last domain controller for a domain. If you select the check box that identifies the domain controller as the last domain controller for the domain, all of the metadata for the domain should be removed from all of the other domain controllers within the forest.

In a perfect world, you would not have to concern yourself with the metadata stored in the database—but as we know, nothing is perfect. You may encounter instances when the metadata for domain controllers or domains is not correctly removed from the database. This could be due to the unsuccessful demotion of a domain controller or because a domain controller failed and you cannot restore it. If this happens, services might try to connect to domain controllers that they think still exist. This can cause problems with replication as well as the Knowledge Consistency Checker.

REMOVING ORPHANED DOMAIN METADATA

To remove a domain's orphaned metadata, follow these steps:

1. Log on to the domain using an account that is a member of the Enterprise Admins group.

2. Make sure that all of the domain controllers have been demoted or taken offline. Also, verify that all of the remaining domain controllers within the forest have successfully replicated.

3. Identify which domain controller holds the Domain Naming Master Operations role. You can do this by opening Active Directory Domains and Trusts, right-clicking on the root node, and selecting Properties. On the context menu, select Master Operations. You will find the Domain Naming Master domain controller within the Current Operations Master box.

4. Open a command prompt, type **ntdsutil**, and press Enter.

5. At the ntdsutil: prompt, type **metadata cleanup** and press Enter.

6. At the metadata cleanup: prompt, type **connections** and press Enter.

7. Type **connect to server** *servername* where *servername* is the name of the domain controller holding the Domain Naming Master Operations role.

NOTE   *If you have not logged on using an account that is a member of the Enterprise Admins group, you can set your credentials at this point by typing* **set creds** *domainname username password and then pressing Enter.*

8. Once you have received confirmation that the connection has been made, type **quit** and press Enter.

9. Type **select operation target** and press Enter.

10. Type **list domains** and press Enter.

11. From the list of domains that appears, locate the domain you want to remove the metadata and the number with which it is associated.

12. Type **select domain** *number* and press Enter.

13. Type **quit** and press Enter.

14. Type **remove selected domain** and press Enter.

15. Once you receive confirmation that the domain metadata has been removed, type **quit** and press Enter.

16. Once you receive confirmation the connection to the Domain Naming Master has been disconnected, type **quit** and press Enter.

REMOVING ORPHANED DOMAIN CONTROLLER METADATA

To remove Domain Controller metadata, you begin by using the same method you used to remove the domain; however, you will need to remove additional data with other utilities to complete the removal. After running NTDSUTIL, you will need to remove the computer account, the File Replication Service (FRS) member, and the trustDomain object using ADSI Edit. The DNS entries using the DNS snap-in and the domain controller object within Active Directory Sites and Services will need to be removed. The steps for all of these procedures are given in the follow sections.

Removing Domain Controller Metadata

1. Log on to the domain using an account that is a member of the Enterprise Admins group.

2. Verify that all of the domain controllers within the forest have successfully replicated.

3. Open a command prompt, type **ntdsutil**, and press Enter.

4. At the `ntdsutil:` prompt, type metadata cleanup and press Enter.

5. At the `metadata cleanup:` prompt, type **connections** and press Enter.

6. Type **connect to server** *servername*, where *servername* is the name of the domain controller holding the Domain Naming Master Operations role.

NOTE *If you have not logged on using an account that is a member of the Enterprise Admins group, you can set your credentials at this point by typing* **set creds** *domainname* *username* *password* *and then pressing Enter.*

7. Once you have received confirmation that the connection has been made, type **quit** and press Enter.

8. Type **select operation target** and press Enter.

9. Type **list domains** and press Enter.

10. From the list of domains that appears, locate the domain that the domain controller is a member of and note the number that is associated with the domain.

11. Type **select domain** *number* and press Enter.

12. Type **list sites** and press Enter.

13. From the list of sites that appears, locate the site the domain controller is a member of and note the number that is associated with the site.

14. Type **select site** *number* and press Enter.

15. Type **list servers in site** and press Enter.

16. From the list of domain controllers that appears, locate the domain controller and note the number that is associated with the domain controller.

17. Type **select server** *number* and press Enter.

18. Type **quit** and press Enter.

19. Type **remove selected server** and press Enter.

20. Once you receive confirmation that the domain metadata has been removed, type **quit** and press Enter.

21. Once you receive confirmation that the connection has been disconnected, type **quit** and press Enter.

Using ADSI Edit to Remove Computer Account

If you are unsuccessful removing a computer account by using Active Directory Users and Computers, you can use this method.

1. Open ADSI Edit.

2. Expand Domain NC.

3. Expand DC=*domain*,DC=*tld*.

4. Expand OU=Domain Controllers.

5. Right-click CN=*domain controller* and click Delete.

Figure 12.7 displays the Domain Controllers node within ADSI Edit and the menu items you can choose.

Using ADSI Edit to Remove the FRS Member

To remove a file replication system member, use these steps.

1. Open ADSI Edit.

2. Expand Domain NC.

3. Expand DC=*domain*,DC=*tld*.

4. Expand CN=System.

FIGURE 12.7
ADSI Edit used to delete domain controller object after metadata has been removed

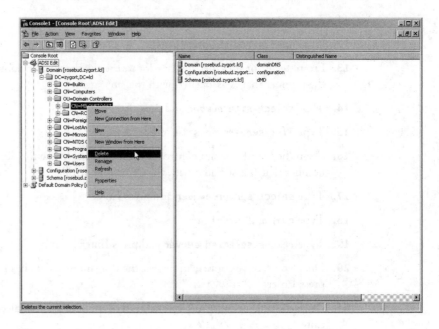

5. Expand CN=File Replication Service.

6. Expand CN=Domain System Volume.

7. Right-click the domain controller you are removing, and click Delete.

Using ADSI Edit to Remove the trustDomain Object

If you need to remove a trust due to the failure of the GUI utilities from performing the operation, you can use these steps.

1. Open ADSI Edit.

2. Expand Domain NC.

3. Expand DC=*domain*,DC=*tld*.

4. Expand CN=System.

5. Right-click the Trust Domain object, and click Delete.

Use DNS Snap-In to Remove DNS Records

DNS records may need to be manually removed. If so, follow these steps.

1. Locate the A record within the zone, right-click the A record and click Delete.

2. Expand the _msdcs container, locate the CNAME record, right-click the CNAME record, and click Delete.

3. If the server was a DNS server, right-click the zone, choose Properties, and then remove the server's IP address from the Name Servers tab.

Using Active Directory Sites and Services to Remove Domain Controller Object

After you have removed the domain controller references, you may have to remove the replication object from Active Directory Sites and Services.

1. Open Active Directory Sites and Services.

2. Expand Sites.

3. Expand the server's site.

4. Expand the Servers node.

5. Right-click the domain controller, and click Delete.

Maintaining Security Accounts

For all of the safeguards that Microsoft has taken to ensure that identical SIDs are not introduced into a domain, there is still the possibility that two accounts could have the same SID. This could occur when an administrator seizes the RID Master role while the original RID Master is offline, but still operational. If the original RID master did not have an opportunity to receive updated replication information and is brought online, it could generate identical RIDs and allow them to be used within the domain. Any time you seize the RID Master role, you should run this check.

In order to check for accounts that may be using identical SIDs, follow these steps:

1. Open a command prompt.

2. Type **ntdsutil** and press Enter.

3. Type **security account management** and press Enter.

4. Type **check duplicate SID** and press enter.

The log file that is created from this check is placed within the directory path where you had started NTDSUTIL. If you had changed directories to the root of the D: partition and then started NTDSUTIL, you would find the **dupsid.log** residing there. If you are lucky, you will not have any entries within the files. If there are entries, note them and delete the duplicate.

To delete the duplicate SID, follow these steps:

1. Open a command prompt.

2. Type **ntdsutil** and press Enter.

3. Type **security account management** and press Enter.

4. Type **cleanup duplicate SID** and press enter.

The object with the newer GUID is removed from the database. You will then need to re-create the account that was removed during this process.

Best Practices for Optimizing AD

Active Directory is the heart of your organization's infrastructure and you need to make sure that is it performing optimally. If you are having problems, you should be familiar with some of the tools that you have at your disposal to troubleshoot and treat the ailment.

◆ When troubleshooting the Directory Services, increase the logging level gradually to isolate the problem if the problem isn't apparent.

◆ Always use the Recover utility in NTDSUTIL to commit all transactions to the database prior to running any other utilities.

◆ Don't run an offline defragmentation on the database unless you have deleted a large number of objects or are planning to move the database and want to reduce its size.

◆ If any domain controller fails during demotion, make sure you remove the associated metadata from the database and remove all of the object information using ADSI Edit.

◆ If the last domain controller for a domain fails during demotion, make sure you remove the associated metadata from the database.

◆ Move the transaction log files to their own drive to increase the domain controller's efficiency.

◆ If the RID Master role is inadvertently seized while the original is still functioning but offline, check for duplicate SIDs when the original is returned to the network.

Next Up

The next chapter concentrates on the Active Directory database as it pertains to an individual domain controller. You will rarely (if ever) find an organization that has only one domain controller. Almost all organizations have multiple domain controllers, and they need to talk to one another in order to share the information they hold in their directory databases. At the same time, this replication traffic may fail or have problems, so it will be up to you to make sure that replication is working correctly and efficiently.

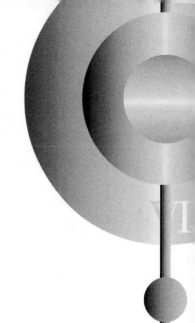

chapter 13

Troubleshooting Active Directory Replication

NOTHING IS MORE STRESSFUL than having domain controllers that are not sharing information. By their very nature, domain controllers are supposed to be multimaster replicas of one another, and you should have identical information on every domain controller within a domain. However, there are some issues that rear their ugly heads and cause you to have the nightmare day of troubleshooting. This chapter is here to help.

Replication Overview

Understanding how something works is the first part of knowing how to troubleshoot a problem. Whereas having troubleshooting methodology will help you ascertain the problem, you will have a better "feel" for where to start looking for problems if you understand the way something works and behaves.

Active Directory replication is probably one of the more obscure things that you will have to learn. Most administrators know why they need it, but they don't know how it goes about its business to get the objects from one domain controller to another. A quick review of the process is in order before we move on to troubleshooting replication problems.

If your DNS infrastructure has issues, Active Directory replication may not work. Verify that your DNS infrastructure is stable and name resolution is working correctly. Chapter 14, "Maintaining DNS," covers some of the options you have when maintaining and troubleshooting your DNS infrastructure.

If DNS is working correctly, domain controllers will have a better chance at replicating the objects between one another. The first thing a domain controller does when replicating objects is to examine the connection objects to other domain controllers. The domain controller will not be concerned about domain controllers other than those to which it has a connection.

Within the Configuration partition, the domain controller will find the domain controllers to which it is connected. Active Directory will return the GUID that is associated with the domain controller defined on the connection object. Each domain controller registers the SRV records for the

Active Directory services it supports and its GUID. If you open the _msdcs zone for the domain, you will find the domain controller GUID. Figure 13.1 shows the GUID for the domain controllers within the zygort.lcl domain. The GUIDs appear as the last two lines within the details pane.

FIGURE 13.1
Domain controller
GUIDs registered
in DNS

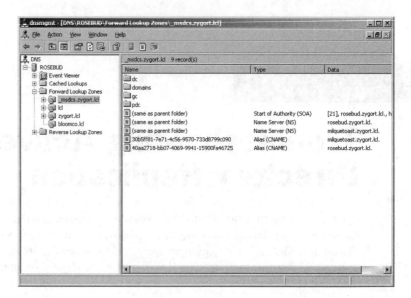

After the domain controller has obtained the GUID for the partner domain controller, it sends a query to DNS to locate the hostname; then using the hostname, it queries for the IP address. Once the domain controller has the IP address of the partner domain controller, it can initiate an RPC connection to the partner and begin the replication process.

Determining DNS Problems

When domain controllers are brought online, they register records within the DNS server they are configured to use. This registration includes the GUIDs that are registered within the _msdcs zone. If the domain controller fails to update its GUID, other domain controllers will not be able to locate it in order to replicate Active Directory objects. To troubleshoot DNS issues, you can use the DNSLint command.

NOTE *The* DNSLint *command can be used to perform other troubleshooting tasks. See Chapter 14, "Maintaining DNS," for more information on the additional uses of* DNSLint*.*

When using DNSLint to troubleshoot Active Directory issues, you need to use the /ad switch. This will force DNSLint to compare the GUIDs within the DNS server to the domain controllers for the domain. The command is issued at the command prompt in the form:

```
Dnslint /ad domain_controller_ip_address /s dns_server_ip_address
```

The /s switch informs DNSLint that you are not going to attempt name resolution to the Internet root domains; instead, you are going to work with specific DNS servers to validate the name resolution information. For instance, if your domain controller is using IP address 10.23.74.1 and the DNS server that you are testing against is using IP address 10.23.77.5, your command line would appear as:

```
Dnslint /ad 10.23.74.1 /s 10.23.77.5
```

Once issued, DNSLint will attempt to bind to the domain controller to retrieve the GUIDs for all of the domain controllers within the domain. If successful, it will then compare the GUIDs to those within DNS by issuing queries to the _msdcs zone looking for the CNAME records. At this point, the DNS server that you identified when using the /s parameter will need to be authoritative for the _msdcs zone. If it is not, the DNS server must have an entry listed within it that will allow DNSLint to locate a DNS server that is authoritative for the zone.

Once the DNS server is located and the GUIDs are queried, if a positive response is returned, DNSLint will attempt to locate the A record for the domain controller based on the host name that is returned from the CNAME record. If everything is successful, you will not receive any errors on the HTML output that DNSLint provides. Otherwise, you will notice errors and have a starting point when trying to determine why replication is not working correctly. Figure 13.2 is an example of the first half of the HTML report that is generated; it shows the GUIDs that were found. Figure 13.3 shows the bottom half of the same report; it details the domain controller entries that were discovered within DNS.

FIGURE 13.2

DNSLint report showing GUIDs of domain controllers

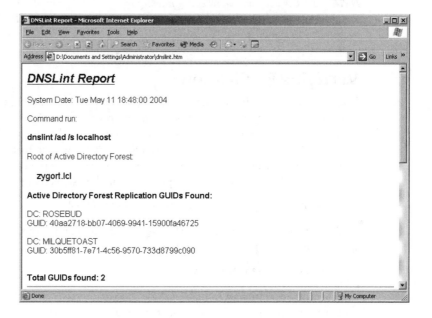

FIGURE 13.3
DNSLint report
showing domain
controller entries
within DNS

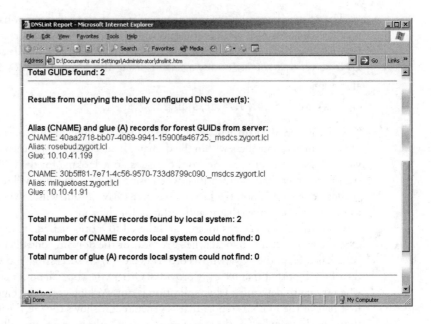

NOTE *To check a domain controller that is configured as a DNS server also, you can issue the command* dnslint
/ad /s localhost. *Doing so will cause* dnslint *to use* 127.0.0.1 *as the IP address of the domain controller and
the internal DNS server as the DNS starting point.*

Verifying Replication

You may want to verify that objects have been completely replicated throughout the domain before
you attempt to run applications or perform administrative management of the domain controllers. In
order to do so, you can use the dsastat.exe utility from the Support Tools. This utility will allow
you to compare the contents of the Active Directory database so that you can determine whether replication has completed. In its most basic form, you can issue the command and specify only the
domain controllers you want to compare, separated by semicolons such as:

    Dsastat -s:*domaincontroller1;domaincontroller2*

When issuing the command in the zygort.lcl domain for the domain controllers rosebud and
milquetoast, the command line would appear as:

    dsastat -s:rosebud;milquetoast

The utility will attempt to make LDAP connections to each of the domain controllers and query
the partition information. It will compare both directory databases and return whether or not they are
identical. Figure 13.4 shows the response that is returned if the databases are identical, and Figure 13.5
shows the response when replication has not completed.

FIGURE 13.4

Response from `dsastat.exe` if replication has completed

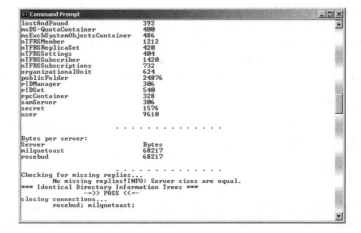

FIGURE 13.5

Response from `dsastat.exe` if replication has not completed

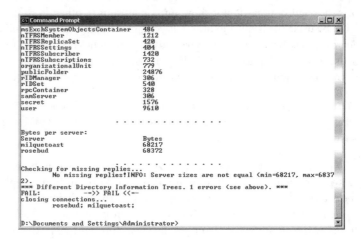

NOTE *The* `dsastat.exe` *utility can also be used to verify that specific portions of the Active Directory structure are synchronized. For more information on the switches available for use with* `dsastat.exe`, *enter* **dsastat /?** *at the command prompt.*

Other tools are available that can also provide information about your Active Directory directory service and tell you whether or not the replicas are up-to-date. The first is the command-line tool `repadmin`, which can be found in the Support Tools. If you are more comfortable using the GUI-based tools, the ReplMon utility is available to perform the same functions. The final tool we will discuss is the DCDiag utility.

Using RepAdmin

The RepAdmin utility can assist you when you are trying to determine the cause of replication problems. Some of its more popular options include checking the status of the Knowledge Consistency Checker (KCC), viewing the replication partners for domain controllers, and viewing which domain controllers have not replicated. If you want to view the KCC status, you can enter the command:

```
repadmin /kcc
```

If you want to view the replication status of the last replication attempt from a domain controllers replication partners, you can enter the command:

```
repadmin /showreps
```

Windows 2000 and Windows Server 2003 will both use the /showreps option, but the RepAdmin utility that is included with Windows Server 2003 Support Tools can also use the /showrepl switch to do the same thing. Windows Server 2003 also uses the /replsummary switch, sometimes abbreviated as /replsum, to allow you to view the failures and replicated objects. You should see a minimum of three connections per domain controller, one connection for each of the directory partitions. If the /showreps or /showrepl options do not show any connections to other domain controllers, you should run the KCC by using the ReplMon utility. If you are working within a Windows Server 2003 environment, you can open Active Directory Sites and Services, right-click the NTDS Settings object, and select All Tasks ➤ Check Replication Topology. If you still receive errors because the KCC did not create the appropriate connection objects, manually create a connection object between the domain controllers.

NOTE If you use the Check Replication Topology option on the domain controller that is the Intersite Topology Generator, you will recalculate the intersite and intrasite replication topology. If you run it from any other domain controller, you will recalculate the intrasite topology.

You can force synchronization for any of the partitions with repadmin tool by using the /sync switch. This will force replication for a specific partition from a replication partner that you use in the command. If you want to force replication between all domain controllers, you can use the option /syncall. By default, the Active Directory replication is *pull replication,* meaning that the domain controller will request the data from its partners. You can change that behavior by using the /P switch, which forces the domain controller to push its objects to it partner domain controllers. The command looks like this:

```
repadmin /syncall domain_controller_FQDN directory_partition /P
```

Using ReplMon

ReplMon is the graphical utility that will allow you to view the connections between domain controllers and troubleshoot issues with Active Directory replication. It will also allow you to view the Update Sequence Number (USN) of the replication partners and the last successful replication time. As seen in Figure 13.6, you can add the domain controllers that you want to monitor within the contents pane of the utility and perform tests on them. Beneath the domain controller, all of the directory partitions are listed. When you expand the partition, you will be shown the replication partner and the replication results for the last replication attempt for that partition.

FIGURE 13.6

ReplMon interface

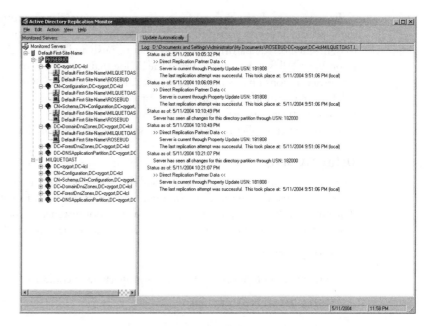

The menu that is shown in Figure 13.7 shows the options that are available when working with a domain controller. You can perform the same functions from this menu that you can from the RepAdmin command-line utility.

FIGURE 13.7

ReplMon menu
options

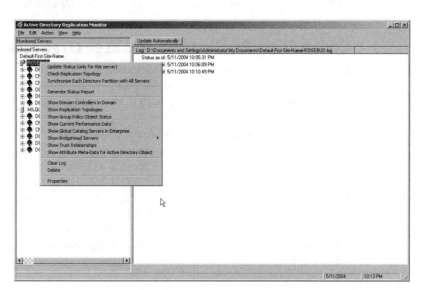

In order to push the changes from one domain controller to another, you need to enable push mode on the directory partition that you want to force to the partners. In order to do so, you need to right-click on the partition that you want to push and select the Synchronize This Directory Partition With All Servers option. From the dialog that appears, you can select the Push Mode option. The other options on this dialog can also come in handy. The option Disable Transitive Replication will force replication to the partner domain controllers only and will not cause them to send out notifications to their partners. The option Cross Site Boundaries will allow you to replicate the data to every domain controller regardless of the site in which they are located.

Using DCDiag

DCDiag is a command-line utility that will run diagnostic tests against the domain controller. It runs several tests, and the output can span many screens. If you want to perform specific tests against the domain controller, you can use the /test: switch. For instance, if you want to make sure that the replication topology is fully interconnected, you can issue the command:

```
dcdiag /test:topology
```

To test that replication is functioning properly, you could issue the command:

```
dcdiag /test:replications
```

To view the status of Global Catalog replication, you can issue the command:

```
dcdiag /v /s:domain_controller_name | find "%"
```

You may have to issue this command a few times from the command line to monitor the progress. As soon as DCDiag has no more output to show, the replication is complete.

Controlling Replication in Large Organizations

In a large organization where you have several domain controllers, you could experience CPU and memory performance problems on bridgehead servers as they attempt to compress the data that needs to be sent between sites. The KCC and ISTG functions run every 15 minutes to calculate and repair the replication topology, which adds an additional load on the domain controller.

In a Windows 2000–based Active Directory forest, even though each directory partition can have a different bridgehead server assigned to replicate it, the KCC can assign only a single bridgehead server to replicate a partition. Windows Server 2003 improved upon this design by allowing the KCC to randomly assign a bridgehead server from the list of available bridgehead servers to replicate a partition. All of the partitions must still be replicated at the same time, however, so the network could still take on a large load if data from all of the partitions were replicated.

The Active Directory Load Balancing (ADLB) tool will allow you to perform advanced load-balancing tasks within the forest. Even though the tool has limitations, it does allow you to load balance Windows 2000 domain controllers, as well as set time staggering on Windows Server 2003 domain controllers.

The limitations are few. However, if you do not specify to retain the ADLB settings, the next time the KCC runs, it will reset the connection objects that ADLB had modified. If you do specify to keep the settings, you will need to make sure that the changes are replicated to the other domain controllers that are acting as partners.

Running ADLB without using the `/commit` parameter will allow the administrator to view the settings that ADLB would like to put into effect. When specifying the bridgehead server that you are running ADLB against, you can use the hostname or the NetBIOS name of the server, depending on the name resolution methods that your network supports. To view the changes for the bridgehead server `rosebud.zyort.lcl` within the Chicago site, you would enter the command:

```
adlb /server:rosebud /site:Chicago
```

The output will detail the connections and changes that ADLB would make if the `/commit` parameter were specified. The ADLB utility can be used by any user who has loaded it from the Windows Server 2003 Resource Kit tools. However, if you want to allow ADLB to make the changes to your replication topology, you need to have Enterprise Admin privileges.

If you want to view the changes that ADLB is recommending, but you want to print them out instead of viewing them at a command prompt, you can specify a log file by using the `/log` parameter and specifying the path to the log file. You can also view additional performance statistics that ADLB uses to make its recommendations by including the `/perf` parameter.

If you are running your domain within the Windows Server 2003 functional level, you can stagger the replication schedule by using the `/stagger` parameter. This will allow you to stagger the updates for each of the directory partitions so that they are not sent at the same time.

The command to create a log file that will allow you to view the performance statistics and recommendations of ADLB when it is set to stagger settings would look like the following command:

```
adlb /rosebud.zygort.lcl /site:Chicago /log:d:\logfiles\adlbtest.log /stagger /perf
```

The `/stagger` option will not modify the connection objects of bridgehead servers in remote sites; you will need to run the utility on each bridgehead server. If you have administrative rights on the remote bridgehead server, and you have Terminal Services configured for administrative use, you can open a session and run the utility. Otherwise, you will have to work in conjunction with an administrator for the remote site.

Best Practices for Troubleshooting AD Replication

If your domain controllers are not replicating objects correctly, users will not be able to gain access to the objects that they need, and may fail to log on at all. The following are tips that you should keep in mind when troubleshooting replication issues.

- ◆ Use the tool you are most familiar with when troubleshooting replication problems.

- ◆ Verify the replication topology to make sure all of the domain controllers from all sites are interconnected.

- ◆ Urgent replication, such as account lockouts, will occur within the site, but will not be replicated to other sites until the site link allows it to replicate. Use RepAdmin to force the change.

- ◆ Create connection objects between domain controllers that hold FSMO roles and the servers that will act as their backup if the FSMO role holder fails. Make sure replication is occurring between the two servers.

Next Up

As we leave Active Directory replication troubleshooting behind, we are going to start looking at DNS. It is one of the technologies that are vital if any type of Active Directory functions are going to be performed. Without DNS, Active Directory replication will not work, and Active Directory will not function at all. The following chapter will introduce you to the new technologies that are available to Windows DNS servers and the tools that you can use to manage and maintain the DNS service.

chapter 14

Maintaining DNS

THERE ARE MANY WAYS to configure your operating systems to perform the tasks that you need them to perform; however, there is one thing that you can't escape: you have to have DNS in place for Active Directory to function. It is true that you can install Active Directory without DNS installed; however, before the directory service will run, you will need to make sure that you have implemented DNS within the organization. Active Directory does not care whether you are running DNS on a Windows-based server or a UNIX system. As long as DNS supports Service Locator (SRV) records, Active Directory will use it.

In Chapter 3, "Domain Name System Design," we looked at the design options that are available when you plan your Active Directory infrastructure. In this chapter, we are going to discuss trouble-shooting and maintaining the DNS infrastructure for your forest. Microsoft has introduced several new options for name resolution, and it is in your best interest to understand how each of the technologies are used so that you can maintain an efficient DNS solution for Active Directory.

DNS Resolution Methods

DNS servers provide name resolution for the DNS zones for which they are authoritative. If a DNS server is not authoritative for a zone, the server should provide the client with an alternative method of resolution. A typical DNS server will host root hints that identify the root DNS servers for the Internet. When the server is not authoritative for a zone and the name that the client is sending the query for has not already been resolved, the DNS server will send an iterative query to one of the root DNS servers. The root DNS server will in turn return an address for a name server that can get the DNS server closer to a DNS server that is authoritative for the zone. If at any time during the iterative process a DNS server has already resolved the name of the host, the address for the host is returned and the client is given a response to its query. The name cache on the DNS server and the client are updated so that they can respond with an immediate response to subsequent queries.

For those DNS servers that sit within your organization's internal network, you may not want them to host the root hints. Some organizations will not allow the internal DNS servers to be accessible from external clients. Those servers typically will not have the root hints installed, so another method of resolution must be configured. Within Windows 2000 DNS servers, you can configure standard forwarders to send resolution requests to other DNS servers. This was a great improvement over Windows NT DNS, which was a very limited DNS service. In Windows NT DNS, if you wanted to allow name resolution for another zone, you had to create a secondary zone for the zone in question and transfer the records from a master DNS server or use a delegation record to redirect queries to DNS servers that are authoritative for zones within the same namespace.

Windows Server 2003 addresses the limitations of simply having standard forwarders by allowing an administrator to configure conditional forwarders and stub zones. Each of these technologies has its advantages as well as disadvantages within your DNS infrastructure. Knowing when to use each one will allow you to use your DNS service efficiently. Each of the options is summarized in the following sections.

Standard Forwarder   A standard forwarder will forward unresolved queries to another DNS sever. A standard forwarder can have multiple DNS servers listed within the DNS server list, and the forwarder will send queries to each one in order, but only if the higher priority DNS server cannot be contacted. Figure 14.1 shows an example of a DNS server's forwarder list. On a Windows 2000 DNS server, the only entry that is available is the standard forwarder entry titled All Other DNS Domains. On a Windows Server 2003 DNS server, conditional forwarders can be also be configured.

Conditional Forwarder   The conditional forwarder sends queries to DNS servers based on the domain name that is included in the query. Windows Server 2003 introduced the ability to configure conditional forwarders. Figure 14.2 shows a DNS server configured to use conditional forwarders. When conditional forwarders are used, they are used prior to a standard forwarder.

Stub Zone   Stub zones are new to Windows DNS, being introduced with Windows Server 2003. A stub zone acts about the same way as a delegation record, but it automates the process of populating the zone information. With a delegation record, the administrator is responsible for identifying the DNS servers that are authoritative for the zone. If those servers change, the DNS administrator will have to change the delegation record accordingly. Stub zones, on the other hand, will retrieve a list of the authoritative DNS servers as they change. As the administrator adds the stub zone, the zone's SOA record is loaded by the stub zone, and the NS and A records for each of the DNS servers that are identified as name servers for the zone are loaded into the stub zone.

Secondary Zone   A secondary zone loads all of the records from the zone so that the queries for records within the zone can be resolved by the DNS server hosting the secondary zone. The records for the zone are transferred from a master server, which can hold the primary zone or another secondary zone.

Delegation Records   Even though delegation records have been used within DNS servers for many years, they are still alive and kicking. For administrators who want to delegate the responsibility of maintaining a subdomain, they can create a delegation record that directs a query to be sent to a DNS server that is authoritative for the subdomain. A delegation record appears within the zone as a gray icon, as seen in Figure 14.3.

FIGURE 14.1
Standard forwarder

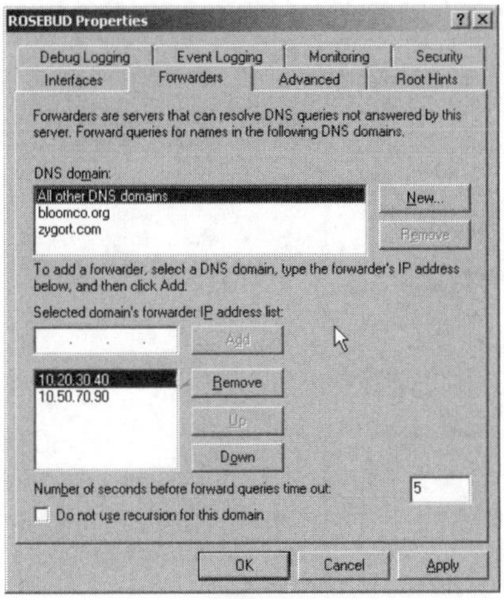

FIGURE 14.2
Conditional
forwarder

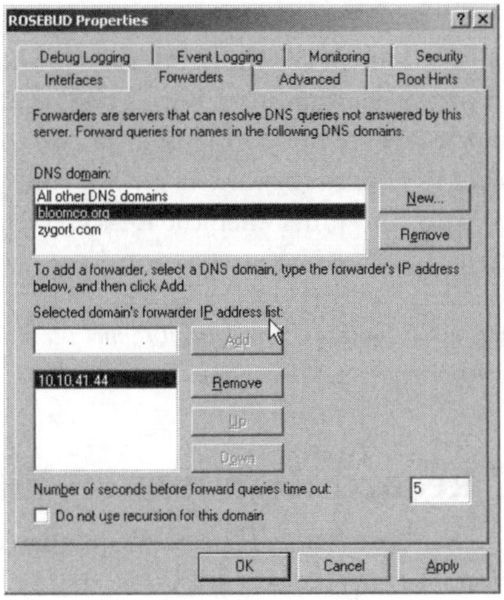

When a query is sent to a DNS server, it will first attempt to resolve the query from its name cache. If the query cannot be resolved from the name cache, the zones that are configured on the DNS server are checked in an attempt to have the DNS server resolve the query. Each of the primary, secondary, and stub zones are checked. If a zone contains a delegation record to the zone in question, the DNS server will respond with the address of a DNS server that is authoritative for the zone. If the stub zone is used for the zone in question, the stub zone will return the IP address of a DNS server that is authoritative for the domain.

FIGURE 14.3
Delegation record

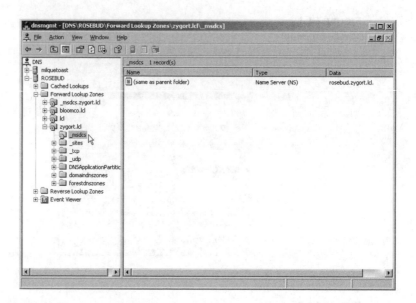

If the zone is not listed on the domain controller, the server will then take advantage of the conditional forwarders, standard forwarders, and root hints. The server will first check the conditional forwarders. If conditional forwarders are not configured for the zone in question, the standard forwarder is used. If conditional and standard forwarders are not configured, the root hints will be used. If the server is not configured with root hints, then the DNS server will return a response specifying that the host cannot be located.

NOTE *Note that if the server hosts a zone within its database, it cannot use a conditional or standard forwarder, nor will the server use the root hints to perform any additional lookups for that hosted zone.*

Root Domain SRV Record High Availability

Windows 2000 DNS servers that host Active Directory–integrated zones hold the records for the zone as Active Directory objects. In a Windows 2000–based domain, when you create an Active Directory–integrated zone, the zone data is stored within the domain partition and is replicated to every domain controller within the domain. In a large domain with several domain controllers, where some of those domain controllers are in remote sites, you may not want to replicate the zone information throughout the organization.

Windows Server 2003–based Active Directory–integrated zones are not required to be stored within the domain partition. A new partition type, known as the *application partition*, can be used to store an Active Directory–integrated zone. An application partition can be stored on any domain controller that is a DNS server within the domain or the forest, or you can create an application partition that is stored on domain controllers that you decide will host the zone.

NOTE   *For more information on creating application partitions, see the section "Active Directory Application Mode" later in this chapter.*

If you are upgrading your Windows 2000–based Active Directory to Windows Server 2003, and you want to make sure that the SRV records that are registered by domain controllers are available to hosts within all of the domains within the forest, you will have to make a couple of changes to the _msdcs subdomain.

In Windows 2000–based domains, if the _msdcs subdomain is to be made available on DNS servers within other domains, a new zone must be created for the _msdcs zone. A delegation record will be created to point to the zone, and then a secondary zone will be used within the other domains' DNS servers.

With the advent of the forest-wide application partition, an administrator now has the ability to use Active Directory–integrated zones within every domain in the forest. To do so, the _msdcs zone is created as an Active Directory–integrated primary zone with a forest-wide scope, as seen in Figure 14.4. The administrator will still need to make sure that a delegation record is created so that the zone can be located when the DNS server receives a query for it. If the administrator has already created the zone as a standard primary zone, the zone only needs to be converted to Active Directory–integrated.

FIGURE 14.4

_msdcs with a forest-wide scope

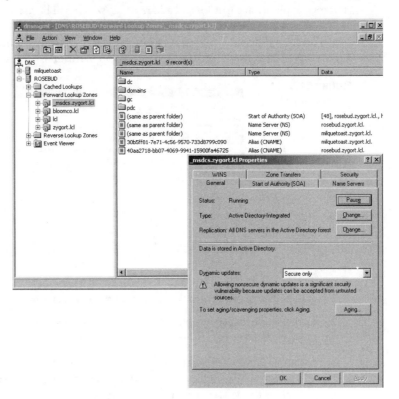

TIP *If your forest root domain is installed using Windows Server 2003, the* _msdcs *zone is created as a forest-wide Active Directory–integrated zone for you and you do not have to reconfigure the zone.*

Limitations abound, and you will need to make sure that your infrastructure can handle the option you choose. For instance, if a firewall blocks TCP port 53, a stub zone will not be able to transfer the zone data. In that case, a delegation record or a forwarder can be configured instead.

Active Directory Application Mode

Active Directory Application Mode (ADAM), or *application partitions* as they are often called, can be used to control where application data is replicated through the forest. You can create partitions that are replicated to all domain controllers or specific domain controllers. Where DNS is concerned, application partitions can be used to host the zone data for Active Directory–integrated zone instead of using the domain partition. Windows Server 2003 will create the application partition for you if you are using domain-wide or forest-wide scopes. There is one other scope option, to replicate to specific domain controllers.

In order to control the replication to specific domain controllers within the forest, you must create your own application partition and add replicas, which will be made part of the replication scope. In order to create an application partition, you will need to use the NTDSUtil tool. This tool will allow you to create and delete application partitions as well as control where the replicas will be held. As seen in Figure 14.5, you can create an application partition by following these steps:

FIGURE 14.5

Creating an application partition

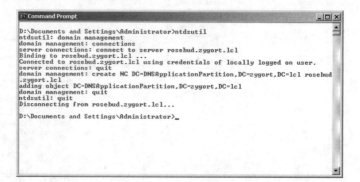

1. Start NTDSUtil, and enter the command **domain management**.

2. At the domain management: prompt, enter the command **connections** to take you to the server connections: prompt.

3. From the server connections: prompt, connect to the server you want to create the application partition by using the command **connect to server** *servername* and then type **quit** to go back to the domain management: prompt.

4. At the `domain management:` prompt, type **create NC *Partition_FQDN servername***.

NOTE *When you add the application partition using this command,* `Partition_FQDN` *will be in the form* `DC=partitionname,DC=domainname,DC=TLDname`.

NOTE *If you are adding the application partition to the system to which you are currently connected, you can use* **NULL** *instead of the server's DNS name.*

After you have added the application partition, you can assign replicas to domain controllers within the forest by performing Steps 1 through 3 and then entering the command **add NC replica *Partition_FQDN servername***, as seen in Figure 14.6.

FIGURE 14.6

Adding a replica of the application partition to a domain controller

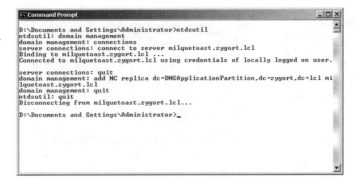

After the replicas are added, the domain controllers that host the replicas of the application partition are the only servers that will participate in replication for the partition. If you want to remove a replica, you can follow Steps 1 through 3 and then enter the command **remove NC *Partition_FQDN servername***. After all of the replicas have been removed, you can remove the application partition completely by performing Steps 1 through 3 and then entering the command **Delete NC *Partition_FQDN***.

You can determine whether the application partition was created by using one of two methods. The first one is to use the `DNScmd` tool to verify that the application partition exists. To do so, open a command prompt and enter the command **dnscmd *domain_controller_name* /directorypartitioninfo *application_partition_name***, as seen in Figure 14.7. When using this command, you do not have to use the fully qualified LDAP name of the domain controller or the application partition, but you should use the fully qualified DNS name of each. Using this command will also allow you to see which domain controllers hold replicas of the application partition.

The other method is to open the properties of an Active Directory–integrated zone and click the Change button next to the Active Directory–integrated zone replication scope. Click the radio button marked To All Domain Controllers Specified In The Scope Of The Following Active Directory Partition, as seen in Figure 14.8. If the application partition appears in the pulldown list, the partition has been created.

FIGURE 14.7
Using DNSCmd
to verify the creation
of an application
partition

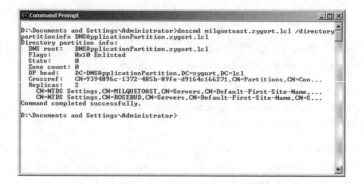

FIGURE 14.8
Application parti-
tion being chosen to
host records for an
Active Directory–
integrated zone

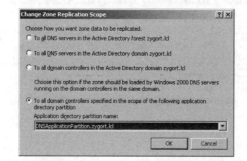

Diagnostic Tools

DNS has been around for a long time, and there are several tools that you can use when attempting to troubleshoot name resolution problems. The standard TCP/IP tools, such as `ping` and `tracert`, will allow you to troubleshoot some basic issues; however, if you want to troubleshoot the DNS server and the zones within, you will want to use the `nslookup` command.

Using `nslookup` will allow you to determine if records have been registered and whether the DNS server is responding to queries correctly. `Nslookup` runs in two modes, interactive and noninteractive. In interactive mode, you can continue issuing commands against the DNS server. In noninteractive mode, you issue individual commands against the server.

To determine if the SRV records for the domain have registered, you can issue the following commands at a command prompt:

1. Type **nslookup** to enter interactive mode.

2. At the > prompt, type **ls -t SRV** *domainname*.

If you are trying to view the SRV records for the domain `zygort.lcl`, you should enter the command **ls -t SRV _msdcs.zygort.lcl**. Figure 14.9 is an example of the output that you would receive.

FIGURE 14.9

Viewing SRV
records with
nslookup

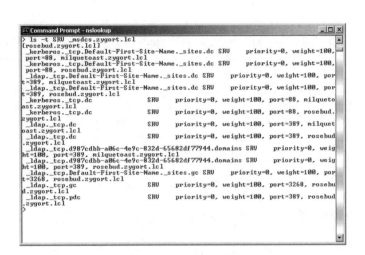

As we mentioned, there are several tools that you can use when troubleshooting DNS, but one of the most useful tools is included with the Windows Server 2003 Support Tools, DNSLint. DNSLint is a command-line tool that will verify your DNS infrastructure and allow you to view the results in an HTML-formatted report. If you use DNSLint without any parameters except for the domain name in question, it will check the DNS servers that are authoritative for the zone and all associated DNS servers. This will give you an easy method to locate lame delegations or delegation records that specify DNS servers that are no longer authoritative for the domain. This is essentially the same thing as using the /d parameter, which will perform lame delegation diagnosis for the domain.

You can use two switches, /ql and /ad, to troubleshoot DNS issues with DNSLint. With the first option, /ql, you can create a text file that will allow you to query against a list of DNS servers for the domain. To create the list, you can issue the command:

```
dnslint /ql autocreate
```

Once you have issued that command, enter the command **Notepad in-dnslint.txt** to open Notepad with the dnslint file that was created using the **autocreate** command.

You will need to edit a few lines within this file. They are as follows;

1. On the sixth line from the bottom of the file, change dns1.cp.msft.net to the fully qualified DNS name of the DNS server you are querying against.

2. Change any instances of Microsoft.com in the last four lines of the file to the domain that you are checking.

3. Change any instances of 207.46.197.100 to the IP address of the DNS server you are querying against.

4. Save the file as **dnslintquery.txt** and close Notepad.

5. At the command prompt type, **dnslint /ql dnslintquery.txt**.

An HTML page will open and you will be able to view the results.

The /ad switch will check the DNS server to make sure the GUID for the domains are registered correctly and will check the records that are registered by the domain controllers, including the NS and A records for the domain.

Windows 2000 and Windows Server 2003 DNS servers have monitoring capabilities built in that will allow you to check the status of simple queries against the computer as well as queries to other servers based on root hints. As long as the system can query against a server within the root hints, it will return a positive result. If root hints are not configured, or the server is blocked from accessing the DNS servers that are listed within the root hints, the query will fail. If you are performing a recursive query test, as seen in Figure 14.10, make sure that your system is not the root of the hierarchy and that it can connect to servers listed within the root hints.

FIGURE 14.10

Results of a DNS monitoring test

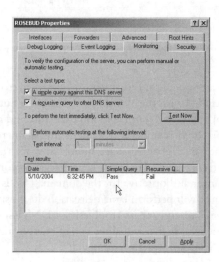

New to Windows Server 2003 is the Debug Logging tab on the DNS server properties, as seen in Figure 14.11. This option should be enabled only if you are having issues with your DNS server and you want to find out more information. The debug logging will produce additional overhead on the DNS server as it monitors itself and writes information into a file. However, you can use this option to determine where problems may be occurring.

If you are experiencing problems with hosts that are resolving against your DNS server, select the Incoming option. If you are experiencing problems with name resolution outside of your zones, enable the Outgoing option. Narrow the problem down by collecting data and then disable debug logging so that you do not affect the performance of your DNS server.

FIGURE 14.11
Debug Logging tab
of DNS properties

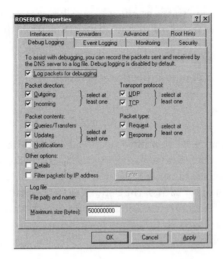

Best Practices for Maintaining DNS

DNS is the lifeblood of your Active Directory infrastructure. Without it, not only will your clients be unable to find the domain controllers, but the domain controllers will not be able to perform replication of the Active Directory objects, the FRS will not function, and several other core features will fail. You should use the following practices to get your DNS up and running.

- ◆ On internal DNS servers that do not provide name resolution to the Internet, remove the root hints and configure forwarders to the DNS server that will provide Internet name resolution.

- ◆ If the root domain of your forest is configured as the root domain for DNS, add your root DNS servers' IP addresses to the root hints of the DNS servers of each of your domains.

- ◆ To automate the process of maintaining the name server records for an external zone, use a stub zone.

- ◆ Use conditional forwarders to direct queries to specific internal and partner zones, and use a standard forwarder for Internet queries.

- ◆ Configure delegation records for zones that are within the same namespace but delegated to other DNS servers.

- ◆ Configure the _msdcs so that it is using the forest-wide application-partition replication scope.

- ◆ If upgrading from Windows 2000, create a new Active Directory–integrated zone for the _msdcs zone, set it to use the forest-wide application partition, and then create a delegation record within the forest root to point to the zone.

- ◆ To reduce the replication traffic as much as possible, create an application partition and configure replicas only on the domain controllers that will use the DNS zone.

- ◆ Only use the debug logging for a DNS server when you need to troubleshoot a problem.

- ◆ Use `DNSLint` to create an output file that you can print.

Next Up

Maintaining DNS is imperative if you want a functional Active Directory infrastructure. With all of the different types of Active Directory environments that exist, you will need to make sure that you are choosing the correct method of name resolution to suit your needs. At the same time, you'll need to make sure you understand how each of the options works so that you can troubleshoot and repair.

Another part of your Active Directory infrastructure that relies on DNS to perform correctly is the File Replication System (FRS). In the next chapter, we are going to look at some of the tools that you can use to make sure FRS is working correctly and how to get it back into an operational state if it is not.

chapter 15

Troubleshooting the File Replication Service

IN CHAPTER 13, "Troubleshooting Active Directory Replication," we discussed Active Directory replication issues. In Chapter 14, "Maintaining DNS," we looked at DNS maintenance and troubleshooting. Both of these chapters are a good preview to this one where we will look at the File Replication Service (FRS). Although we will use some of the same tools, the issues that spring up with the FRS require different solutions to repair.

File Replication Service Overview

FRS is responsible for replicating objects from the Sysvol folder so that all of the domain controllers have the same Group Policy Objects and scripts. FRS is also responsible for synchronizing the files within Distributed File System (DFS). It is up to FRS to determine when changes have occurred in the replicas of the folder. Because FRS allows for multimaster replication, any of the domain controllers can update the files within the Sysvol folder, and it is then up to FRS to synchronize all of the partners.

Just as Active Directory relies on DNS, so does FRS. If you are having problems with your DNS implementation, you will probably experience problems with FRS as it attempts to perform its duties. FRS also relies on Active Directory replication to be working so that the Active Directory objects that make up GPOs are replicated among the domain controllers. Active Directory's domain partition replication topology is used when determining the replication topology for FRS. Doing so will allow you to update both the Active Directory object and Sysvol objects that correspond to one another.

The Sysvol folder is actually shared as two names that you can access: Sysvol and NETLOGON. They are actually DFS links that are used to store the data that users need for GPOs and scripts. For this reason, the DFS service will automatically start and you should not stop the DFS service on a domain controller; otherwise, you will terminate the replication of any Sysvol data.

TIP   *Although we are concentrating on* Sysvol *synchronization problems in this chapter, DFS troubleshooting can use the same utilities that are mentioned here.*

FRS Problems

There are some common problems that you may encounter with FRS. These common issues can cause plenty of headaches, but knowing the way to work through them will allow you to leave work on time and spend the night free of phone calls. Some common problems include journal wrap, morphed directories, staging area problems, and parallel version vector joins.

Journal Wrap

When changes are made to NTFS objects, entries are written into the NTFS Change Journal. FRS uses the NTFS Change Journal to identify the objects that have changed. If an object that FRS needs to replicate is changed, the object is copied into the staging area and compressed, making it ready to be replicated to the other domain controllers. If the NTFS Change Journal is too small, several changes can occur before FRS checks with the journal. If too many changes occur and the oldest changes are purged before FRS can see them, FRS does not replicate them to the other domain controllers.

Windows 2000 SP2 and earlier uses a very small NTFS Change Journal size of 32K. Windows 2000 SP3 increases the size to 128KB, while Windows 2000 SP4 and Windows Server 2003 have a Journal size of 512KB. If you are still having problems due to the amount of changes that are occurring within your environment, you can increase this even more by editing the following Registry entry on your domain controller:

```
HKEY_LOCAL_MACHINE\System\CurrentControlSet\Services\NtFrs\Parameters
```

You will need to create a new REG_DWORD key called:

```
NTFS Journal Size In MB
```

Add the size of the journal as a decimal value.
At a command prompt, type **net stop ntfrs** followed by **net start ntfrs**.

WARNING   The journal size can be increased. However, to decrease it, all volumes that contain FRS content must be reformatted. See Knowledge Base Article Q292438 for more information.

Morphed Directories

When you create an object on two domain controllers before they have a chance to replicate, the domain controller will rename the new item with a prefix of _NTFRS_*xxxxxxxx*, where *xxxxxxxx* is a random number to uniquely identify the object. When this happens, FRS will not replicate the duplicate object; instead, it will hold the object until the administrator can decide what to do with it. If you notice that there are duplicate entries due to the names of the files, you will need to decide whether you are going to delete the object with the correct name and rename the morphed object, or whether you will delete the morphed object retaining the correctly named object.

Usually, morphed entries are caused by administrators who manually copy files into the replicating folder because they do not think the system replicated the files, or because two administrators copy the same information into folders on two different domain controllers. Morphed folders can also occur when you make one of your domain controllers authoritative for the data that is configured to replicate and you did not make the other domain controllers nonauthoritative. Make sure you understand how FRS treats replicated files before you start changing the behavior of the domain controllers or start copying files.

NOTE   For more information about configuring the BurFlags registry value on a domain controller so that you can control the authoritative copy of the `Sysvol` *data, read Knowledge Base articles 315457 and 328492.*

Staging Area Problems

When an object that FRS maintains is changed, it is copied into the staging area where it will reside until all of the partner domain controllers have pulled it. If you are having replication problems with FRS and one of the partner domain controllers does not pull the objects, they could stay in the staging area and cause a backlog.

With Windows 2000 SP3 and later systems, including Windows Server 2003, if the staging area reaches 90 percent capacity, the domain controller will remove the oldest files until the directory is down to 60 percent capacity. You should monitor the staging directory to see if it is filling up to an excessive amount and determine what is causing so many object changes.

1. If you need to increase the size of your staging area, you can do so by editing the following Registry key:

   1. `HKEY_LOCAL_MACHINE\System\CurrentControlSet\Services\NtFrs\Parameters`

2. Right-click on Staging Space Limit In KB, and select Modify.

3. Add the size of the staging area as a decimal value.

4. At a command prompt, type **net stop ntfrs** followed by **net start ntfrs**.

NOTE   For more information about staging area space recommendations, see Knowledge Base article 329491.

Parallel Version Vector Joins

When a domain controller is added to the domain, a version vector is created that notifies all of the domain controllers of the add and the latest version of the `Sysvol` data. Pre-SP3 versions of Windows 2000 will perform a parallel update, pulling the `Sysvol` information from all of the partner domain controllers. This could cause a tremendous amount of replication traffic. Windows 2000 SP3 and later and Windows Server 2003 will perform a serial update, requesting the `Sysvol` information from each domain controller in turn. This way, after the first domain controller replicates the `Sysvol` data, the others are queried, and if there are no discrepancies no further replication will occur.

FRS Troubleshooting Tools

The tools that were mentioned in the past two chapters can assist you when trying to troubleshoot problems associated with FRS replication. Remember that Active Directory replication and the DNS infrastructure are key to FRS working properly. There are a couple of very useful tools that you can use when working with FRS; `FRSDIAG.EXE` from the Windows 2000 and Windows Server 2003 Resource Kit tools, and a freely downloadable utility called Ultrasound.

Using *FRSDIAG.EXE*

The FRSDiag tool will help you determine which of your domain controllers is having problems with FRS replication. When you load this tool, you can include specific domain controllers that you want to run tests against. As you can see in Figure 15.1, the domain controllers are listed within the summary window, and each one has its own tab that you can use to find out additional information from the tests that are run against it. On the left side of the tool, there are several tests that you can select to run against all of the domain controllers that you have identified. Notice that the tests that run with this utility are also used when troubleshooting Active Directory replication such as RepAdmin.

FIGURE 15.1
The FRSDiag utility

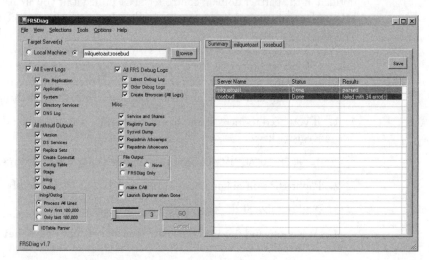

Once you select the test you want to run, you can click the Go button and be presented with information about each domain controller. A file will be created within a subfolder of where the tool is installed.

This utility will also run a propagation test that will place files within the staging area to determine how long it takes for files to replicate between all of the partner domain controllers.

One nice feature of this tool is the ability to force replication between the domain controllers with which you are working. If the domain controllers are not in sync, and the NTFS Change Journal has rolled over so that FRS does not realize it is supposed to replicate the data, you can force the issue using this tool. To do so, you can go to the Tools menu and select Force Replication On Target Servers, or use the Ctrl+F key combination.

Using Ultrasound

This freely downloadable utility will proactively monitor your FRS service on your domain controllers. It relies on client software that needs to be loaded on each domain controller, and requires a database to hold the resulting data. The database can be either Microsoft SQL Server or Microsoft MSDE 2000. Once you have the database ready, and you install Ultrasound, you can specify the domain controllers you want to monitor and Ultrasound will push the client software onto the domain controllers.

The client software actually installs Windows Management Instrumentation (WMI) providers that are used to gather FRS status information so that it can be relayed back to the control console. Figure 15.2 shows the control console. Notice the tabs that are available. From them, you can get detailed information about the status of FRS. The Health tab is a quick view of the status of each domain controller you are monitoring. From there, you can quickly see if a domain controller has warnings or errors, and you can double-click on the entries to see what is happening with the domain controller.

FIGURE 15.2

Ultrasound control console

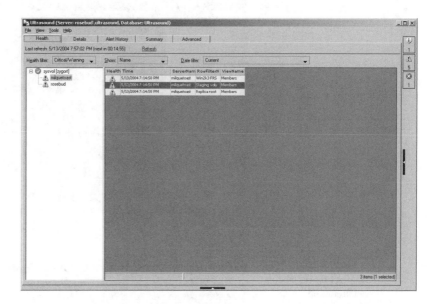

The Details tab allows you view the status of the domain controller in relation to its partners, along with the results of propagation tests that you have ran. As seen in Figure 15.3, the Details tab has four views that control the information that appears. The Topology view lists the domain controllers you are monitoring. When you select one from the Members list, the replication partners for both Inbound and Outbound connections appears. The Topology Changes tab will show the latest connection changes due to new domain controllers that were added, and it will show changes to the topology when the KCC ran.

The Files view on the Details tab will show the files that have been placed within Sysvol. This includes the logon scripts and System Policies as well as the GPO templates. You can look on this page to determine the number of files that are on each replication partner and also determine which GPO templates are stored in the Sysvol. If you know the GUID of the GPO, you can match it up against the GPO template that is stored here.

The Alert History tab shows you exactly that—the alerts that have been issued within the time frame you have specified. If you are concerned only about warnings and errors within the last 24 hours, you can show that time frame, or you can change it to any of the time frames shown in Figure 15.4. Notice that the alerts are also shown summarized on the right-hand side of the utility so that you can double-click them at any time to learn more about the warning or error. When you do so, you will receive a dialog box similar to the one shown in Figure 15.5. The dialog tells you what the alert is for, and it will also suggest how to fix the problem.

FIGURE 15.3
Details tab for Ultrasound

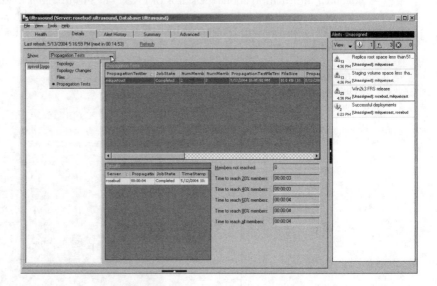

FIGURE 15.4
Alert History tab for Ultrasound

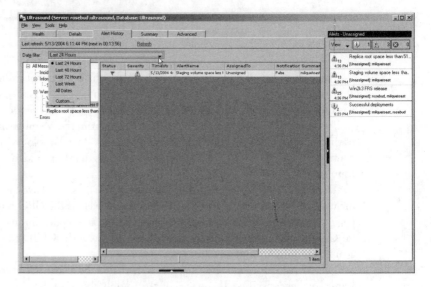

FIGURE 15.5
Alert dialog

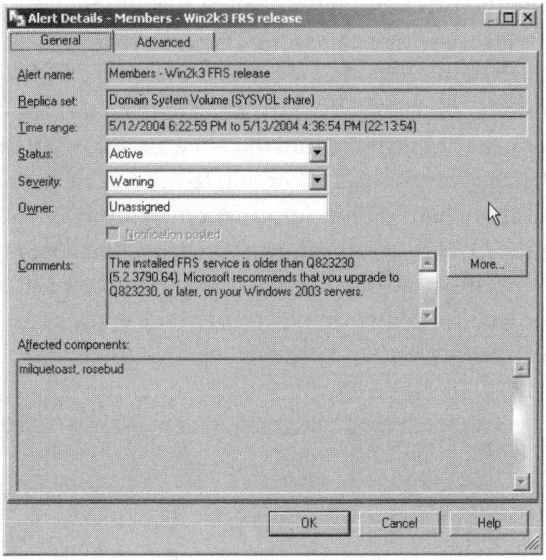

The Summary tab shows summarized information about the domain and the domain controllers you are monitoring. This tab is useful to get a bird's eye view of the condition of your replication topology. None of the items within this view will return any additional information if you click on them. However, as you can see in Figure 15.6, you can see immediately what the condition of each partner is.

FIGURE 15.6
Summary tab of
Ultrasound

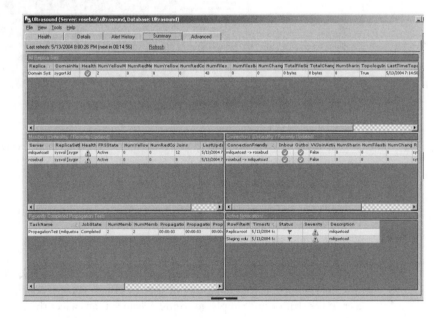

Figure 15.7 shows the Advanced tab and all of the options that are available to select. Notice that several monitored items are within this view. You can see nearly every aspect of your FRS replication topology and any of the data that is being extracted from the WMI filters that are installed when the client software installs on the domain controller. You have a lot of control over how this tab displays the data. Clicking any of the entries within the Views window on the left-hand side of the utility and then selecting the Change button will allow you to modify the data that the view will show. You can also click the Details button to receive information about the view. You can then customize what is displayed by using the Date Filter dropdown to change the date range. You can view data based on information within specific rows or columns by using the Row Filter and Columns Filter dropdowns. If the Row Filter or Column Filter do not contain the entries you want to view, you can select the ellipses button next to either one and create your own filter.

FIGURE 15.7

Advanced tab of Ultrasound

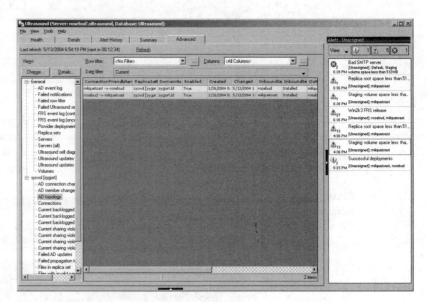

The Incident Log is displayed at the bottom of the screen, as shown in Figure 15.8. In this area, you can enter information concerning the alerts and how you took care of them (or information about the steps you are currently taking to fix problems). This way, any technician who is working on problems can view what has been attempted or resolved.

You can configure alert notifications as either e-mail notifications or messages. Use Tools ➤ Default Notifications to enter the e-mail address of a technician or Help Desk account to which e-mails will be sent in case of an alert. You can also send messages on the network, assuming that the messenger service is running on your systems. When you set default notifications, the accounts that are listed will receive all alert messages that are at the error level. If you have specific personnel who are responsible for taking care of specific issues, you can configure notifications on any of the alert types that occur. Simply go to the Advanced tab, select the row or column filter you want to set a notification for, and then change the alert setting on the Alert tab of the filter properties. By default, the accounts listed within the Default Notifications will receive the messages; however, entering an account in this area will override that setting.

FIGURE 15.8

Incident Log

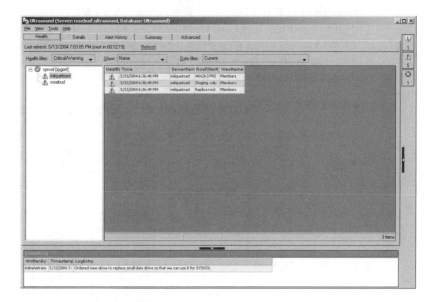

Microsoft Operations Manager

If you are using Microsoft Operations Manager (MOM), you can add the FRS Management Pack and start using the real-time monitoring capabilities that MOM offers. MOM can log information into a database and send alerts. MOM takes advantage of the Ultrasound database to monitor FRS. Using MOM for monitoring purposes allows you to centralize all of the monitoring within your organization and take advantage of the rules that are built into MOM that analyze the data coming from all of the monitored servers and services. For more information on using MOM, see Microsoft's website at http://www.microsoft.com/mom.

ULTRASOUND HELP

As you can tell, I am very impressed with the Ultrasound utility. But as impressed as I am with the utility itself, the Help file that accompanies it is even more impressive. Nearly every detail of FRS is contained within this file. If you want to become an expert on FRS—and in a large Active Directory infrastructure you should have a team that is—you will want to study this file. This file includes complete details as to how FRS works, best practices for supporting FRS, troubleshooting tips, and a complete list of events that are registered to the Event Viewer as FRS events occur.

Common FRS Problem Resolution

You will find events within the File Replication Service Event Log such as those seen in Figure 15.9. Some of the events that you will see are easily corrected. You will note that events 13508 and 13509 are in this log. If you find event 13508, wait for a 13509 to appear. Event 13508 specifies that the domain controller could not replicate to a partner. This could be a temporary problem, and if the 13509 appears within a few hours, you should not have any problems. If the 13509 does not appear within approximately 4 hours after the 13508, you should start investigating what is causing the two domain controllers to be unable to start RPC sessions between them.

FIGURE 15.9

File Replication Service Event Log

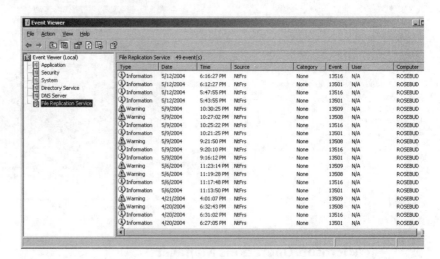

You may also encounter an Event ID 13511. This indicates that the FRS database is out of disk space. If you run into this problem, you should free up space on the partition, or move `Sysvol` to another partition where you are not likely to run out of space. This error is usually found on a system using DFS, but it can occur on a system that was not properly sized to hold the Active Directory database and all of the associated files.

An Event ID 13522 denotes that the staging area is full. Within a pre–SP3 Windows 2000 domain controller, you will need to manually clear the files from the staging area. The domain controllers that are running SP3 or later, or Windows Server 2003 domain controllers, will automatically reduce the files within the staging area when it reaches 90 percent capacity.

Event ID 13548 is found in the Event Viewer when the clocks on the domain controllers are skewed. Domain controllers will not authenticate computer accounts whose clocks are off by more than 30 minutes. If the clocks on the domain controllers are off by more than 30 minutes, you will need to synchronize the clocks. If this persists, it could be a problem with the PDC Emulator, because it is responsible for maintaining time synchronization within the domain.

If other events appear in the FRS Event Log, refer to the Help file within Ultrasound, or search the Microsoft website for more information.

Best Practices for Troubleshooting FRS

FRS is a very mysterious service for many administrators, mainly because Microsoft has been slow in releasing details on how this service functions. If you want a functional FRS, you should consider the following practices to keep replication of your Sysvol running efficiently.

◆ Keep all domain controllers at the same service pack level so that the NTFRS.EXE file is the same revision level.

◆ For large environments, increase the USN journal size so that you do not overwrite USN entries that have yet to replicate.

◆ Allow the replicator to perform its job, do not create the same object on multiple domain controllers.

◆ Monitor the FRS service for failures so that you can resume synchronization quickly.

Next Up

As we move away from the replication issues that plague Active Directory infrastructures, we will move on to another troublesome issue, logon failures. Several things can cause logon failures within an Active Directory environment. Understanding what causes most logon failures is in your best interest. Once you have a good handle on the symptoms of the most common failures, you will be able to pinpoint problems easily and resolve them quickly.

chapter 16

Troubleshooting Logon Failures

NOTHING IS MORE FRUSTRATING for users than to attempt to log on first thing on a Monday morning, only to receive an error. Immediately their work week is off to a bad start, and they are on their way to having a bad day. Troubleshooting is your realm, so it's up to you to determine what is causing the problem and set things back on track. Within an Active Directory domain, several things could be at fault.

If you are using a Windows Server 2003–based domain, the default password policy uses complex passwords. Although this is a good policy to use from the standpoint of most of your security auditors, you will find that it can cause additional headaches. Complex passwords, while more secure, are also more difficult for users to remember. You will probably end up unlocking users' accounts and changing their passwords for them more often than you would with simpler passwords. You will also run into the problem of users writing their passwords down and leaving them close to their systems where they are readily available. Controlling passwords, monitoring authentication, and maintaining a sensible password and lockout policy will help you minimize logon problems, but you will still be forced into troubleshooting these issues.

Auditing for Logon Problems

As with any troubleshooting, you should start with checking out the event logs on the client system and the domain controllers within their site. Although many administrators criticize the event logs, you can find out some interesting and useful information from them. If you have enabled auditing of account logon and logon events, you will receive events in the security log that pertain to accounts as they authenticate, or fail to authenticate. In order to watch for failures, you will need to start auditing the failure of authentication within an audit policy. Once you do, you can peruse the audit log for specific entries if users start having difficulty authenticating.

Figure 16.1 shows an example of a GPO that is being used to implement auditing for the domain. When you choose the options to audit and you want to see information concerning authentication, you should set the options seen in Table 16.1.

TABLE 16.1: AUDIT SETTINGS FOR MONITORING DOMAIN LOGON PROBLEMS

AUDIT OPTION	SETTING
Account Logon	Failure
Account Management	Success
Logon	Failure

FIGURE 16.1
Audit Policy in GPO

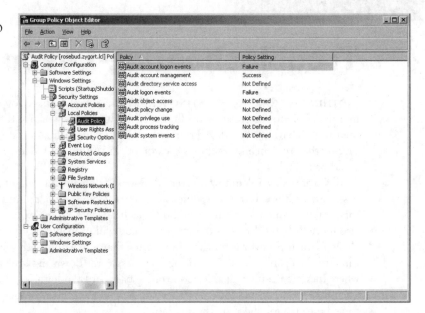

Setting Failure for Account Logon will tell the system to send an event to the security log any time a domain user account fails to authenticate. Doing the same thing for Logon will audit a local account authentication failure. Successful changes to any account, whether it is a password reset or the unlocking of an account, will be registered by the Audit Account Management setting.

Once these settings are enacted, you will be able to view the security logs for common events. On domain controllers, you can look for information concerning account lockouts and changes to the accounts. Event ID 675 will show you the IP address of a client computer from where the bad password originated. If this IP address is not the computer from which the client normally authenticates, it may be an indication of an attack on the account. Event ID 644 will appear if the Audit Account Management auditing option is set for Successful. This event is generated any time an account is locked out due to improper credentials.

You can also view the security logs on client systems and search for common Event IDs. Event 529 is recorded if the system does not have the user account that is attempting to log on. This could be due to the user accidentally pressing the wrong keys when they are logging on, but it could also be an indication of someone trying to hack into a system by guessing an account name. Event

ID 531 indicates that the account that was attempting to authenticate is locked out, or has been disabled by an administrator.

Table 16.2 is a list of the Event IDs that you will encounter as you troubleshoot logon failures and account lockouts.

TABLE 16.2: LOGON EVENT IDs

EVENT ID	DESCRIPTION
528	Successful interactive logon.
529	Failed logon. Due to either unknown account or bad password.
530	Failed logon. Time restrictions prohibited authentication.
531	Failed logon. Account disabled.
532	Failed logon. Expired account.
533	Failed logon. Computer restrictions do not allow logging on to the chosen computer.
534	Failed logon. Disallowed logon type.
535	Failed logon. Expired password.
536	Failed logon. NetLogon is not available to accept authentication request.
537	Failed logon. The logon attempt failed for other reasons. The reason for the logon failure may not be known.
538	The logoff process was not completed.
539	Failed logon. Account locked out.
540	Successful network logon.
541	The local computer and its partner completed the main mode Internet Key Exchange (IKE) authentication or quick mode has established a data channel.
542	Data channel terminated.
543	Main mode was terminated.
544	Main mode authentication failed due to invalid certificate or the signature was not validated.
545	Main mode authentication failed due to Kerberos failure or invalid password.
546	IKE security association establishment failed due to invalid proposal.
547	IKE handshake failure.
548	Failed logon. The security identifier (SID) from a trusted domain does not match the client's account domain SID.
549	Failed logon. SIDFiltering filtered out all SIDs that correspond to untrusted namespaces during an authentication across forests.
550	A denial-of-service (DOS) attack may have occurred.

Continued on next page

TABLE 16.2: LOGON EVENT IDs *(continued)*

EVENT ID	DESCRIPTION
551	User logged off.
552	A user successfully logged on to a computer using explicit credentials while currently logged on as a different user.
672	Kerberos successfully issued and validated an authentication service (AS) ticket.
673	Kerberos successfully granted a ticket-granting service (TGS) ticket.
674	An AS ticket or TGS ticket was renewed.
675	Preauthentication failed. The KDC generates this event if an incorrect password is entered.
676	Authentication ticket request failed. This event is not generated in Windows XP or in the Windows Server 2003 family.
677	A TGS ticket was not granted. This event is not generated in Windows XP or in the Windows Server 2003 family.
678	An account was successfully mapped to a domain account.
681	Failed logon. A domain account logon was attempted. This event is not generated in Windows XP or in the Windows Server 2003 family.
682	A user has reconnected to a disconnected terminal server session.
683	A user disconnected a terminal server session without logging off.

Figure 16.2 shows an example of an event that was generated as a user attempted to log on to a system. Take note of the data within the event, especially the Logon Type entry. You can determine the kind of logon attempt that was attempted. Table 16.3 describes the logon types and the code that is entered into events.

TABLE 16.3: LOGON TYPE CODES

TYPE	REASON RECORDED	CODE
Interactive Logon	User logged on directly on a computer.	2
Network Logon	User connected to the computer from a remote computer.	3
Batch	Account was authenticated when used from a batch queue.	4
Service	Account used by a service when the service was started by a service controller.	5
Unlock	Credentials entered in order to unlock a locked account.	7
NetworkClearText	Account was authenticated with a cleartext password.	8

Continued on next page

TABLE 16.3: LOGON TYPE CODES (continued)

TYPE	REASON RECORDED	CODE
NewCredentials	Account connected to the system after password was changed.	9
RemoteInteractive	Account authenticated from a remote system, but the account is used interactively through a terminal services session.	10
CachedInteractive	The user was logged onto the computer using cached credentials.	11

FIGURE 16.2
Logon event

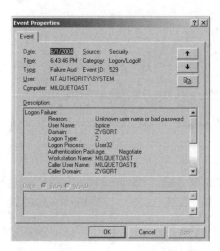

Acctinfo.dll

The `acctinfo.dll` file is actually part of the Account Lockout and Management Tools that you can download from Microsoft, which we discuss later in the Account Lockout Problems section. Once added into your system, `acctinfo.dll` adds an additional property page to the user account properties. As seen in Figure 16.3, this additional property page will allow you to determine when the account's password was set, when the password expires, when the user last logged on or off the domain, and additional lockout information.

One of the best features of `acctinfo.dll` is that it allows you to change a user's password on a DC within the site where the account is used. This allows you to make the change on a domain controller close to the user so that you do not have to wait until replication passes the password change across the site links. Figure 16.4 shows the screen that appears once you have clicked the Set Password On Site DC button. You'll still have the option to reset the password normally, but you will also have the additional site-level options.

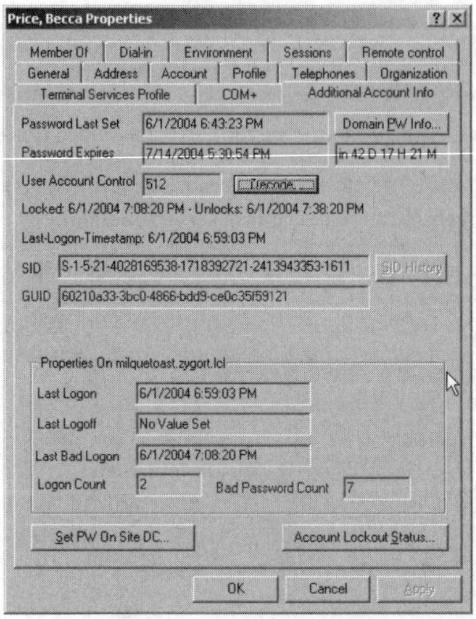

FIGURE 16.3
Acctinfo.dll
property page

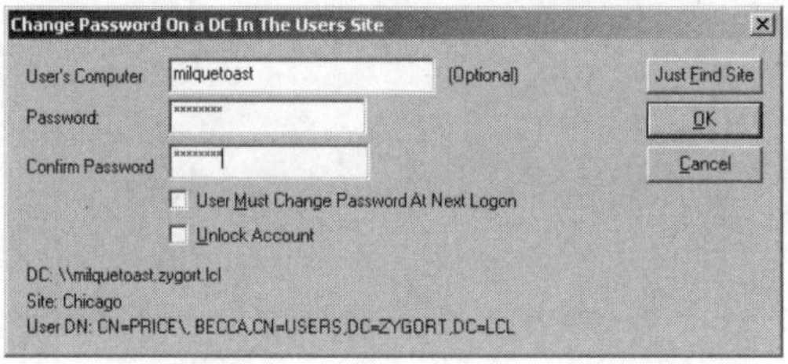

FIGURE 16.4
Set Password
On Site DC

Kerberos Logging

You can have the system present more detailed information concerning authentication by turning on Kerberos logging. To do so, either you can edit the Registry manually or you can run a script provided within the Account Lockout and Management Tools (see the Account Lockout Problems section for more information). If you plan to edit the Registry on a domain controller in order to enable Kerberos logging, you will need to open regedt32 and navigate to the following Registry key:

    HKLM\System\CurrentControlSet\Control\LSA\Kerberos\Parameters

You will need to add the REG_DWORD entry LogLevel. If you set the value of this entry to 1, you will be able to monitor the system event log for Event ID 4. If Event ID 4 appears in the log, it will indicate that a bad password was sent to the Kerberos service for authentication or the account was locked out. If the error code within this event specifies 0x18 KDC_ERR_PREAUTH_FAILED, the password was incorrect. An error code of 0x12 KDC_ERR_CLIENT_REVOKED indicates that the account was locked out.

Native Mode Logon Problems

Once you have switched your domain out of Windows 2000 Mixed Mode, you will be required to have Global Catalog servers available. Windows 2000 native and Windows Server 2003 functional levels require that a Global Catalog server be available so that a user's universal group membership is checked prior to authentication. Universal security groups do not exist within a Windows 2000 Mixed Mode domain. However, once you have changed your domain to support them, each user's universal group membership is checked to make sure that the user is not a member of a universal group that has been denied permission to a resource.

Problems occur when you have replication issues between domain controllers and the universal group membership is not replicated to the local Global Catalog. A user who is a member of a universal group could be denied access to a resource since the replicated information has not arrived at the domain controller to which the user is authenticating. The same is true about having access to resources to which the user should be explicitly denied access. If the Global Catalog has not received the new group membership, the user could access resources that you want to prevent them from accessing.

As important as it is to know which resources the user should be able to access, the requirement of having a Global Catalog server online can cause logon issues for some administrators. Take for instance an organization that has remote offices and due to bandwidth restrictions the administrative staff has decided not to use any of their domain controllers as Global Catalogs within those offices. Global Catalog queries are sent to a nearby site that has a Global Catalog. However, if the users attempt to log on and they cannot contact a Global Catalog in the nearby site, whether due to down WAN links or unavailable Global Catalog servers, those users will not be able to log on to the domain.

Windows Server 2003 has addressed this limitation with a feature known as Universal Group Membership Caching. You enable this feature on a per-site basis and any Windows Server 2003–based domain controller will start using it. As users authenticate, the domain controller servicing the request will query a Global Catalog server within another site for the user's universal group membership and then cache the details.

WARNING   *Global Catalog caching will support a maximum of 500 users per site. Also, the cache is only updated once every 8 hours. You should not consider using this option if you have frequent group updates or many users.*

If your domain does not have any Windows Server 2003–based domain controllers, either you will have to configure a domain controller within the office as a Global Catalog server or you will need to turn off the universal group membership requirement. The latter is not a recommended solution, however, because the user could be allowed to access resources that they should not have permission to use. The inverse could also occur; the user could be denied access to resources that they need to use. If you want to turn off group membership checking when Global Catalog servers are unavailable, you can navigate to the following Registry entry:

```
HKEY_LOCAL_MACHINE\SYSTEM\CurrentControlSet\Services\NTDS\Parameters
```

From there, you will need to add a new key by the name of IgnoreGCFailures. This will tell the domain controller to authenticate a user even though the universal group membership is not evaluated for the user's access token. Again, let me stress that this is not a secure way to run your organization.

However, if you are not using universal groups, or you are desperately seeking a way to allow your remote users to authenticate when WAN link failures occur, you can implement this fix.

Account Lockout Problems

Having the ability to lock out accounts when they are being attacked can be a great security feature, but at the same time, you may find that this policy can cause you some definite headaches. If the settings are too restrictive, users will lock themselves out by mistyping their passwords. If they are not restrictive enough, you potentially open up a security hole that will allow accounts to be attacked. Another potential problem occurs if you have the settings too restrictive and you do not reset the bad password count when the user authenticates; their account could become locked out due to scripts that map drives because the scripts have the wrong password associated with them. The most common causes of account lockouts are discussed here:

Programs   Several programs store a user's credentials so that the program can access resources that it requires. If the user changes their password but the program still has the credentials cached, the user's account could become locked out by the program trying to authenticate.

Reset Account Lockout Counter After Setting   You should consider keeping this setting at the default level of 30 minutes or higher. If this setting is too low, you could cause a false lockout as programs attempt to access resources. Cached credentials, or mapped drives that attempt to connect with invalid credentials, could also cause lockouts if this setting is too low.

Persistent Drive Mappings   If a user has a persistent drive mapping, and that mapping has an incorrect or old password, the account that is associated with the mapped drive could become locked out as the user attempts to access it.

Outlook and Outlook Web Access   If you are using e-mail clients to access mail stored on an Exchange server, and the client has cached the password for the account, the multiple attempts that are made to access the user's mail could result in a locked out account.

Disconnected Terminal Server Sessions   Terminal server sessions that a user has disconnected from will remain running on the server. If the user changes his or her password while the session is running, the session still uses the original password. If applications running within the session attempt to access resources, they could cause the account to become locked out

Microsoft has addressed these issues with Windows 2000 SP4 and Windows Server 2003. Domain controllers are instructed to deny the last two passwords that a user has used; if these two passwords happen to be used, they will not increment the bad password count. Most of the common account lockout problems can be resolved by installing the latest service pack from Microsoft.

If you still have issues with locked-out accounts, Microsoft has released a set of tools that you can use when troubleshooting account lockout problems. These tools are collectively known as the Account Lockout and Management Tools. You can download them from the Microsoft website at the following location:

```
http://www.microsoft.com/downloads/details.aspx?FamilyId=7AF2E69C-91F3-4E63-8629-
B999ADDE0B9E&displaylang=en
```

LockoutStatus.exe   As seen in Figure 16.5, `LockoutStatus.exe` will display information concerning a locked out account. Use this tool to determine which computers were involved in the lockout by the account and when the lockout occurred. You need to copy this tool to the same directory as `acctinfo.dll` if you want to have access to it from the user account properties. This tool is also available from the Windows Server 2003 Resource Kit.

FIGURE 16.5
`LockoutStatus`
`.exe` showing information about a user account

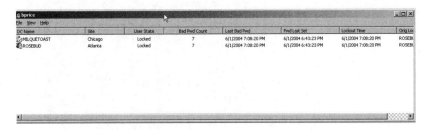

Alockout.dll   This tool, when configured on a system, will monitor the account authentication attempts and deliver the results to a file named `Alockout.txt` that is stored in the `winnt\debug` directory. In order to use this tool, you will need to copy the `alockout.dll` and `appinit.reg` files that are included in the Account Lockout and Management Tools tool set to the `systemroot\system32` folder. Once they are copied, double-click on the `appinit.reg` file to embed the Registry entries into the local Registry of the computer and reboot the system to activate the changes.

Aloinfo.exe   If you want to view all of the accounts and the associated password age, you can run this command at the command line. This will allow you to view the accounts that are about to have their passwords expire so that you can anticipate the flood of calls that will occur right after the new passwords go into effect.

Acctinfo.dll   As mentioned previously, `acctinfo.dll` will add an additional property page to the user's account properties within Active Directory. Figure 16.6 shows the password policy screen that appears when you click the Domain Password Policy button from the Additional Account Info property page shown in Figure 16.7. To install `acctinfo.dll`, you will need to type **regsvr32 acctinfo.dll** at a command prompt or from the Run line. You will need to close and reopen Active Directory Users and Computers for the change to take effect. You will also need to have `lockoutstatus.exe` loaded for the full benefits of this new property page.

FIGURE 16.6
Domain Password Policy

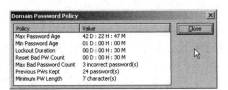

FIGURE 16.7
Property page added
by `acctinfo.dll`

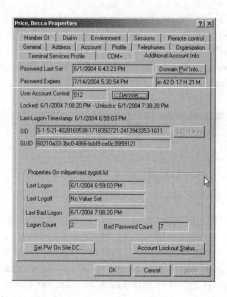

EventCombMT   This tool will search through the event logs on several systems looking for events that you have specified. The default events that the tool will search for are 529, 644, 675, 676, and 681. You can add additional Event IDs if you know which events you want to search. You can also control how many threads are used during the search so that you do not consume too many resources within the domain. The fewer threads you specify, the longer the search will take.

EnableKerbLog.vbs   This is a script that changes the Registry in order to enable Kerberos logging. Once it has been run, additional events are sent to the event log so that you can monitor what the Kerberos service is doing during account authentication.

NLParse   NLParse is used to find NetLogon status codes that have been dumped to the `netlogon.log` file when NetLogon logging has been enabled. It will dump the data that it finds into a comma-separated value file that you can pull into a spreadsheet or database. Several codes can be searched on, but `0X0000006A` and `0x0000234` are the default options.

Any time you are troubleshooting logon and account lockout problems, you should start by enabling NetLogon logging and then view the logs in an attempt to determine which domain controllers may be involved. NetLogon logging has been available since Windows NT 4, and it was used to check the PDC within the domain. You can still use this tool in order to view the interaction between the domain controllers and the PDC emulator. To enable NetLogon logging, you will need to open a command prompt and enter the command **`nltest /dbflag:0x2080ffff`**. This will create a log file within the *systemroot*\Debug directory called `netlogon.log`.

TIP   *After running the* `nltest` *command to enable NetLogon logging, if the* `netlogon.log` *file does not exist, stop and restart the NetLogon service.*

When you view the `netlogon.log` file on the PDC emulator, you can look for instances of event 0xC000006A for authentication requests that have been passed to the PDC emulator from other domain controllers. You can differentiate between authentication requests that are sent directly to the PDC emulator and those that are passed to it from other domain controllers by the reference within the entries that show transitive network logons and the domain controller that passed the request. Looking at the log file, any line that shows the entry "via" displays the computer where the user was attempting the logon and the domain controller that they were authenticating against. If the password is not valid on the domain controller, the user's credentials are sent to the PDC emulator to verify that the user's password has not been changed recently, but the password has not been replicated to the domain controller yet.

TIP   Due to the additional overhead that is consumed when you are logging the NetLogon service, you should turn off the logging when you are finished troubleshooting. To do so, run the command **nltest /dbflag:0x0**.

Because the `netlogon.log` files can be up to 10MB in size, you may want to use the NLParse utility to ease your searching woes. With NLParse, you can select the codes that you want to search for and have the utility load the results into a comma-separated value (`.csv`) so that you can view the results in a spreadsheet. Even though you have several options to choose from, you should start by taking the default options of searching for status codes 0xC000006A and 0xC0000234. These two codes will give you the authentication attempts and the domain controller that locked out the account. Using the resulting CSV file will help you determine if the lockout was due to a program or service, because they would send several attempts within a matter of a second or two. If the attempts came from a user account, there would be a few seconds in between each attempt. Table 16.4 details the status codes that you will find in a `netlogon.log` file and that you can search for with NLParse.

TABLE 16.4: NLParse Status Codes

STATUS CODE	DESCRIPTION
0x0	Successful logon.
0xC0000064	User does not exist.
0xC000006A	Incorrect password.
0xC000006C	Password policy not met.
0xC000006D	Bad username.
0xC000006E	User account restriction prevented successful logon.
0xC000006F	Time restrictions prevented user from logging on.
0xC0000070	Workstation restrictions prevented user from logging on.
0xC0000071	Password has expired.
0xC0000072	The user account is currently disabled.
0xC000009A	Insufficient system resources.
0xC0000193	User's account has expired.

Continued on next page

TABLE 16.4: NLParse Status Codes *(continued)*

STATUS CODE	DESCRIPTION
0xC0000224	User must change password before the first logon.
0xC0000234	The user account has been locked.

Remote Access Issues

If you are using Routing and Remote Access Service (RRAS) as a remote access server, you will need to make sure that the remote access policies are configured correctly. Several layers of control are associated with these policies, and a user could be stopped from authenticating even before they connect to the network.

Remote access policies are not stored within Active Directory; they are configured on a per-server basis. With this in mind, you should make sure that all of the RRAS servers to which a user will connect have the same policy parameters. Otherwise, the user's connection attempts could be erratic.

The only way to guarantee that the RRAS servers are using the same policy is to configure an Internet Authentication Service (IAS) server with a policy and make each RRAS server a client of the IAS server. This still does not store a copy of the policy within Active Directory, but you do have a central repository for the remote access policies.

Are You Being Attacked?

Account lockout policies are not simply for administrators to test the patience of their users; they are used to protect an organization's resources against attack. Companies that are very paranoid, or that have very sensitive data, can set the lockout count to between 3 and 5, but most of the companies that I have talked with or worked with have a policy setting that falls between 5 and 7. This should be sufficient when your users mistype their passwords, and at the same time, it should protect the network.

If you are not sure whether you are under attack or if you have a user problem, look through the NetLogon log files on your domain controllers to determine the extent of the problem. Your PDC emulator will be a central location for the events to be recorded. Any time a bad password is entered, the PDC emulator is checked to validate the attempt. If you see several accounts with bad passwords, and there are 15 to 20 attempts on each account, chances are that an attack is occurring, either internal from a virus or Trojan program, or from an external source attempting to hack an account.

Check the computer that appears in the status code to determine if a rogue program is attempting to authenticate. If the computer that is listed within the status code is a remote access server, an external account could be attempting to attack the network.

Controlling WAN Communication

Typically, a user will log on within the same site a majority of the time. At the same time, when a user changes a password, they do not have to worry about logging on to another system within another site prior to their password change replicating to other domain controllers throughout the organization.

If your users typically log on to the same site, you could reduce the replication traffic that is sent between remote sites and the site where the PDC emulator is located.

To do so you need to add the AvoidPdcOnWan value under the `HKEY_LOCAL_MACHINE\System\CurrentControlSet\Services\Netlogon\Parameters` Registry key. If you set the value to 1, the domain controller will ignore sending password updates as a critical update when the PDC emulator is located in another site. A setting of 0 restores normal operation.

When you turn this value on, the PDC emulator receives the password change during the normal replication cycle. Do note that if the user does travel to another site prior to the replication of the password change, they may be denied access to the network if they use the new password.

Best Practices for Logon and Account Lockout Troubleshooting

Nothing frustrates administrators and users alike more than logon issues. The calls that erupt right after a mandatory password change can be frustrating, but if you follow the information in this chapter, and especially these tips, you may be able to reduce some of your headaches.

◆ Only enable Universal Group Membership Caching if you want to reduce the replication across a WAN link and you have a small number of users who will be affected.

◆ Only turn off Universal Group Membership Enumeration for a native mode domain unless you are not using universal security groups.

◆ Turn on auditing for account logon and account management so that you can identify logon failures and can determine the causes.

◆ Take advantage of the new Account Lockout and Management Tools to aid in troubleshooting account lockout.

◆ Monitor the PDC emulator for authentication attempts. All attempts with a bad password are forwarded to the PDC emulator.

◆ Turn off logging when it is not necessary so that it does not consume additional resources.

Next Up

Due to the multimaster replication that is at the heart of Active Directory, you may find that logging on to the domain can be a troublesome process, as well as difficult to troubleshoot. Users who have changed their passwords, or have just had their password changed by an administrator, can cause additional network traffic due to validation of the password. The PDC emulator is very important in this scenario because it is notified of password changes anywhere in the domain. Making sure this master operation is available is an important part of an Active Directory administrator's responsibilities. In the following chapter, we are going to look at the master operations. I'll give you some troubleshooting tips to monitor their operational status, and we'll examine ways to keep them online.

chapter 17

Troubleshooting FSMO Roles

BACK IN CHAPTER 4, "Sites, Flexible Single Master Operations, and Global Catalog Design," we discussed the Flexible Single Master Operations (FSMO) roles and where you should place each one. Because there can be only one domain controller holding each of the roles, you need to make sure that you keep them operational. Of course, with some of these roles, getting them up and operational is more important than it is with others; however, you should still know what is required to get them into an operational state.

This chapter is going to deal with making sure you know which of the FSMO roles you need to repair immediately, and which ones you can probably leave offline for a while. It will also look at how you can move the roles to other domain controllers and how you can have another domain controller take over the role in case of an emergency.

FSMO Roles and Their Importance

Each of the FSMO roles is important within the forest. Without them, you will not have a means of identifying objects correctly and data corruption can occur if two or more administrators make changes to objects within the forest. As we move through this section, I am going to introduce each of the FSMO roles and how important it is to get each one back online immediately. If you are familiar with the FSMO roles, you may want to skip this section and head directly to the "Transferring and Seizing FSMO Roles" section later in this chapter.

For efficiency's sake, you should identify another domain controller that could be used as the role holder if the original role holder were to fail. You have to do very little to configure another system to become the standby server. Realistically, you should have the role holder and the standby on the same network segment, and they should be configured as replication partners of one another. This will give you a higher probability that all of the data is replicated between the two systems in case there is a failure of the role holder.

Schema Master

The Schema Master controls all of the attributes and classes that are allowed to exist within Active Directory. Only one Schema Master can reside within the forest. The domain controller that holds the Schema Master role is the only domain controller that has the ability to make changes to schema objects within the forest. Once changes are made to a schema object, the changes are replicated to all other domain controllers within the forest.

You should not be too concerned if the Schema Master goes offline. The only time that you will need the Schema Master is when you need to make changes to the schema, either manually or when installing an application that modifies the schema. The forest can exist and function for an extended period of time without the Schema Master being online. If you cannot repair the Schema Master and you need to make a change to the schema, you can seize the role on the standby domain controller.

Domain Naming Master

As with the Schema Master, there can be only one Domain Naming Master within the forest. This is the domain controller that is responsible for allowing the addition and deletion of domains within the forest. When Dcpromo is executed and the creation of a new domain is specified, it is up to the Domain Naming Master to verify that the domain name is unique. The Domain Naming Master is also responsible for allowing deletions of domains. Again, as Dcpromo is executed, the Domain Naming Master is contacted, and the domain that is being deleted will then be removed from the forest by the Domain Naming Master.

Losing the Domain Naming Master should not affect the day-to-day operations of the organization. The only time the Domain Naming Master is required to be online is when a domain is added or removed from the forest. As with the Schema Master, you can allow the Domain Naming Master to remain offline as you try to recover the domain controller. If the Domain Naming Master is still offline when you need to add or remove a domain, or if the original role holder is not recoverable, you can seize the role on the domain controller that has been identified as the standby server.

Infrastructure Master

If you are working in a multiple-domain environment, the Infrastructure Master can be your best friend or your worst enemy. It is the Infrastructure Master's job to make sure that accounts from other domains that are members of a group are kept up-to-date. You do not want an account to have access to resources that it is not supposed to, and if changes are made to users and groups in other domains, you will need to make sure that the same changes are reflected in your domain. For instance, the administrator of `bloomco.lcl` has just added two accounts to a global group and removed one from the group. Within the `bloomco.lcl` domain, the changes are replicated throughout. Within your domain, there is a domain local group that contains the global group. Because the changes are not replicated to domain controllers within your domain, the user who was removed from the group might still have access to resources within your domain and the two new accounts might not.

The infrastructure master needs to be able to maintain the differences between domains so that the correct group membership can be applied at all domain controllers. This is why the Infrastructure Master should not be on a domain controller that is acting as a Global Catalog. The Infrastructure

Master will contact a Global Catalog and compare the member attributes for the groups with the attributes that are contained within its domain. If there is a difference, the Infrastructure Master updates the attributes to keep everything synchronized. If you want to change the default scanning interval for the Infrastructure Master, you can set the following Registry value from two days to whatever value works best in your environment.

```
HKEY_LOCAL_MACHINE\System\CurrentControlSet\Services\NTDS\Parameters\Days per
database phantom scan
```

NOTE *For more information on the Infrastructure Master and how to control the scanning interval, see Knowledge Base article 248047 at* `http://support.microsoft.com/default.aspx?scid=kb;EN-US;248047`.

Loss of the Infrastructure Master is a little more severe than the previous two Master Operations roles. If the Infrastructure Master is offline for an extended period of time, the data cannot be synchronized and users could have access or be denied access to the wrong objects. If you cannot resolve the problem with the Infrastructure Master, you may want to seize the role on the standby server.

Relative Identifier Master

Whenever a security principle, such as a user, group, or computer account, is created within, it has an associated security identifier (SID). A SID consist of the domain's SID and a relative identifier (RID) that is unique to the security principle. Allocating and keeping track of all of the RIDs for the domain is the RID Master's responsibility. Having the RID Master allows you to sleep better at night knowing that a duplicate SID will not be generated within the domain. Even if the security principle associated with a RID is deleted, the RID will still not be regenerated and used again.

If you take a look at a SID, you will notice that it is an alphanumeric combination that is not easy to understand. There is a logic behind the madness, however. If you take a look at the SID or a user account it may look like this:

```
S-1-5-21-1068514962-2513648523-685232148-1005
```

Broken down, the sections that make up the RID fall into these categories:

S The initial character S identifies the series of digits that follow as a SID.

1 This is the revision level. Every SID that is generated within a Windows environment has a revision of 1.

5 This third character is the issuing authority identifier. A majority of the SIDs will have the Windows NT issuing authority number of 5, but some of the well-known built-in accounts will have other values.

21 The fourth character set represents the sub-authority. The sub-authority identifies the service type that generated the SID. SIDs that are generated from domain controllers will contain the characters 21, while built-in accounts may have other characters, such as 32.

1068514962-2513648523-685232148   This long string of characters is the unique part of the SID for a domain. If you are working with local accounts, it represents the unique SID for the computer.

1005   The last set of characters represents the RID for the account. The RID Master starts at 1000 and increments by 1 for every RID it allocates to the domain controllers.

Due to the fact that any domain controller within a native mode domain can generate a RID to an account, you must make sure that only one domain controller is allocating and controlling the RIDs. For this reason, make sure that you do not seize the RID role on a domain controller when the original role holder is just temporarily unavailable. You could cause yourself a nightmare trying to troubleshoot permission problems.

This is a role that you might miss sooner than some of the others. The RID Master allocates blocks of RIDs to the domain controllers within the domain. If a domain controller uses up its last RID while creating a security principle, it will no longer be able to create security principles. Another drawback to losing the RID Master is you cannot promote another domain controller without the RID Master online. For these reasons, you should attempt to recover the original RID Master role holder as quickly as possible or seize the role on the standby server.

Primary Domain Controller Emulator

The PDC emulator is probably the busiest of the master operations, and yet it is the only one that is not known by the name "master." This is also the role that confuses new administrators, because they think that this role is needed only until all of the NT 4 BDCs are taken offline. This is far from the truth. Microsoft should consider changing the name of this master operation to reflect the other functions it provides.

First off, the PDC emulator allows for replication of directory information to Windows NT 4 BDCs while the domain is still in mixed mode. This is also the only domain controller that will create security principles while the domain is in mixed mode, due to the fact that is has to act like a Windows NT 4 PDC. You should make sure that you place this role holder in a location that will create the most accounts.

This is also the only domain controller that is allowed to change passwords for legacy operating systems, such as Windows 98 and Windows NT. They will look for the PDC of the domain, and the PDC emulator fulfills that roll. Another password function that this role holder provides is that it has the final say whenever there is a password change. Whenever an account's password is changed, the PDC emulator is notified immediately. After a user types in their password for authentication, the domain controller that is attempting to authenticate the user will check with the PDC emulator to make sure the user's password has not been changed before notifying the user that they typed in the wrong password.

Two other functions, time synchronization and global policy centralization, are functions of the PDC emulator. All of the other domain controllers within the domain will look to this role holder as the official timekeeper within the domain. You should set the PDC emulator to synchronize with an external time source so that all of the other domain controllers will have the correct time. This is also the domain controller that is used as the default location for changing group policies. Making one domain controller the default GPO holder allows you to control policy changes and minimize conflicting changes within the domain.

NOTE   *In a multiple-domain forest, the PDC emulator for the forest root becomes the Time Master for all PDCs within the forest.*

Due to the amount of responsibilities that the PDC emulator has, it will probably be the master operation that you will miss the most if it fails. When it fails, you should immediately assess how long it is going to take to recover the domain controller holding this role. If it looks like the domain controller is going to be offline for an extended period of time—let's say more than a couple of hours— you should seize the role on the standby server. While the other roles may cause problems for administrators, users will be affected by a loss of the PDC emulator, and they will let you know that they see something wrong!

Transferring and Seizing FSMO Roles

Transferring a FSMO role to another system is a rather painless process. Because all of the domain controllers within a domain have identical data within the Active Directory database, when you transfer a FSMO role, you are simply changing a flag that specifies that one domain controller can control the master operation and the other cannot.

Seizing a FSMO role has serious implications. If you are going to take this drastic step, you must commit yourself and make sure that the original role holder is never reintroduced onto the network. Doing so could cause serious problems within your Active Directory infrastructure.

In the following sections, you will find the methods you can use to identify the systems that currently hold the Master Operations roles and the methods you can use to make sure the domain controller that is identified as the standby server can take over the role.

Identifying the Current Role Holder

There are several ways that you can identify which domain controller is holding a FSMO role. With some of these options, you will be able to see all of the role holders at one time; with others, you are forced to view them separately.

BUILT-IN ACTIVE DIRECTORY TOOLS

You can view the roles for four of the five roles by using the Active Directory Users and Computers (ADUC) and Active Directory Domains and Trusts (ADDT) snap-ins. Using ADUC, you can identify the PDC emulator, RID Master, and Infrastructure Master role holders. ADDT will allow you to identify the Domain Naming Master. In order to get to the screen shown in Figure 17.1, you need to open ADUC and right-click on the domain name and select Operations Masters.

Figure 17.2 shows the Domain Naming Master as found when you choose the Operations Masters option from the context menu that is available when you right-click the Active Directory Domains and Trusts label within the ADDT snap-in.

FIGURE 17.1
FSMO roles listing
in Active Directory
Users and Computers

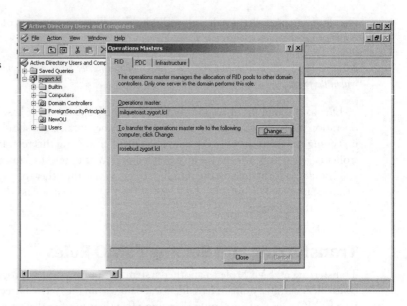

FIGURE 17.2
Domain Naming
Master role as seen in
Active Directory
Domains and Trusts

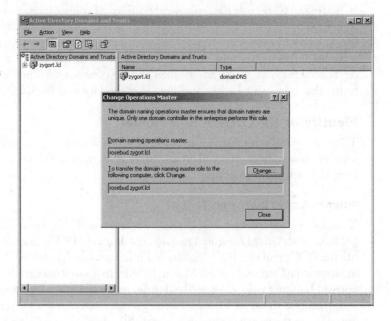

ACTIVE DIRECTORY SCHEMA

The Active Directory Schema snap-in is listed separately because it is not available by default. In order to access this snap-in, you must register its associated DLL. To do so, type **regsvr32 schmmgmt.dll** at the run line or a command prompt. After you receive a message stating that the DLL is registered, you can add the snap-in to an MMC. You can view the Schema Master role holder as seen in Figure 17.3, by right-clicking the Active Directory Schema container within the MMC and selecting Operations Master.

FIGURE 17.3

Schema Master role as seen in Active Directory Schema snap-in

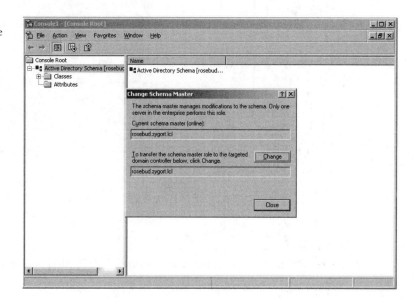

REPLMON

This tool was discussed in Chapter 13, "Troubleshooting Active Directory Replication." In addition to the benefits that we introduced in that chapter, ReplMon also has the ability to view the role holders within the domain. When you add a monitored server to the console, you can view its properties by right-clicking on the server and choosing Properties. As seen in Figure 17.4, you can view all five of the role holders from the FSMO Roles tab. Note the naming convention for the RID Master and Domain Naming Master.

COMMAND LINE OPTIONS

Some command-line utilities will allow you to identify the role holders. The first, netdom, will show you all of the role holders at the same time. The second, dsquery, will allow you find individual roles when you ask for them. The DCDiag utility will show you all of the roles. The final utility is from the Resource Kit, dumpfsmos.cmd.

FIGURE 17.4
Identifying the roles
using Replication
Monitor

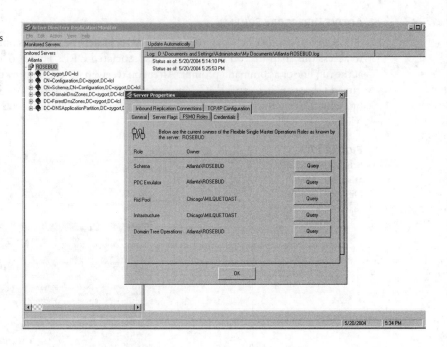

netdom

The netdom command syntax that will report the role holders is as follows:

```
netdom query fsmo /domain:zygort.lcl
```

Of course, you would replace zygort.lcl with your domain name. This will return a list of all of the role holders.

dsquery

In order to find individual role holders with the dsquery command, you would use the following commands:

◆ To find the Schema Master:

```
dsquery server -hasfsmo schema
```

◆ To find the Domain Naming Master:

```
dsquery server -hasfsmo name
```

◆ To find the Infrastructure Master:

```
dsquery server -hasfsmo infr
```

◆ To find the RID Master:

```
dsquery server -hasfsmo rid
```

◆ To find the PDC emulator:

```
dsquery server -hasfsmo pdc
```

DCDiag

The DCDiag utility is used as:

```
dcdiag /test:knowsofroleholders /v
```

Because the verbose switch (/v) is used, this command will return the role holders and give you information on each.

dumpfsmos.cmd

The dumpfsmos.cmd utility from the resource kit is a small script that actually starts NTDSUTIL and issues the appropriate commands to return a list of the role holders. The syntax for this command is

```
dumpfsmos.cmd zygort.lcl
```

Of course, you would want to replace zygort.lcl with the name of the domain you are querying against.

Transferring the Role to Another Domain Controller

If you are demoting a role holder, you should make sure that you transfer the role to another domain controller, preferably the domain controller you have designated as the standby role holder. Doing so will guarantee that you are transferring the role to the appropriate domain controller instead of allowing Dcpromo to choose another domain controller on its own. Remember, it is always better to have control over these things than to allow random chance to control your organization.

NOTE *If you are permanently taking a domain controller offline, whether it is a role holder or not, you should demote it so that the references to the domain controller are removed from Active Directory.*

Transferring the role to another domain controller is a very simple process. Using the snap-ins that we discussed in the "Identifying the Current Role Holder" section, you can simply connect to the domain controller that you want to be the new role holder, choose the Operations Master option to view the role holder, and click change. Look back at Figure 17.1 and note that the snap-in is currently connected to the domain controller rosebud.zygort.lcl. The RID Master role is currently held by milquetoast.zygort.lcl. When you click the Change button, the role will be transferred to milquetoast.zygort.lcl.

You can also use NTDSUTIL to transfer the roles. To do so, you need to start a command prompt and enter the ntdsutil command. Once the ntdsutil: prompt appears, you can enter the following commands:

1. At the ntdsutil: prompt, type **roles** to enter into fsmo maintenance.

2. At the `fsmo maintenance:` prompt, type **connections** to enter into `server connections`.

3. At the `server connections:` prompt, type **connect to server *domain_controller***, where *domain_controller* is the name of the domain controller to which you are going to transfer the role.

4. At the `server connections:` prompt, type **quit** to enter into `fsmo maintenance`.

5. At the `fsmo maintenance:` prompt, type one of the following to transfer the appropriate role:

   ◆ To transfer the Schema Master:

      transfer schema master

   ◆ To transfer the Domain Naming Master:

      transfer domain naming master

   ◆ To transfer the Infrastructure Master:

      transfer infrastructure master

   ◆ To transfer the RID Master:

      transfer rid master

   ◆ To transfer the PDC emulator:

      transfer PDC

After you have transferred the role, type **quit** twice to exit NTDSUTIL. You can then use one of the aforementioned utilities to verify that the role was transferred to the appropriate domain controller.

Seizing the Role on the Standby Domain Controller

You should have already designated another domain controller as the standby server in case a role holder becomes unavailable. If you have configured the original role holder and the standby as replication partners, there is a very good chance that they are completely synchronized with one another. If the original role holder becomes unavailable and you deem it necessary to have the standby server become the role holder, you can seize the role on the standby server. Again, this is a drastic measure and should be performed only if you are certain the original role holder is not going to be reintroduced on the network.

In order to seize a role, you need to follow Steps 1 through 4 as outlined in the previous section, "Transferring a Role to Another Domain Controller." Once you have connected to the domain controller that will become the role holder, you can use one of the following commands from the NTDSUTIL `fsmo maintenance:` prompt:

- To seize the Schema Master:

  `seize schema master`

- To seize the Domain Naming Master:

  `seize domain naming master`

- To seize the Infrastructure Master:

  `seize infrastructure master`

- To seize the RID Master:

  `seize rid master`

- To seize the PDC emulator:

  `seize PDC`

Now that the role has been seized, type **quit** twice to exit NTDSUTIL. Verify that the role has been taken over by the new role holder. If the original system is repaired and could be used again, make sure you reformat the system and reinstall the operating system. This will guarantee that you will not introduce problems within your Active Directory from having a rogue role holder in place.

NOTE *The PDC emulator and Infrastructure roles are designed for "graceful seizure." This means that the old role holders can be brought back online after a seizure with no ill effects.*

NOTE *If a domain controller does go offline and you are not going to reintroduce it to the network, make sure you remove all references to the domain controller within Active Directory. See Chapter 12, "Optimizing the Active Directory Database," for information concerning how to remove orphaned objects.*

Best Practices for Troubleshooting FSMO Roles

Just a few pointers here, but they are good tips to remember.

- Do not seize a role unless you are absolutely positive that you will never reintroduce the original role holder to the network.

- If demoting a role holder, transfer the role to another domain controller first.

- Keep documentation that identifies the role holders and the domain controllers that are designated as the standby servers.

Next Up

Understanding how to manipulate the FSMO roles is important if you want to keep Active Directory 100 percent available. Some of the roles are not as critical to have online as others, and you need to know when you will be required to take action in order to make the role available. One of the roles, the PDC emulator, is a highly critical role that you should not leave offline for long. Part of the reason is that it is the central repository for Group Policy Objects. In the following chapter, we are going to look at the problems you could encounter while using GPOs, along with some troubleshooting tips to help you fix your problems.

chapter 18

Group Policy

So far in Part III of this book, "Maintenance and Administration," we have covered how to troubleshoot several different areas of Active Directory, from DNS to Active Directory replication. This final chapter is going to cover one of the most beneficial, and sometimes the most frustrating, parts of your Active Directory infrastructure, Group Policy.

As we saw in Chapter 5, "Organizational Unit Design," designing Group Policy so that it is both efficient and effective can be a daunting task. You will find that troubleshooting GPOs is also a difficult proposition due to the many settings and options you can use. A methodic approach to any type of troubleshooting is always a good thing, but when it comes to Group Policy troubleshooting, it is a necessity.

This chapter is the last chapter of Part III for a good reason. Most of the other troubleshooting techniques that we have looked at up to this point will come into play when you are attempting to troubleshoot problems with your Group Policy infrastructure. Group Policy relies on Active Directory and Active Directory replication to be functioning correctly, and they rely on a functional DNS. The File Replication System (FRS) has to be functioning correctly for the Group Policy template to be replicated to all of the domain controllers.

If you look through the previous chapters of this part of the book, you will find the troubleshooting tools to help you when you are working with each of the underlying technologies upon which the Group Policy infrastructure relies. In this chapter, we are not going to rehash the information that has already been presented, but we will point you back to the appropriate chapters when necessary.

We need to cover several areas within this chapter. As you have found in previous chapters, I cover the basic points quickly and cover the advanced topics in greater detail. The first section will cover troubleshooting tools that are available in Windows 2000– or Windows Server 2003–based domains, and the second section will cover how to use the new Group Policy Management Console. If you want to pursue Group Policy beyond the confines of this chapter, see *Group Policy, Profiles, and IntelliMirror* by Jeremy Moskowitz (Sybex, 2004) for a detailed treatment of the topic.

Troubleshooting Tools

Several tools have been developed to assist you with your Group Policy woes. These tools can be used in either version of Active Directory. If you are only using Windows 2000 or prior operating systems within your organization, you will need to have a good feel for these tools because you do not have Group Policy Management Console available. If you want a tool that will provide the same functionality as the GPMC, you can check out the FAZAM Group Policy Management tool by Full Armor.

TIP   The GPMC will function in a Windows 2000 domain, but you must have a Windows Server 2003 or Windows XP system to run the GPMC.

NOTE   A reduced-functionality version of FAZAM is included in Windows 2000 Server.

Microsoft-provided tools include the following:

◆ Group Policy Results Tool (`GPResult.exe`)

◆ Group Policy Verification Tool (`GPOTool.exe`)

◆ Software Installation Diagnostics Tool (`addiag.exe`)

◆ Replication Monitor (`ReplMon.exe`)

◆ Domain Controller Diagnostics (`DCDiag.exe`)

Two of these tools, ReplMon and DCDiag, were discussed in Chapter 13, "Troubleshooting Active Directory Replication." The other three are available from the Windows 2000 Server Resource Kit or are included as part of Windows Server 2003.

Group Policy Results Tool

One version of `GPResult.exe` ships with the Windows 2000 Server Resource Kit, and the other version is included with Windows Server 2003. As you might guess, if you are running all Windows 2000 servers and workstations, the version supplied in the Resource Kit will suffice. However, if you have Windows Server 2003 or Windows XP in your environment, you should use the newer version.

NOTE   To download the Windows Server 2003 Resource Kit, go to `http://www.microsoft.com/windowsserver2003/techinfo/reskit/tools/default.mspx`.

NOTE   To download the Windows 2000 Server Resource Kit, go to `http://www.microsoft.com/windows2000/techinfo/reskit/tools/default.asp`.

GPResult will provide you with information concerning the operating system in use, such as user information and computer information. For the operating system section of the report, you will find the following information:

◆ Type of system: Professional, Server, or domain controller

◆ Build number

◆ Service Pack

◆ Whether Terminal Services is installed and the mode it is in

You will find information that is generated about the user:

◆ Username

◆ Active Directory location

◆ Site name

◆ Profile type and location of profile if roaming

◆ Security group membership

You will find information that is generated about the computer:

◆ Computer name

◆ Active Directory location

◆ Domain name

◆ Domain type

◆ Site name

To use GPResult.exe, run it from a command line. If you want to direct the output to a file, you can issue the command gpresult >filename. You can then open the output file in any text editor to view the information that was gathered. Figure 18.1 shows part of the output that is generated from running GPResult.exe from the command prompt.

Some switches that are associated with GPResult allow you to control the output. If you are interested in only the computer settings, you can use the /c switch to suppress any user-level information. The same is true for user information; you can use the /u switch to prevent the computer information from being displayed.

If you want more detailed information within the report, you can use the verbose (/v) or super verbose (/s) switches. Verbose mode will allow you to see details on the user's security privileges, the extensions that are used within the Group Policy and the Group Policy details. Super verbose mode will report the applications that will be displayed in Add/Remove Programs due to software installation actions, GPO version numbers for both the Group Policy template and Group Policy container, and the binary values on Registry settings.

FIGURE 18.1
Sample output from
GPResult.exe

Group Policy Verification Tool

Another utility that is available from the Windows 2000 Server Resource Kit or the Windows Server 2003 Resource Kit is GPOTool.exe. GPOTool can come in very handy in domains where you have more than one domain controller, or when you have a policy that needs to be replicated to more than one domain. GPOTool has switches, as seen in Table 18.1, that allow you to control how it behaves and what information it will display. Any of the switches in this table can be used in conjunction with one another.

TABLE 18.1: GPOTool Switches

SWITCH	DESCRIPTION
/gpo	Policies to verify. You can use a GUID or friendly name, and partial matches are accepted. All GPOs are assumed if not used. Used in the form gpotool /gpo:*GPOName*. Note: the GUID and friendly name entries are case sensitive.
/domain	Used to specify the fully qualified DNS name of the domain that hosts the policies. Current domain is used if not specified. Used in the form gpotool /domain:*DomainName*. Not case sensitive.
/dc	List of domain controllers that will be checked. If not used, all domain controllers are checked. Used in the form gpotool /dc:*DomainControllerName*. Not case sensitive.

TABLE 18.1: GPOTOOL SWITCHES *(continued)*

SWITCH	DESCRIPTION
/checkacl	Verifies that the Sysvol access control list is valid and the operating system can access the files.
/verbose	Generates additional information that can assist in troubleshooting.

Software Installation Diagnostics Tool

As of the time of the writing of this book, Microsoft has not made addiag.exe available for download; however, if you purchase the Windows 2000 Server Resource Kit, it is available for use. Used at the command line without any switches, Addiag will present information concerning the Active Directory location data for the user, the GPOs that apply the software, and which MSI packages are installed on the system. You can also view the applications that are applied to the computer by using the /user:false switch.

You can use this tool to determine which applications are being pushed down to the user by a Group Policy and which ones are installed locally on the system. Within the output, you will see entries for any application that is installed locally using an MSI file or through a Group Policy. This will aid you in determining if the problems are because a user installed a local copy of an application or if a GPO is not applying as it should.

Troubleshooting with the Group Policy Management Console

Although not included with the base operating system, the Group Policy Management Console (GPMC) is freely available for you to download and add onto a Windows XP Professional or Windows Server 2003 member of Active Directory. As seen in Figure 18.2, there are two options that you can use within the GPMC that will allow you to view how GPOs are applied to systems. The first option is the Group Policy Modeling and the other is Group Policy Results. Both of these present you with an HTML report that you can view in the GPMC or print out or save.

FIGURE 18.2
GPMC showing Group Policy Modeling and Group Policy Results containers

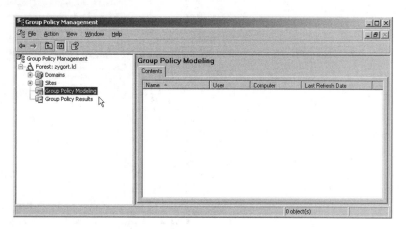

To gain access to either one of the wizards, right-click on the appropriate container and select Group Policy Modeling Wizard or Group Policy Results Wizard. You will need to make sure that you have the appropriate permissions in order to start either wizard. Members of the Domain Admins group from a domain have the ability to run either wizard, but you can delegate the ability to run either wizard by adding an account to the Delegation tab of an OU, site, or domain, as seen in Figure 18.3.

Group Policy Modeling

This container is used to build reports that will show what would happen if you were to apply GPOs. There are several options that you can select that will help you determine what will happen when GPOs are applied under specific circumstances. Use this tool if you want to plan the application of GPOs. You can manipulate the Active Directory location of a user or computer, and you can check out what will be applied to a specific user or computer or any user or computer within an Active Directory location. You can also determine the affects of slow links, loopback settings and WMI filters.

Although you will not typically use the Group Policy Modeling Wizard when you are trying to troubleshoot GPO application problems, it does come in handy if you want to see what is supposed to be applied according to the GPOs that are configured. You can compare the report to the output that is shown from the Group Policy Results Wizard, which is discussed next.

Group Policy Results

When troubleshooting GPO problems, Group Policy Results is the preferred tool used to determine what is applied or denied against the user and computer accounts. The report that is generated when you input the data into the wizard is representative of the settings applied the last time the user logged onto a computer. Of course, those last few words are the key—the user has to have logged on to the computer you are checking against.

FIGURE 18.3
The Delegation tab controls administrative access to the wizards.

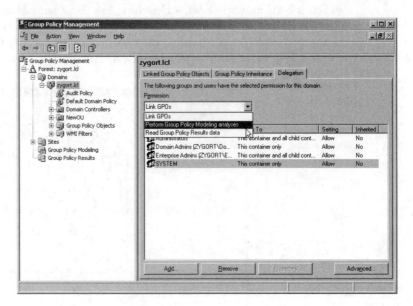

If the user has not logged on to the system you are checking against, you will not receive the correct results in the report. You will need to make sure that the user has successfully authenticated to the computer, and that the computer is either a Windows XP Professional or Windows Server 2003–based system. If you are still running other client operating systems, you will need to purchase the full version of FAZAM from Full Armor, or an equivalent utility.

The Group Policy Results Wizard simply asks you for the name of the computer to which the user logged on, and then the name of the user you want to validate settings. That's it. As soon as the wizard has completed, you will see an HTML report that allows you to view the settings, as seen in Figure 18.4, and all of the options that are configured within the GPOs that apply.

FIGURE 18.4
GPMC results

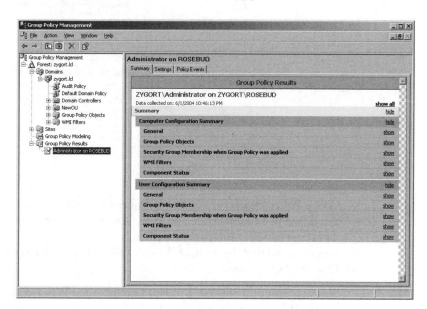

The three tabs on this report (Summary, Settings, and Policy Events) will give you information as to how the settings were applied.

SUMMARY TAB

If you look at the Summary tab, as shown in Figure 18.5, you will see listings for both the Computer and User Configuration Summaries. I expanded the sections from the Computer Configuration Summary. The same sections are available from the User Configuration Summary section.

General The General section contains brief information concerning the computer. Use this section to determine if the computer is in the correct site and the last time the GPO was processed. Remember that the client-side extensions (CSE) run at logon to determine the initial settings for the session, but they process again during the refresh interval only if the settings have changed. Of course, this is the default behavior; you can change how the CSEs process by making changes to a GPO that is applied to the client system.

FIGURE 18.5
Computer Configuration Summary

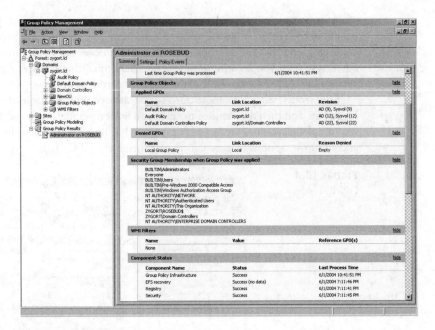

Group Policy Objects The Group Policy Objects section displays the GPOs that were applied and denied to a computer account. The GPO name, where the GPO was linked, and the revision number of the GPO, both the Active Directory and Sysvol, are displayed in the Applied GPOs section. You will find the name of the GPO that was denied and the reason for the denial in the Denied GPOs section.

Security Group Membership When Group Policy Was Applied The Security Group Membership When Group Policy Was Applied section allows you to determine if the user is a member of a group that may have allowed or denied the GPO. This can aid you when you are trying to determine whether the proper permissions are set on GPOs.

WMI Filters The WMI Filters section will show the WMI filters that are in place for GPOs. Remember that only Windows XP and Windows Server 2003 can take advantage of WMI filters, so if the user logs on to any other operating system, the WMI Filters will be ignored.

Component Status Component Status reveals the last time the client-side extension (CSE) processed. This section will indicate when each section of the GPO was processed last, allowing you to determine if a policy setting that you had just changed was enforced.

SETTINGS TAB

Figure 18.6 is a partial display of the settings that are in place once all of the GPOs have been processed. This is the view that you will use to determine what settings have been applied and the GPOs that applied the setting. As you already know, GPOs are processed according to a predetermined order. The site-level GPOs are processed first, then the domain-level GPOs, and finally the OU-level

GPOs. Child OUs are processed from the parent down. As you move down the list, each lower level will override the upper level if there are conflicts within the settings. This behavior can be modified by using the Enforced (No Override) and Block Inheritance options. For more information on how the settings are applied, see Chapter 2, "Active Directory Domain Design."

FIGURE 18.6
GMPC Settings tab

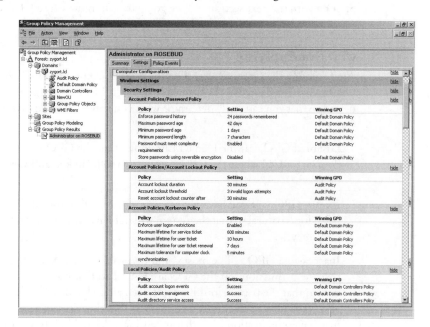

When you look at the Settings tab, note that the Policy option that has been applied will show up in each of the sections. The setting that has been configured and the GPO that applied the policy setting is listed next to it. If you have problems with a policy setting that is applying when it shouldn't or that does not apply when you think it should, open the Settings tab and look for the setting. You can then look at the Winning GPO to determine where the setting was applied. This will give you a starting point from which to figure out why the setting is applying incorrectly.

POLICY EVENTS TAB

This tab is a look into the Event Viewer, but it displays only the events that are relevant to Group Policy processing. You can use this tab to look over the GPO processing events instead of filtering the events within Event Viewer.

Troubleshooting Methodology

When using the GPMC to troubleshoot Group Policy problems, you should start by asking yourself some basic questions in order to narrow down the possible issues. Using a systematic approach will allow you to determine the probable causes and will help you expeditiously come to a solution.

First, you should determine whether the GPO was applied to the user or computer. Although this may seem to be what you want to happen, there are cases where you do not want policies applied to specific users or computers. When they are applied, you'll need to determine why. The following sections present troubleshooting tips. When to use them depends on whether the GPO is applied or not. Starting with the next section, we are going to determine why a GPO did not apply when it was supposed to.

GPO Not Applying

After running the Group Policy Results Wizard, you should look in the report to determine if the GPO is listed as denied in the Denied List. In the Denied List, you will find the reason the GPO was denied so that you can easily determine what you may need to do in order to allow the GPO to process correctly.

Disabled GPO   If the Denied List shows that the GPO is disabled, you can look at the site, domain, or OU where the GPO is supposed to be linked and view whether the link was explicitly disabled.

Empty GPO   If you have not set any options within the GPO, it will be implicitly denied. This behavior is natural so that the system will not have to scan through all of the GPO settings at every refresh cycle.

Inaccessible GPO   The most common problem that causes this entry within the Denied List is that the permissions on the GPO are not set so that the GPO can be read or applied. If you are certain that the permissions have not been altered and are sufficient, check network connectivity and availability of the domain controllers that the user can access. If everything is functional, you may have a replication issue that is causing a deleted link to exist while waiting for replication to remove it.

Security Filtering   Any computer or user with a GPO that is supposed to be applied to them will need to have both Read and Apply Group Policy permissions. Within the GPMC, any users or computers that you have added to the Security Filtering field should have the GPO applied to them. However, either of these permissions can be denied, so make sure you check the permissions for an explicit denial.

WMI Filters   WMI filters apply only to Windows XP and Windows Server 2003 operating systems. Windows 2000–based systems ignore WMI filters and only apply GPOs that are allowed through security filtering. WMI queries are based on Boolean decisions that are evaluated according to the results of a WMI query language (WQL) test. Make sure the syntax of the query is valid; otherwise, the WMI filter will not be applied to the correct systems.

If the GPOs are not applying to the computer or user and they are not listed in the Denied List, you will need to make sure that the GPOs are correctly configured. One of the most common errors is not having the GPO linked to the correct site, domain, or OU. GPOs only apply to users who are members of the containers where the GPO is applied. If you think that you have linked the GPO to the appropriate container, then check to make sure that replication has updated the domain controller where the user is getting their policies. If replication has not completely converged, the GPO may not be allowed to process. Network connectivity issues could keep replication from reaching the domain controller and site link schedules. Check to make sure that the network infrastructure is not causing a replication problem and that replication has completely converged.

The other issue that you could be facing is the refresh interval. If the user has already logged onto their system and you made a change to the GPO, it will not apply until the user's or computer's refresh interval has occurred. To compound the problem, the replication cycle may hit after the refresh interval, which means the client will not receive the updated GPO settings until the next refresh interval.

NOTE *Folder redirection and software installation settings are applied only to a user when the user logs on to the system, and software installation settings for the computer are applied only when the computer starts. Changes made to a GPO that affect these settings will not be refreshed during the refresh cycle.*

GPO Applying When It Should Not

When you use the Group Policy Results Wizard, the resulting report will show that the setting is listed in a GPO or that the setting is missing from the GPO. Either way, you will need to determine why the setting is being enforced. The former is usually easier to troubleshoot than the latter, but either scenario can lead to ulcers and sleepless nights.

If the setting is listed, you need to determine which of the following is the underlying reason: asynchronous processing, client-side extensions, GPO inheritance, GPO refresh cycle, or loopback processing.

Asynchronous Processing   If asynchronous processing has been enabled, the computer can start up and the user can log on before the GPOs have been completely processed. This could cause problems with some settings as the user tries to perform actions while the policy processes and tries to restrict them from performing the action.

WARNING *Enabling Asynchronous Processing will speed up logon time, but be aware of the consequences.*

Client-Side Extensions   Client-side extensions are responsible for processing the specific settings within the GPO. If the client-side extension is corrupt or has been disabled, the settings will not be processed for the user.

GPO Inheritance   Settings within GPOs are inherited at the child levels unless the GPO is blocked. Open the listing for the setting in the resulting report and look at the Winning GPO column to determine which GPO is applying the setting.

GPO Refresh Cycle   The GPO may have been changed, but if the user is logged on and the user or computer refresh cycle has not occurred, the settings will not be applied. Run GPUPDATE in order to refresh the policy.

Loopback Processing   Loopback processing can be configured to apply the user settings from the OU where the computer is located instead of from a user's settings from the user's OU. This allows you to enforce specific settings on a computer no matter who logs on. Make sure the computer is really supposed to be added to the OU where loopback is configured, or determine if loopback is necessary.

If the setting is not listed within the resulting report, there are a few things that could be causing this behavior. You will need to determine if it is due to the GPO refresh cycle, operating system support, replication, or slow link processing restrictions.

GPO Refresh Cycle   The GPO may have been changed, but if the user is logged on and the user or computer refresh cycle has not occurred, the settings will not be applied. Run GPUPDATE in order to refresh the policy.

Operating System Support   Some GPO settings will affect only specific operating systems. Some GPO settings that apply to Windows XP do not apply to Windows 2000 or Windows Server 2003. At the same time, some of the settings that apply to those operating systems are not applied to the other operating systems. When you are setting the options, make sure you verify that they will apply to the systems you are supporting.

Replication   If the GPO has not replicated to the domain controller where the user is getting their settings applied, they may not get the correct settings. By default, the changes to GPOs are made on the PDC emulator. Make sure the replication has occurred between the PDC emulator and the domain controller the user is contacting, or you could change the focus of the GPMC so that it is effecting its changes on the domain controller that the user is connecting to.

NOTE   *You can view the replication status between domain controllers with GPOTool.*

Slow Link Processing Restrictions   When a slow link is detected, under 500 Kbps, then some of the client-side extensions are not processed. This is the normal behavior of Group Policy processing. If you want to make sure that the settings are applied no matter what the speed of the link, you will need to change the slow link processing speed or use a Group Policy to change which client-side extensions are enabled over a slow link.

User Environment Logging

One tool that will assist you in troubleshooting either version of Active Directory is User Environment (UserEnv) logging. Once it is enabled, you will be able to view detailed information about the Group Policy processing that occurs on a system. This is not enabled by default because, just like any other logging, enabling it will trade off performance for the logging that occurs.

To enable UserEnv logging, you will need to add a Registry value under HKEY_LOCAL_ MACHINE\Software\Microsoft\WindowsNT\CurrentVersion\WinLogon. Add a REG_DWORD value named UserenvDebugLevel and set it to 0x10002. Once added, the system will automatically create a log file named userenv.log under the %systemroot%\debug directory.

Several levels of logging can be used. Each level provides more detailed information than the previous one. Table 18.2 shows the values you can set when you configure the logging level. Some of these levels can be combined to allow for additional logging capabilities. For instance, when you configured the Registry key in the previous paragraph, you set the logging level to 0x10002. This actually informed the system that you wanted to use the verbose logging level and create a logfile. Simply enabling the logging by using a 0x2 would have sent more detailed information to the application event log, but it would not create the userenv.log file.

TABLE 18.2: USER ENVIRONMENT LOGGING LEVELS

LOGGING LEVEL	DESCRIPTION
NONE	0x00000000
NORMAL	0x00000001
VERBOSE	0x00000002
LOGFILE	0x00010000
DEBUGGER	0x00020000

The application event log contains events that are generated due to Group Policy processing, but it does not receive all of the data that is contained in `userenv.log`. This is by design. In order to reduce the events that are recorded, and to keep the application log from becoming flooded with events, the `userenv.log` file is used for the additional detail. Figure 18.7 shows a partial sample of the entries that are entered into the log file after logging has been enabled.

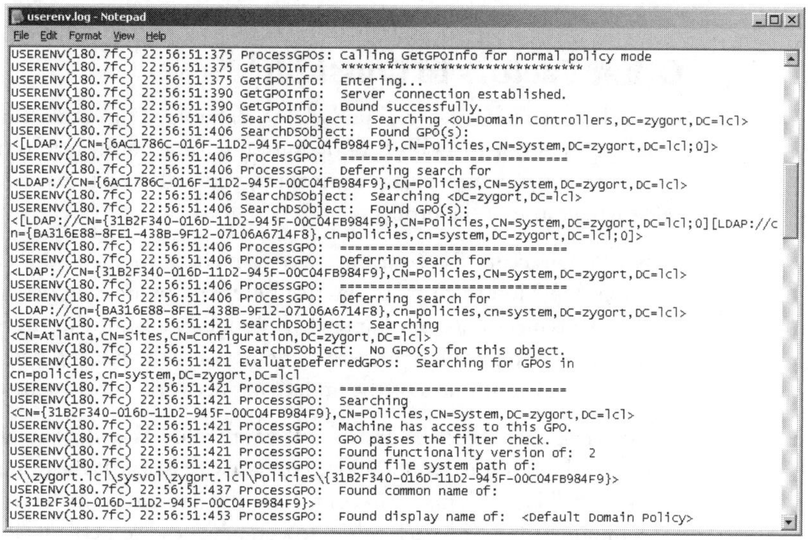

```
userenv.log - Notepad
File Edit Format View Help
USERENV(180.7fc) 22:56:51:375 ProcessGPOs: Calling GetGPOInfo for normal policy mode
USERENV(180.7fc) 22:56:51:375 GetGPOInfo:  ********************************
USERENV(180.7fc) 22:56:51:375 GetGPOInfo:  Entering...
USERENV(180.7fc) 22:56:51:390 GetGPOInfo:  Server connection established.
USERENV(180.7fc) 22:56:51:390 GetGPOInfo:  Bound successfully.
USERENV(180.7fc) 22:56:51:406 SearchDSObject:  Searching <OU=Domain Controllers,DC=zygort,DC=lcl>
USERENV(180.7fc) 22:56:51:406 SearchDSObject:  Found GPO(s):
<[LDAP://CN={6AC1786C-016F-11D2-945F-00C04fB984F9},CN=Policies,CN=System,DC=zygort,DC=lcl;0]>
USERENV(180.7fc) 22:56:51:406 ProcessGPO:  ==============================
USERENV(180.7fc) 22:56:51:406 ProcessGPO:  Deferring search for
<LDAP://CN={6AC1786C-016F-11D2-945F-00C04fB984F9},CN=Policies,CN=System,DC=zygort,DC=lcl>
USERENV(180.7fc) 22:56:51:406 SearchDSObject:  Searching <DC=zygort,DC=lcl>
USERENV(180.7fc) 22:56:51:406 SearchDSObject:  Found GPO(s):
<[LDAP://CN={31B2F340-016D-11D2-945F-00C04FB984F9},CN=Policies,CN=System,DC=zygort,DC=lcl;0][LDAP://c
n={BA316E88-8FE1-438B-9F12-07106A6714F8},cn=policies,cn=system,DC=zygort,DC=lcl;0]>
USERENV(180.7fc) 22:56:51:406 ProcessGPO:  ==============================
USERENV(180.7fc) 22:56:51:406 ProcessGPO:  Deferring search for
<LDAP://CN={31B2F340-016D-11D2-945F-00C04FB984F9},CN=Policies,CN=System,DC=zygort,DC=lcl>
USERENV(180.7fc) 22:56:51:406 ProcessGPO:  ==============================
USERENV(180.7fc) 22:56:51:406 ProcessGPO:  Deferring search for
<LDAP://cn={BA316E88-8FE1-438B-9F12-07106A6714F8},cn=policies,cn=system,DC=zygort,DC=lcl>
USERENV(180.7fc) 22:56:51:421 SearchDSObject:  Searching
<CN=Atlanta,CN=Sites,CN=Configuration,DC=zygort,DC=lcl>
USERENV(180.7fc) 22:56:51:421 SearchDSObject:  No GPO(s) for this object.
USERENV(180.7fc) 22:56:51:421 EvaluateDeferredGPOs:  Searching for GPOs in
cn=policies,cn=system,DC=zygort,DC=lcl
USERENV(180.7fc) 22:56:51:421 ProcessGPO:  ==============================
USERENV(180.7fc) 22:56:51:421 ProcessGPO:  Searching
<CN={31B2F340-016D-11D2-945F-00C04FB984F9},CN=Policies,CN=System,DC=zygort,DC=lcl>
USERENV(180.7fc) 22:56:51:421 ProcessGPO:  Machine has access to this GPO.
USERENV(180.7fc) 22:56:51:421 ProcessGPO:  GPO passes the filter check.
USERENV(180.7fc) 22:56:51:421 ProcessGPO:  Found functionality version of:  2
USERENV(180.7fc) 22:56:51:421 ProcessGPO:  Found file system path of:
<\\zygort.lcl\sysvol\zygort.lcl\Policies\{31B2F340-016D-11D2-945F-00C04FB984F9}>
USERENV(180.7fc) 22:56:51:437 ProcessGPO:  Found common name of:
<{31B2F340-016D-11D2-945F-00C04FB984F9}>
USERENV(180.7fc) 22:56:51:453 ProcessGPO:  Found display name of:  <Default Domain Policy>
```

FIGURE 18.7
`Userenv.log` file output

NOTE *The* `userenv.log` *file has a maximum file size of 1MB. If the log file hits this limit, it will automatically save the existing file as* `userenv.bak` *and then start a new logfile.*

The `userenv.log` file is very handy when investigating client-side extensions failures, but it will not show detailed information on all of the CSEs. It will show whether the CSE ran successfully or not, whether the policy was changed, and to which site the user authenticated. For Administrative Templates, it will show missing or corrupt `ntuser.pol` or `registry.pol` files, and it will indicate whether or not the policy information could be read from the Sysvol folder. However, for some of the CSEs, you will need to enable additional logging.

Folder Redirection   If you cannot determine the folder redirection problem from the events in the application log, you should enable FDeploy logging to get more detailed information. This can be performed by adding the REG_DWORD value `FDeployDebugLevel` to `HKEY_LOCAL_MACHINE\ Software\Microsoft\WindowsNT\CurrentVersion\Diagnostics` and setting it to `0x0f`.

Security   If you want to view more detailed information than the application log provides, you can increase the `winlogon.log` diagnostic level by setting the value at `HKEY_LOCAL_MACHINE\ Software\Microsoft\WindowsNT\CurrentVersion\CurrentVersion\Winlogon\GpExtensions\ {827d319e-6eac-11d2-a4ea-00c04f79f83a}\ExtensionDebugLevel` to `0x2`.

Scripts   There are two script settings that you can apply, one for the user scripts and the other for machine scripts. This is not a method to increase the logging level. However, by looking at the Registry values at the following keys, you can determine where the scripts are supposed to be located. For user scripts you can navigate to `HKEY_CURRENT_USER\Software\Policies\Microsoft\ Windows\System\Scripts`, and for computer scripts you can navigate to `HKEY_LOCAL_MACHINE\ Software\Policies\Microsoft\Windows\System\Scripts`.

Other Factors to Consider

Group Policy relies on several underlying technologies in order for it to function correctly. If the problem is not due to a GPO configuration setting, but instead is due to a problem within your network infrastructure or domain controllers, you will need to use additional tools to determine the underlying cause of the problem.

Active Directory Replication   You can check to make sure GPOs are replicating correctly by using ReplMon to check the Active Directory replication between domain controllers and the FRS tools mentioned in Chapter 15, "Troubleshooting the File Replication Service," to make sure the Sysvol is replicating properly. These tools will help you determine if the problem is related to the domain controllers or the underlying network infrastructure.

Network Infrastructure Issues   If your troubleshooting points you to network problems, you can use NetDiag to troubleshoot connectivity issues at the domain controller or the client. DNS issues will keep clients from contacting the domain controllers and the domain controllers from communicating with each other, so you may need to perform some of the DNS troubleshooting, as covered in Chapter 14, "Maintaining DNS."

Trust Relationships   Although you are allowed to administer GPOs within any forest or domain that has the appropriate trust relationship and to which you have been granted permissions, you will not be able to link GPOs from remote forests into your local forest. You can, however, link GPOs from one domain to another. If you experience a broken trust relationship, the GPO from the remote domain will not apply against the user or computer.

Moving Accounts   If you are moving accounts from one OU to another, you will need to make sure the computer is restarted or the user logs out and logs back in. If they fail to do so, the policies that they are supposed to be under will not apply.

Loopback   This is one topic that throws most administrators. By default, when a computer is started, the computer settings within the computer's OU apply and then the user settings from the user's OU apply. By enabling loopback, the user settings from the computer's OU will be applied instead of those configured at the user's OU. Loopback has two options: replace mode and merge. Replace mode completely replaces the user's OU policies with those from the computer's OU. Merge joins the settings from both OUs, and the computer settings having precedence if there are any conflicts.

WMI Filtering   If you delete a WMI filter and do not remove the links within GPOs, the GPO will not be processed by clients. For this reason, make sure you know the GPOs that fall under the control of a WMI filter before removing it.

Security Filtering   You can control the accounts to which a GPO applies by adding them to the access control list (ACL) of the GPO and setting the Read and Apply Group Policy permissions. In the GPMC, just add the accounts to the Security Filtering option of the GPO. You can filter an account by not applying the Apply Group Policy permission to it or by explicitly denying it. Filter accounts with caution, because troubleshooting permissions can be difficult. You should also make sure that any account that does not need to have the policy applied to it has the Read permission filtered as well as the Apply Group Policy. Just make sure that anyone who manages the GPO has the Read permission. Each account that is a member of the site, domain, or OU where the policy applied will still enumerate the settings within the GPO even if it is not applied against its account.

Asynchronous Processing   Windows XP does not process GPOs in the same manner as Windows 2000 or Windows Server 2003. Windows XP is "optimized for logon" speed. This can be problematic for some Active Directory installations because Windows XP processes the GPOs in asynchronous mode, which means that the policies are applied after the user has logged on and their Desktop is created. Some policy settings apply only when the computer is starting or the user is logging on, and they will only apply before the Desktop is generated. Due to the asynchronous processing of Windows XP, any settings that have changed in relation to software installation and folder redirection will not take effect at the next logon. However, a flag is set within the operating system so that it will start in synchronous mode so that those settings are applied at the next logon.

In order to change the processing type, modify a GPO to include the setting that you want within the `Computer Configuration\Administrative Templates\System\Logon` entry.

Handy Dandy Scripts

Included with the GPMC is a host of scripts that will allow you to perform some quick checks against your Group Policy environment and perform some administrative tasks. These sample scripts can also be a good starting place for you to start writing your own scripts.

After installing the GPMC, the scripts will be located in a subdirectory named `scripts` in the path where you installed the GPMC. In this directory, you will find the scripts and also the GPMC Help file. The Help file includes information concerning each script, the function it performs, and the syntax to run the script. Some interesting scripts that are included are shown in Table 18.3.

TABLE 18.3: GPMC SCRIPTS

SCRIPT	FUNCTION
`ListAllGPOs.wsf`	Lists all of the GPOs in a domain. The `/v` switch is used for verbose output.
`DumpGPOInfo.wsf`	Lists information about a specified GPO.
`FindDisabledGPOs.wsf`	Lists all of the GPOs that are completely disabled or that have either the user or configuration sections disabled.
`FindOrphanGPOsInSYSVOL.wsf`	Lists all of the GPOs within the Sysvol folder that do not have an associated container object within Active Directory.
`FindDuplicateNamedGPOs.wsf`	Lists all of the GPOs within a domain that contain the same friendly name.
`FindGPOsWithNoSecurityFiltering.wsf`	Lists all GPOs that do not have any Apply Group Policy permissions set to allow.
`FindUnlinkedGPOs.wsf`	Lists all GPOs within a domain that are not linked to a site, domain, or OU.
`FindGPOsBySecurityGroup.wsf`	Lists all of the GPOs that have a security group with Apply Group Policy permissions set to allow.

Other scripts are available that will allow you to configure who is allowed to create or link GPOs within the domain, set security filtering on GPOs, and generate reports that detail the settings for GPOs.

Best Practices for Group Policy

Try to keep these tips in mind when you are working with and troubleshooting GPOs.

- ◆ Use the GPMC as a starting point for troubleshooting.

- ◆ If the GPMC is not available, use the limited use version of FAZAM that is included with Windows 2000.

- ◆ Use the advanced options for Group Policy (No Override (Enforced), Block Inheritance, Security Filtering) sparingly.

- ◆ Understand how to use all of the tools, including the network diagnostic tools, replication tools, and DNS troubleshooting tools.

- ◆ Disable any diagnostic logging that you are performing when the testing is complete.

Next Up

Group Policy has proven to be the most difficult to implement and troubleshoot of the Active Directory technologies. With the inclusion of the Group Policy Management Console, troubleshooting issues with GPOs became easier—yet they still cause many administrators sleepless nights. As we move on to the next unit, we leave behind the troubleshooting headaches and prepare for the migraine known as security. Microsoft has attempted to rectify some of the security issues that have plagued them in the past. However, there are still some issues that you should be aware of and some security measures that you should take whenever you implement Active Directory in your environment.

Security in Active Directory

part4

In this part:

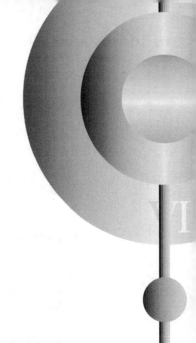

chapter 19

Securing the Base Operating System

ONE OF THE MOST important steps to ensure the stability of your domain is often the most over-looked. Most administrators will take steps to secure Active Directory, but most fail to take the extra steps to secure their domain controllers. A security breach of a domain controller means a breach of your entire Active Directory infrastructure, including all user accounts, domain information, etc.

People can gain physical or remote access to your domain controller. In this chapter, I will talk about preventive measures you can take to guard against physical and remote access to your domain controllers. I will also talk about steps you can take to make sure you can track information on these attacks to see who is attempting the attack or who was successful.

Securing the Domain Controller from a Physical Access Attack

Probably the most overlooked area in security is physical access to the domain controllers. I am cur-rently on a team that engages in "social engineering" in order to try to find weaknesses in our client's networks. We were hired by the company's executives to try to gain access to the network.

Of all the processes that we try, I was very surprised to find that the physical access test is more successful that I had originally anticipated. This test does not have a very high success rate, but it is higher than I had thought it would be.

The steps you can take to deny physical access to a server include more than just putting a lock on the server room door. Every layer of security adds time to an intrusion attempt, and possibly adds to the frustration level of the person making the attempt. If someone gains access to your server room, you shouldn't have your entire bounty lying there waiting for them to take. Even Indiana Jones had to go through many tests to obtain his treasure. Even after success, he still had to deal with that big boulder chasing him.

Locking the server room door is great, and a lot of people do that, but many other layers are often missed. Put all of your servers in racks that lock. To prevent someone from booting your DC into an alternative operating system, you can also remove the floppy and CDRom or CDRW drives from the server. You should also disable external ports (serial, SCSI, USB, etc.) that are not being used. Plug-and-Play technology makes it very easy for external drives to be connected and easily configured without a reboot. Many USB "pen drives" can hold over 1GB of information. If someone gains physical access to these machines, a wealth of information could walk out the door in someone's pocket.

NOTE *If you enable Syskey, you may need to keep a floppy drive located on the domain controller, depending on the level of Syskey you decide to use. Syskey will be discussed later in the chapter.*

Guarding Against Remote Access Attacks

There are many steps you can take to prevent remote access attacks. You can secure and/or delete certain built-in accounts, secure your password information with the Syskey utility, relocate the Active Directory database files, and even block ports with IPSec so communication between domain controllers is encrypted. In this section, we will look at each of these settings individually.

Domain Controller Auditing Policy Settings

In this section, I will explain the audit policy that should be configured for domain controllers, which can be seen in Figure 19.1. We will look at each of these settings individually.

Audit Account Logon Events This setting should be configured to Success/Failure. An event will be logged each time a user attempts to log on to a domain controller.

Audit Account Management This setting should be configured to Success/Failure. Events are created when security principal accounts are created, deleted, or modified. Events are also created if an attempt to create, delete, or modify account management is unsuccessful.

FIGURE 19.1
Auditing options for domain controllers

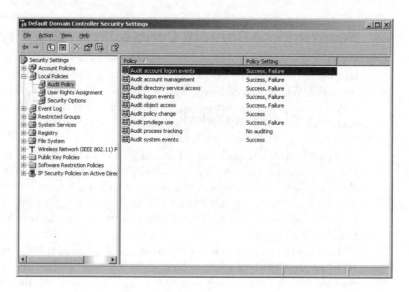

Audit Directory Service Access   This setting should be configured to Success/Failure. When an Active Directory object with a system access control list is accessed, an event will be generated.

Audit Logon Events   This setting should be configured to Success/Failure. Events are recorded when a user attempts to interactively log on to a domain controller or authenticates to a domain controller to retrieve a logon script or policy.

Audit Object Access   This should be set to Success/Failure. An event will be created each time an attempt is made to access objects such as files, folders, and Registry keys.

Audit Policy Change   This setting should be configured to Success. Changes to user rights assignments policies, audit policies, or trust policies will generate a policy change event.

Audit Privilege Use   This should be set to Success/Failure. An event will be created for each instance of a user exercising a user right.

Audit Process Tracking   This should be set to No Auditing.

Audit System Events   This setting should be configured to Success. System events, such as a restart or shutdown of the domain controller, and security events will be recorded in the event log.

Configuring User Rights Assignments

By default, user rights assignments are defined at the domain controller's OU and are defined by the Default Domain Controller Policy. Certain items that are required to be in the Default Domain Controller Policy can be tightened. Editing the existing policy is not recommended though, because you may want to recover the Default Domain Controller Policy. You can, however, create a new policy and link it to the domain controller's OU. This policy is known as the Domain Controller Baseline Policy (DCBP), and it takes precedence over the Default Domain Controller Policy.

Microsoft has included three `.inf` files to be used for the DCBP. The three files are listed here:

Legacy Client   `domain controller.inf`

Enterprise Client   `domain controller.inf`

High Security   `domain controller.inf`

When you are configuring the security for your domain controllers, some settings will not have to be enforced on member servers. The Network Security: Do Not Store LAN Manager Hash Value On Next Password Change setting should be enabled on your domain controllers.

Member servers will typically have this setting for all three security environments. The DCBP disables this policy for the Legacy Client, but leaves it enabled for the Enterprise client and High Security Client. Windows 9x clients would not be able to log on after a password change if this policy setting were enabled.

The following services are also defined in the Domain Controller Baseline Policy. Defining the service startup mode in a Group Policy prevents the service from being configured by anyone besides an administrator. It also prevents users, even administrators, from accidentally disabling the service. All of the following services are defined in the baseline policy for the Legacy Client, Enterprise Client, and High Security Client to start automatically:

- Distributed File System Service

- DNS Server Service

- File Replication Service

- Intersite Messaging Service

- Kerberos Key Distribution Center Service

- Remote Procedure Call (RPC) Locator Service

Domain Controller Security Options

The following list contains the recommended settings for the Domain Controller Security Options Policy. The Security Options section of the policy determines behavior with Active Directory, network, file system, and user logon security.

We will look at each of the settings individually. Some of them are found in Figure 19.2. Each setting is different depending on whether the forest is in a Windows 2000 Mixed Mode or Windows 2003 Native Mode. We will compare the two. Each setting in the Windows 2003 Native Mode is a recommended change for the Windows 2000 Mixed Mode.

FIGURE 19.2

Security options for domain controllers

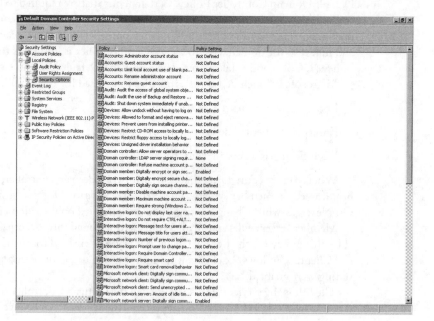

The security options that are relevant to securing your domain controllers, along with their recommended settings, are listed here:

Audit: Audit The Access Of Global System Objects   Disable this setting to prevent the creation of default SACL on system objects, such as events, semaphores, and MS_DOS devices.

Audit: Audit The Use Of Backup And Restore Privilege   Disable this setting to disable auditing for the use of user privileges, including backup and restore operations.

Audit: Shut Down System Immediately If Unable To Log Security Events   Disable this setting so your domain controller will not shut down if it cannot record an event log.

Devices: Allow Undock Without Having To Log On   Disable this setting, as it is very unlikely your domain controller is a laptop.

Devices: Allowed To Format And Eject Removable Media   This setting should be configured for Administrators. This will allow administrators to accomplish this task, yet keep others from stealing important information.

Devices: Prevent Users From Installing Printer Drivers   This setting should be set to Enabled so only Administrators and Server Operators can install printer drivers. Malicious users can perform disk space attacks by submitting large print jobs.

Devices: Restrict CD-ROM Access To Locally Logged On User Only   Keeps the CD-ROM from being accessed over the network. Only interactive sessions can access the CD-ROM.

Devices: Restrict Floppy Access To Locally Logged On User Only   Keeps the floppy from being accessed over the network. Only interactive sessions can access the floppy drive.

Devices: Unsigned Driver Installation Behavior   This should be set to Do Not Allow Installation so that you can prevent untrusted and unsigned drivers from being installed on the server.

Domain Controller: Allow Server Operators To Schedule Tasks   Set this to Disabled to restrict the number of users who can schedule tasks, because tasks usually run at an elevated level.

Domain Controller: Refuse Machine Account Password Changes   This setting should be changed to Disabled because it is much more secure to have machine accounts change their passwords on a regular basis.

Domain Member: Digitally Encrypt Or Sign Secure Channel Data (Always)   Change this setting to Enabled to ensure that all domain controllers are at least Windows NT 4 SP 6a. Make sure that all security fixes have been made.

Domain Member: Disable Machine Account Password Changes   Change this setting to Disabled so machine accounts can regularly change their passwords.

Domain Member: Maximum Machine Account Password Age   Configure this setting for 30 days. A best practice is to have machine accounts reset their passwords on a regular basis.

Domain Member: Require Strong (Windows 2000 Or Later) Session Key   This setting should be set to Enabled. This eliminates negotiated key strength and requires a 128-bit encrypted secure channel so the most secure connection is always used.

Interactive Logon: Do Not Display Last User Name   This should be set to Enabled. As I mentioned earlier in the chapter, you shouldn't give away part of the puzzle to a would-be hacker. If this setting is enabled, users will have to enter both a username and a password to access the domain controller.

Interactive Logon: Do Not Require Ctrl+Alt+Del   This should be set to Disabled to ensure that the users have a secure logon.

Interactive Logon: Number of Previous Logons To Cache (In Case Domain Controller Is Not Available)   This should be set to 0 Logons. This will prevent the domain controller from caching any previous logons and requires authentication at each logon.

Interactive Logon: Prompt User To Change Password Before Expiration   Change this setting to 14 days. This will notify the users that their passwords are about to expire so they can come up with another strong password in that time.

Interactive Logon: Require Domain Controller Authentication To Unlock Workstation   Set this to Enabled so changes made to an account are enforced immediately. If cached credentials are used to unlock the console, changes to the account are not enforced.

Interactive Logon: Require Smart Card   If you have a PKI infrastructure in place, you should set this to Enabled to take advantage of that level of security.

Interactive Logon: Smart Card Removal Behavior   Set this to Force Logoff to prevent administrators from walking off and keeping their session open on the server. A domain controller should never be left alone logged into the network with administrator credentials.

Microsoft Network Client: Send Unencrypted Password To Third-Party SMB Servers
Change this setting to Disabled to prohibit the SMB redirector from sending plaintext passwords to servers that do not support password encryption. You do not want to disable this setting if your servers must communicate with non-Microsoft SMB servers.

Microsoft Network Server: Disconnect Clients When Logon Hours Expire   When this setting is Enabled, client sessions are disconnected to keep clients from staying logged in during disallowed times.

Network Access: Do Not Allow Storage Of Credentials Or .NET Passports For Network Authentication   Change this setting to Enabled. If someone accesses a logged-in session on a domain controller, this can keep that user from accessing any information or websites that may be stored with the administrator's credentials.

Network Access: Restrict Anonymous Access To Named Pipes And Shares   Change this setting to Enabled. Administrators can define which Named Pipes and Shares can be accessed by changing the following settings: Network Access: Named Pipes That Can Be Accessed Anonymously, and Network Access: Shares That Can Be Accessed Anonymously.

Network Security: LDAP Client Signing Requirements   Set this to Require Signing if all of your domain controllers are at Windows 2000 Service Pack 3 or higher, or at Windows 2003.

Recovery Console: Allow Automatic Administrative Logon   Change this to Disabled. This requires an administrator password to gain access to the domain controller.

Recover Console: Allow Floppy Copy And Access To All Drives And Folders   This should be set to Disabled to prevent unauthorized users from manipulating the Active Directory database and other files on the domain controller.

Shutdown: Allow System To Be Shut Down Without Having To Log On   This setting should be set to Disabled. Domain controllers should be shut down only by an authenticated service account.

Shutdown: Clear Virtual Memory Pagefile   Change this setting to Enabled to prevent memory data from going into the `pagefile` on shutdown in case a user gains access to the `pagefile`.

System objects: Strengthen Default Permissions Of Internal System Objects (E.G. Symbolic Links)   Change this setting to Enabled to enable users who are not administrators to read shared objects. The users will not be able to modify the shared objects.

System Settings: Optional Subsystems   The Posix subsystem is the only subsystem that is enabled by default. If you do not need Posix, you can change this policy and remove Posix so your list will be empty.

System Settings: Use Certificate Rules On Windows Executables For Software Restrictions Policies   If you are using PKI in your environment, you can enable this setting to check CRLs to check the validity of the software certificate and the signature.

Protecting Systems During Installation

Most administrators dread the thought of installing the operating system on a new system and will instead take measures to automate the installation. The most popular methods of automating the installation include creating an image, using an automated installation file, or using Microsoft's RIS service. There are pros and cons to each of the installation types, but all of them are more efficient than installing by hand.

NOTE   *For more information about the automated installation methods, review Chapter 8, "Deployment."*

Use Operating System Best Practices

A domain controller's base operating system should be as secure as possible so that you do not risk it being susceptible to common attacks. You should follow these guidelines to make sure that you have your bases covered:

Format the drives with NTFS.   The NTFS file system is the only file system that protects files locally, as well as across the network.

Load only TCP/IP.   TCP/IP should be the only protocol loaded onto the domain controller. You should not have any applications that require any other protocols to be loaded onto your domain controllers, and your clients should use only TCP/IP when connecting using the domain controller's services. Additional protocols invite an additional method of access and potentially an additional attack approach.

Apply service packs.   You should apply all of the latest service packs and security patches before you promote the domain controller. This adds an additional level of security by closing up the known security holes.

Secure DNS.   Make sure DNS is already configured and set up securely before promoting your domain controller. See Chapter 20, "Securing DNS," for tips on securing DNS servers.

Do not install IIS.   Domain controllers do not require IIS to function. Windows Server 2003 does not install this service as a default part of the operating system, but Windows 2000 does. If you accepted the default options when you installed your Windows 2000 server, uninstall IIS before putting it into production. To make sure that IIS is not installed as part of the Windows 2000 installation, use an unattended installation file that contains the line `iis_common = off` in the `[Components]` section of the answer file.

Secure Installation Location

As you build domain controllers, make sure you are working in a secure location where the automated installation files and media can be protected. Unattended installation files and automated promotion files used in Dcpromo can include passwords for the administrator account used to promote the domain controller or sensitive information about the system.

If you are using the advanced version of Dcpromo, you should make sure that you destroy the media that includes the System State of the original domain controller after you finish promoting the domain controller. The System State is valid only for the tombstone lifetime, and Dcpromo will not use a System State that is out of date.

Disable 8.3 Auto-Name Generation

Typically, when a file is created with a long filename, the system will automatically generate an associated 8.3 version of the filename so that the file can be used by 16-bit programs. Several viruses have been written as 16-bit programs that take advantage of the 8.3 version of the filename. Because domain controllers do not typically have additional programs running on them, you can safely turn off the auto-name generation by editing the Registry and changing the value of `HKEY_LOCAL_MACHINE\ SYSTEM\CurrentControlSet\Control\FileSystem\NtfsDisable8dot3NameCreation` to 1.

Securing Well-Known User Accounts

When a malicious user attempts remote access to a server, they often use a brute-force password attack. The first accounts they attempt to use are the built-in administrator and guest accounts. These accounts cannot be deleted, but they can be renamed. If these accounts are not renamed, you have done 50 percent of a would-be hacker's work; they will only need to determine the passwords for these accounts.

The built-in account guest is disabled by default. Make sure this account is still disabled, and I strongly recommended that you do not enable it for any reason.

The built-in administrator account should be changed immediately upon configuration of the server. Aside from just renaming the account, you should also modify the description of the administrator account. You can easily rename the administrator account to *jsomebody*, but if you leave the description field as "Built-in account to administer the domain," anyone who has viewing rights to ADUC will be able to see which account is the administrator account.

An added step in securing your administrator account is to create a new account that has all of the same rights, and then disable the built-in administrator account. Many programs are available on the Internet that will scan for an administrator SID on the system. The built-in administrator SID always ends in 500, and these programs will find those SIDs.

Securing Service Accounts

Domain account passwords are stored in the Local Security Authority (LSA) secrets. If a domain controller is physically compromised, these LSA secrets can be dumped, and all domain account passwords can easily be obtained. This is the number one reason that services should never be set to run under the security context of a domain account.

Using the Syskey Utility to Secure Password Information

All domain passwords are stored in the Active Directory database. As you read previously, these passwords can easily be obtained if the domain controller is physically compromised. You can encrypt the passwords on a system by using a utility called Syskey. The System Key is used to encrypt the password data in the database on the domain controller.

Syskey can operate at three different levels.

Level 1 Level 1 is enabled on all Windows 2003 Servers by default. A system key is randomly generated, and an encrypted key is stored locally on that server.

Level 2 Level 2 operates in the same manner as Level 1, but the administrator selects an additional password to enter into the system when the computer is starting up. Unlike Level 1, this password is not stored locally.

Level 3 Level 3 requires much more administrator interaction. The computer randomly generates a key and stores it on a floppy disk. The computer will not start unless the administrator has the floppy disk to put into the system during bootup.

Level 2 and Level 3 are suggested for areas where the domain controller is subject to a physical attack (for example, in an unlocked room). Keep in mind that with Level 2 or Level 3, administrator interaction on-site is required for the server to boot properly. Losing the floppy disk or forgetting the password will render a domain controller useless. There is no way to recover the domain controller; it will have to be rebuilt.

You can run Syskey from a command prompt or from the Run dialog box. Simply type **syskey**, and click OK. Select Encryption Enabled, and then click Update. Click the desired option, and then click OK.

Defining Domain Controller Communication with IPSec Filters

Defining the IPSec filters is an added level of security that is really only recommended for a very high security environment. Microsoft recommends that you create the IPSec filters found in Table 19.1 on all domain controllers in a high security environment.

TABLE 19.1: HIGH SECURITY IPSEC FILTERS FOR DOMAIN CONTROLLERS

SERVICE	PROTOCOL	SOURCE PORT	DESTINATION PORT	SOURCE ADDRESS	DESTINATION ADDRESS	ACTION	MIRROR
CIFS/SMB Server	TCP	ANY	445	ANY	ME	ALLOW	YES
	UDP	ANY	445	ANY	ME	ALLOW	YES
RPC Server	TCP	ANY	135	ANY	ME	ALLOW	YES
	UDP	ANY	135	ANY	ME	ALLOW	YES
NetBIOS Server	TCP	ANY	137	ANY	ME	ALLOW	YES
	UDP	ANY	137	ANY	ME	ALLOW	YES
	UDP	ANY	138	ANY	ME	ALLOW	YES
	TCP	ANY	139	ANY	ME	ALLOW	YES
Monitoring Client	ANY	ANY	ANY	ME	MOM Server	ALLOW	YES
Terminal Services Server	TCP	ANY	3389	ANY	ME	ALLOW	YES
Global Catalog Server	TCP	ANY	3268	ANY	ME	ALLOW	YES
	TCP	ANY	3269	ANY	ME	ALLOW	YES
DNS Server	TCP	ANY	53	ANY	ME	ALLOW	YES
	UDP	ANY	53	ANY	ME	ALLOW	YES
Kerberos Server	TCP	ANY	88	ANY	ME	ALLOW	YES
	UDP	ANY	88	ANY	ME	ALLOW	YES
LDAP Server	TCP	ANY	389	ANY	ME	ALLOW	YES

Continued on next page

TABLE 19.1: HIGH SECURITY IPSEC FILTERS FOR DOMAIN CONTROLLERS *(continued)*

SERVICE	PROTOCOL	SOURCE PORT	DESTINATION PORT	SOURCE ADDRESS	DESTINATION ADDRESS	ACTION	MIRROR
	UDP	ANY	389	ANY	ME	ALLOW	YES
	TCP	ANY	636	ANY	ME	ALLOW	YES
	UDP	ANY	636	ANY	ME	ALLOW	YES
NTP Server	TCP	ANY	123	ANY	ME	ALLOW	YES
	UDP	ANY	123	ANY	ME	ALLOW	YES
PredefinedRPC Range	TCP	ANY	57901–57950	ANY	ME	ALLOW	YES
DC Comms	ANY	ANY	ANY	ME	Domain Controller	ALLOW	YES
DC Comms	ANY	ANY	ANY	ME	Domain Controller 2	ALLOW	YES
ICMP	ICMP	ANY	ANY	ME	ANY	ALLOW	YES
All Inbound Traffic	ANY	ANY	ANY	ANY	ME	BLOCK	YES

Modifying the Default Services

Most domain controllers will not need to have all of the default services enabled. These services do not provide any additional functionality on most domain controllers, and they become an additional attack point. You should consider disabling unused services or at the very least, configuring them to start manually, just in case another service may depend on the service. Table 19.2 shows the services you should consider disabling or setting to start manually.

TABLE 19.2: UNNECESSARY SERVICES

SERVICE	DEFAULT SETTING 2003	DEFAULT SETTING 2000 SECURE SETTING	RECOMMENDED SETTING
Application Management	Manual	Manual	Consider setting to Disabled or Manual
Automatic Updates	Automatic	Automatic	Consider setting to Disabled or Manual
Background Intelligent Transfer Service	Manual	Manual	Consider setting to Disabled or Manual

Continued on next page

TABLE 19.2: UNNECESSARY SERVICES *(continued)*

SERVICE	DEFAULT SETTING 2003	DEFAULT SETTING 2000 SECURE SETTING	RECOMMENDED SETTING
Computer Browser	Automatic	Automatic	Consider setting to Disabled or Manual
DHCP Client	Automatic	Automatic	Consider setting to Disabled or Manual
Distributed Link Tracking Client	Manual	Automatic	Disabled
Distributed Link Tracking Server	Disabled	Automatic	Disabled
DNS Server	Automatic	Automatic	Consider setting to Disabled or Manual
Error Reporting Service	Automatic	Automatic	Consider setting to Disabled or Manual
Fax	Automatic	Automatic	Disabled
IIS Admin Service	Automatic	Automatic	Disabled
Indexing Service	Disabled	Manual	Disabled
Internet Connection Firewall (ICF)/ Internet Connection Sharing (ICS)	Disabled	Manual	Disabled
License Logging	Disabled	Automatic	Disabled
Microsoft Software Shadow Copy Provider	Manual	Manual	Consider setting to Disabled or Manual
NetMeeting Remote Desktop Sharing	Disabled	Manual	Disabled
Performance Logs and Alerts	Manual	Manual	Consider setting to Disabled or Manual
Portable Media Serial Number Service	Manual	Manual	Disabled
Print Spooler	Automatic	Automatic	Consider setting to Disabled or Manual
Remote Access Auto Connection Manager	Manual	Manual	Consider setting to Disabled or Manual

Continued on next page

TABLE 19.2: UNNECESSARY SERVICES *(continued)*

SERVICE	DEFAULT SETTING 2003	DEFAULT SETTING 2000 SECURE SETTING	RECOMMENDED SETTING
Remote Access Connection Manager	Manual	Manual	Consider setting to Disabled or Manual
Remote Procedure Call (RPC) Locator	Manual	Manual	Consider setting to Disabled or Manual
Removable Storage	Manual	Automatic	Consider setting to Disabled or Manual
Shell Hardware Detection	Automatic	Automatic	Disabled
Simple Mail Transfer Protocol (SMTP)	Automatic	Automatic	Disabled
Special Administrator Console Helper	Manual	Manual	Disabled
Telephony	Manual	Manual	Consider setting to Disabled or Manual
Telnet	Disabled	Manual	Disabled
Terminal Services	(Manual)	Manual	Consider setting to Disabled or Manual
Uninterruptible Power Supply	(Manual)	Manual	Consider setting to Disabled or Manual
Upload Manager	Manual	Manual	Disabled
Utility Manager	Manual	Manual	Disabled
Volume Shadow Copy	Manual	Manual	Consider setting to Disabled or Manual
Windows Audio	Automatic	Automatic	Disabled
Wireless Configuration	Automatic	Automatic	Consider setting to Disabled or Manual

Best Practices for Securing Domain Controllers

When planning security for your domain controllers, follow these tips to secure the base operating system from attack.

- ◆ Secure the server from a physical attack. Lock the server room door, lock the server rack, lock the server's case, remove writable drives, and disable unused physical ports (SCSI, serial, and USB).

- ◆ Secure the server from a remote access attack. Configure auditing on the domain controller to audit events to the Schema, the Configuration Directory Partition, and Domain Controller

Partitions. You should also configure the Audit Policy settings in the Default Domain Controller Security Policy, as well as User Rights Assignments and Security Options.

◆ Account management should be scrutinized by securing well-known accounts and securing service accounts.

◆ Use the Syskey utility to protect password information.

◆ Change the default services within a domain controller so that they cannot be a point of attack.

◆ Secure server-to-server communication with IPSec filters.

Next Up

In this chapter, we covered many of the options you have to secure your domain controllers. You can take many preventive steps to guard against a physical or remote access breach of your domain controller. We also studied the steps you can take to monitor a system to determine which users are making changes to the system.

Depending on the functional level of your forest, a lot of these settings may already be in place in your environment. A Windows 2003 Forest Functional Level is much more secure than a Windows 2000 Mixed or Native forest. If you are running at any 2000-level forest functional level, I recommend the changes listed in this chapter.

Now that you have a good understanding of some of the methods of securing the domain controllers within your organization, you should be ready to move on to securing other aspects of your network infrastructure. One of the most important services within any Active Directory implementation is DNS. DNS supports the Active Directory infrastructure, and it is the primary method of name resolution within networks of any size. For you to keep your DNS infrastructure available at all times, you will need to make sure that you secure it from outside influences, and at the same time keep it available and communicating with the proper entities. As we move on to next chapter, we will delve into securing DNS.

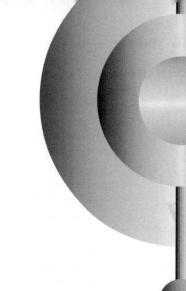

chapter 20

Securing DNS

As YOU MAY HAVE already noticed, DNS has played an important role throughout this book. This is the third chapter on the topic, and nearly every other chapter has had a reference to DNS. DNS is a very important service that needs to function correctly in order for your Active Directory infrastructure to work properly.

DNS has been a popular service to attack because so many clients rely on it in order to locate the host systems that they are attempting to contact. Without DNS, you would not be able to locate http://www.microsoft.com. You could call the web server by its IP address, but how many of us have the IP address of the server memorized?

Two methods of attack are usually attempted against DNS servers: denial of service (DoS) attacks and abusing the name resolution. With denial of service attacks, the attacker attempts to block the DNS server from answering client queries, thereby reducing its effectiveness to clients. When abusing the name resolution that a DNS server provides, either the attacker will cause the DNS server to return incorrect results to the client, or the attacker will gather information about a company from the data that the DNS server returns.

In this chapter, I am going to discuss some of the security options that are available to use in order to protect your DNS servers. You may not need to implement each of the methods identified here, but you should identify the systems that are at risk and use every precaution to make sure that your systems are protected from attack.

Keeping the System Going

Without a functional DNS, nearly all of the topics that I have discussed throughout this book will fail. Understanding just how important DNS is to a company's infrastructure, the designers of DNS built the service to be redundant and able to withstand attacks that attempt to take down the DNS servers that support a company.

Nevertheless, some attackers will try to knock down your DNS so that they can reduce the effectiveness of your implementation, annoy your clients as they attempt to perform their jobs, and just plain dampen your spirits. Denial of service attacks can be devastating, but you can take steps to put yourself at ease.

Limit the Dynamic Updates

I am going to assume that you are working in an Active Directory environment because that is the main thrust of this book. An Active Directory–integrated DNS server can be configured so that it accepts dynamic update requests only from authorized systems. Once you configure a zone as Active Directory–integrated, change the dynamic updates so that only secure updates are allowed. At that point, only members of Active Directory can update the zone records. Once secure updates are turned on, an attacker will not be able to add false records to your database that could cause the domain controller to become overloaded as it tries to replicate the changes.

In a Windows Server 2003–based domain, you can take this one step further by making sure that the DNS data is replicated only to domain controllers that are DNS servers or by specifying that the records are replicated only to the DNS servers that are included within the scope of an application partition. For more information on how to control the Active Directory replication for application partitions, see Chapter 14, "Maintaining DNS."

Monitor for Traffic

If the DNS server appears to be overloaded and you believe the resource overhead is due to an attack, you can use a monitoring tool, such as Microsoft's Network Monitor, or a product, such as Sniffer, to detect where the traffic is originating. If the traffic is from outside of your company, you can assume that you are being attacked. If this is the case, you can attempt to quell the traffic by putting firewall rules into place that will reject packets that originate from the addresses that you identify from the network trace. Most firewalls can be configured to drop spoofed packets. Check with your firewall administrator to determine what you can do with the firewalls in your infrastructure.

If you do put rules into place, that does not mean you will stop the attack. The attacker was probably spoofing their address in the first place, so you may end up being attacked again from the same entity but through another address. Some firewalls have intrusion-detection capabilities, and you may be able to have the firewall dynamically drop packets if they are deemed an attack.

Separate Namespaces

If you support both an Internet and intranet presence, you should keep the two parts of your organization separate so that someone gaining access to Internet resources will not be able to attempt an attack on your internal resources. In Chapter 2, "Active Directory Domain Design," and Chapter 3, "Domain Name System Design," we reviewed the options you have when creating the domain and DNS naming strategy. In both chapters, separating the two namespaces was recommended from an administration standpoint, but there are also security benefits to this design.

When you use a different namespace for your internal organization, you are essentially hiding the namespace from would-be intruders and attackers. This technique is sometimes referred to as "security through obscurity." If you decide to have different namespaces, the internal network should still utilize a naming convention that makes sense to users. If systems that exist within the external namespace are attacked, they should not give up information concerning the systems within the internal network.

Set Quotas

In Windows Server 2003–based Active Directory domains, you have the ability to set quotas on the number of objects that a user is allowed to create within the partitions. You can set quotas differently on each partition because each partition is evaluated separately. By using quotas, you are able to effectively control the number of objects that can be created by an account, thereby quelling any attempt to flood an Active Directory–integrated zone with too many false objects.

You can set a quota limit on either user accounts or group accounts. An account that has been explicitly added to the quota list that is also a member of a group that has quotas applied to it will be able to create as many objects as the least restrictive of the quota policies will allow. When a user attempts to create an object within the container where a quota limit has been set, the existing objects are compared against the quota limit. If the user has not met the quota, the object can be created, but the user will be denied the ability to create the object if the quota has been met.

NOTE   *The quota limit includes tombstoned objects. If the user has objects that are tombstoned and waiting to be purged, new objects may not be created until the tombstone lifetime has expired. If you want to ignore tombstoned objects, you can use the* dsmod partition *command with the* -qtmbstnwt *switch. If you specify a value of 0, then all tombstoned objects will be ignored when objects are evaluated against a user's quota.*

NOTE   *For more information on setting the tombstoned object weight, see the command-line reference within Help and Support Center.*

The command dsadd is used in order to create a quota limit for an Active Directory partition. You can set quotas on any of the partitions, schema, configuration, domain, or any application partitions. However, the quota can only be created or modified on a Windows Server 2003 domain controller because Windows 2000 domain controllers are unfamiliar with the command-line utilities that are used to work with the Active Directory partitions.

Figure 20.1 shows the switches that are available when you are using the dsadd quota command. In its most basic form, you can use it to simply set a quota on a partition. For example, the command dsadd quota -part zygort.lcl -acct zygort\jprice -qlimit 10 would restrict the account jprice so that it is able to create only 10 objects within the zygort.lcl domain partition.

If at a later time you want to modify the number of objects that jprice could create, you could use the dsmod quota command. The syntax for dsmod quota is shown in Figure 20.2. Notice that you will have to know the fully distinguished name for the quota entry before you can change the quota limit. You can use the dsquery quota command to list the quotas that are set. As you can see in Figure 20.3, nearly all of the same options that are available from dsadd are also available from dsquery.

To find the quota entry for the jprice account, you would enter dsquery quota -acct zygort\jprice at the command prompt. If you want to start your search at a specific partition, you can enter the partition's fully distinguished name in the command by using the startnode option.

Once you know the quota entry, you can issue the dsmod quota "CN=zygort_jprice,CN=NTDS Quotas,dc=zygort,dc=lcl" -qlimit 15 command, which will set a new quota of 15 objects for the jprice account. Note that when you have a space within the fully qualified name of an object, you need to enclose the entire name in quotes.

FIGURE 20.1
Syntax of the `dsadd quota` command

```
D:\Documents and Settings\Administrator>dsadd quota /?
Adds a quota specification to a directory partition. A quota specification
determines the maximum number of directory objects a given security principal
can own in a specified directory partition.
dsadd quota -part <PartitionDN> [-rdn <RDN>] -acct Name
-qlimit <Value> | -1 [-desc <Description>]
[{-s <Server> | -d <Domain>}] [-u <UserName>] [-p {<Password> | *}]
[-q] [{-uc | -uco | -uci}]
-part <PartitionDN>           Required. Specifies the distinguished name of the
                              directory partition on which you want to create a
                              quota. If the distinguished name is omitted, it
                              will be taken from standard input (stdin).
-rdn <RDN>                    Specifies the relative distinguished name (RDN)
                              of the quota specification being created. If the
                              -rdn option is omitted, it will be set to
                              <domain>_<accountname>, using the domain and
                              account name of the security principal specified
                              by the -acct parameter.
-acct Name                    Required. Specifies the security principal (user,
                              group, computer, InetOrgPerson) for whom the
                              quota specification is being specified. The -acct
                              option can be provided in the following forms:
                                DN of the security principal
                                domain\SAM account name of the security
                                principal
-qlimit <Value> | -1
                              Required. Specifies the number of objects within
                              the directory partition that can be owned by
                              the security principal. To specify an unlimited
                              quota, specify -1 as the value.
-desc <Description>           Specifies a description for the quota
                              specification you want to add.
{-s <Server> | -d <Domain>} Connects the computer to either a specified
                              server or domain. By default, the computer is
                              connected to a domain controller in the logon
                              domain.
-u <UserName>                 Specifies the user name with which user will log
                              on to a remote server. By default, the logged on
                              user name is used. You can specify a user name
                              using one of the following formats:
                                 user name (such as, Linda)
                                 domain\user name (such as, widgets\Linda)
                                 user principal name (UPN) (such as,
                                 Linda@widgets.microsoft.com)
-p {<Password> | *}           Specifies use of a specific password or a * to
                              log on to a remote server. If you type *, then
                              you are prompted for a password.
-q                            Suppresses all output to standard output (quiet
                              mode).
{-uc | -uco | -uci}           Specifies that output or input data is formatted
                              in Unicode. The -uc value specifies a Unicode
                              format for input from or output to pipe.
                              The -uco value specifies a Unicode format for
                              output to pipe or file. The -uci value specifies
                              a Unicode format for input from pipe or file.
/?                            Displays help at the command prompt.
```

FIGURE 20.2
Syntax of the `dsmod quota` command

```
D:\Documents and Settings\Administrator>dsmod quota /?
Modifies attributes of one or more existing quota specifications in the
directory. A quota specification determines the maximum number of directory
objects a given security principal can own in a specific directory partition.
dsmod quota <QuotaDN ...> [-qlimit <Value>]
[-desc <Description>] [{-s <Server> | -d <Domain>}] [-u <UserName>]
[-p {<Password> | *}] [-c] [-q] [{-uc | -uco | -uci}]
<QuotaDN ...>         Specifies the distinguished names of one or more quota
                      specifications to modify. If values are omitted, they
                      are obtained through standard input (stdin) to support
                      piping of output from another command to input of this
                      command.
-qlimit <Value>
                      Specifies the number of objects within the
                      directory partition that can be owned by the security
                      principal to which the quota specification is assigned.
                      To specify an unlimited quota, use -1.
-desc <Description>   Sets the description of the quota specification to
                      <Description>.
{-s <Server> | -d <Domain>}
                      Connects to a specified remote server or domain. By
                      default, the computer is connected to a domain
                      controller in the logon domain.
-u <UserName>         Specifies the user name with which the user logs on to
                      a remote server. By default, -u uses the user name with
                      which the user logged on. You can use any of the
                      following formats to specify a user name:
                        user name (for example, Linda)
                        domain\user name (for example, widgets\Linda)
                        user principal name (UPN)
                          (for example, Linda@widgets.microsoft.com)
-p {<Password> | *}   Specifies to use either a password or a * to log on to
                      a remote server. If you type *, you are prompted for a
                      password.
-c                    Specifies continuous operation mode. Errors are
                      reported, but the process continues with the next
                      object in the argument list when you specify multiple
                      target objects. If you do not use -c, the command quits
                      after the first error occurs.
-q                    Suppresses all output to standard output (quiet mode).
{-uc | -uco | -uci}   Specifies that output or input data is formatted in
                      Unicode.
                      -uc   Specifies a Unicode format for input from or
                            output to a pipe (|).
                      -uco  Specifies a Unicode format for output to a
                            pipe (|) or a file.
                      -uci  Specifies a Unicode format for input from a
                            pipe (|) or a file.
Dsmod quota only supports a subset of commonly used object class attributes.
```

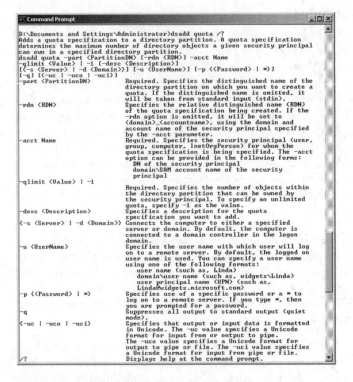

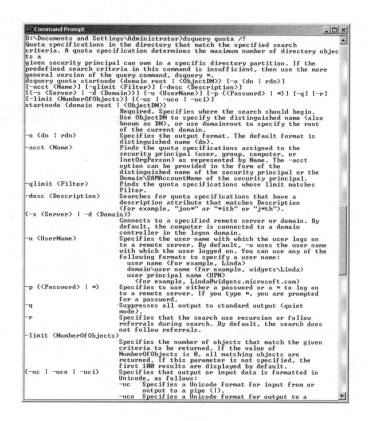

NOTE *If you are familiar with ADSI scripting, you can also manage quota limits on Active Directory partitions.*

Disable Recursion

The typical behavior for a DNS server is to take over the name resolution process whenever a client is attempting to resolve a host name. Clients typically send an iterative query to their DNS server, and the DNS server starts the recursion process to locate a DNS server that can identify the IP address for the host name in question. An attacker can take advantage of this scenario and start attacking the DNS server with several queries in an attempt to limit its ability to respond to valid queries.

When you disable recursion on a DNS server, you are essentially telling it that it will no longer be a slave to the client, and it should only return a referral to the client. In this scenario, the DNS server takes on far less of a load, but the client will incur more of the work. As the clients send queries to their DNS servers, the DNS servers will check their zone data for a match. If the DNS server is not authoritative for the zone and has not cached the entry, the DNS server will refer the client to another DNS server to contact.

In order to disable recursion, you can open the properties of the DNS server and select the option Disable Recursion (Also Disables Forwarders), as seen in Figure 20.4.

FIGURE 20.4
Disabling recursion

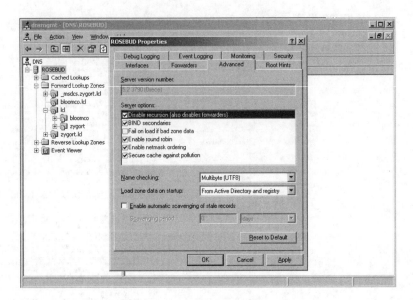

This takes most of the resolution responsibility off of the DNS server; however, you should note that DNS servers that have been stripped of their recursive abilities cannot be configured to forward, by using either a standard or conditional forwarder. This is due to the recursive nature of forwarding. The DNS server would normally send a recursive query to the server listed within the Forwarders tab of the DNS server properties.

Use Appropriate Routing

As mentioned in Chapter 3, there are several ways to resolve a query when it is sent to a DNS server. If the query and the DNS server that receives the query cannot be resolved from a zone in which the DNS server is authoritative, the server will attempt to locate the host name within the query by asking other servers. As long as you have not disabled recursion, you can still configure a server to act as a forwarder. You can also configure any Windows Server 2003 DNS server with a stub zone.

Which routing method should you choose when you are attempting to maintain a secure system? If you are worried about a denial of service attack, you should use the method that is the least resource intensive. Conditional forwarding is the most resource intensive of the routing methods, because it has to process the conditions before it decides where to forward the query. However, if you have implemented a firewall to block traffic, you may need to use another method besides a stub zone, because stub zones require access to remote systems by using TCP and UDP port 53.

Keeping the System Accurate

Attacks are not always attempts to stop the system from responding. Sometimes attacks are meant to discover information about a company or to redirect clients to incorrect hosts. Two of the most common attacks on a DNS implementation are *database manipulation* and *cache poisoning*. In either of these scenarios, data in entered into the DNS server that does not correspond to the correct host with which the client is attempting to communicate.

To alleviate attacks on your system, you should take steps to help guarantee that the DNS database can be modified only by authorized entities and to ensure that the DNS resolver cache does not contain invalid records. The options discussed in the following sections will help you protect your systems and alleviate problems for your users.

Use IPSec

If you want to make sure that you have control over the systems that are able to connect to your DNS server and ensure that those systems are authorized to do so, you could implement IPSec and use a policy that requires the clients to have IPSec in order to communicate with the DNS servers. You could even go so far as to configure policies that are specific to certain clients in order to allow only a subset of clients to connect to a DNS server. Clients from remote sites, or outside of a specific department, may not have the appropriate settings to allow them to connect to a DNS server, while authorized clients are allowed to update records within the zone and communicate with the DNS server in order to query for other hosts.

You can create your own IPSec policies that have rules in place that will allow only the appropriate clients to access the DNS server. At the same time, you can include a rule that will allow all of the DNS servers that need to communicate with one another to do so. If you are using Active Directory–integrated DNS servers, make sure the IPSec rules that govern the domain controllers are configured to allow any replication partner the ability to connect and communicate.

Use Secure DDNS

As mentioned before, if you want to make sure the records that are entered within your DNS zones are valid records, you can implement the Secure Only option from the General tab of the zone properties, as seen in Figure 20.5. Once enabled, the only clients that can enter records within the zone are clients that are members of your Active Directory.

The greatest benefit of using only secure updates is that you can be guaranteed that the records that are entered are valid. An attacker would not be able to register records that would redirect the client to an invalid host or bad records that would cause the failure of the client's access attempt.

The only way you would be able to make the zone more secure would be to completely disable the ability to use dynamic updates. Usually, this is not an option because the administrative staff would have to manually enter every record within the zone. This could be a very time-consuming task, and it would be prone to human error, which could cause the same problems you are trying to alleviate.

If you implement secure updates, make sure that the clients that need to register within your zone are still able to do so. You might need to allow DHCP to register on behalf of some of the clients within your network, and you might have to manually create the records for others.

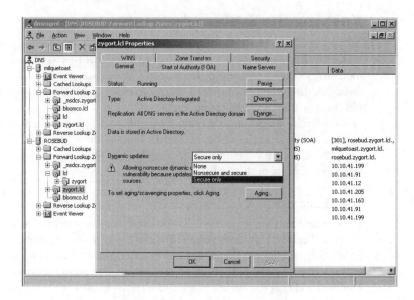

Avoid Cache Poisoning

An attacker could attempt to populate the cache on your DNS server with incorrect information in an attempt to either stop name resolution or to redirect clients to incorrect systems. If an attacker were able to populate the cache with an entry that would redirect a client to the wrong DNS server, the client could receive a response to their query that redirected them to a compromised host.

To make sure that the entries within the DNS cache are complete and accurate entries that are part of the name resolution path that the DNS server has obtained during resolution, you can enable the Secure Against Cache Pollution option, as seen in Figure 20.6. You can reach this option by opening the properties of your DNS server and selecting the Advanced tab.

Once enabled, your DNS server will ignore records that were not obtained from the DNS server that is authoritative for the zone in question. This will place additional resource requirements on the DNS server because it will need to perform more queries due to the dropping of records that are not obtained from authoritative DNS servers. However, it will allow you to guarantee the authenticity and accuracy of the records.

Allow Appropriate Access

Keeping attackers away from the data contained in your database should be of high concern. If an attacker is able to access the records, or able to damage the database so that it no longer responds correctly to queries, either your clients will become victims of redirection attacks or they will not have the ability to access the hosts with which they were intending to communicate. The following sections cover options that you should consider when you are attempting to secure both Active Directory–integrated and non–Active Directory–integrated zones.

FIGURE 20.6

Securing against
cache pollution

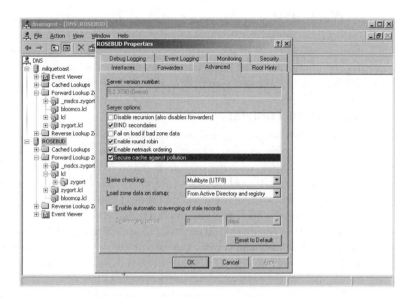

ACTIVE DIRECTORY–INTEGRATED ZONES

By default, members of the domain's Administrators group, Domain Admins, Enterprise Admins, and DNS Admins groups have the ability to manage DNS zones. If you want to control the administrative staff who can manage a zone, you can configure the permissions on the zone within the DNS console. If special groups are responsible for specific zones, make sure you remove the other administrative groups from the zones' access control lists. If you don't, a rogue administrator could make unauthorized changes to the zones.

NON–ACTIVE DIRECTORY–INTEGRATED ZONES

Stub zones, secondary zones, and primary zones that are not Active Directory–integrated do not have access control lists associated with them. This is not necessarily a bad thing for stub and secondary zones because the records contained within them cannot be modified directly. The primary zone is the only one that can be modified directly. Non–Active Directory–integrated primary zones are at risk, however. You should make sure that you monitor the accounts within the groups that have the ability to work on the DNS server, and you should consider turning off the dynamic update option.

Zone data is stored within a file on the DNS server when the zone is not Active Directory–integrated. These zone files are protected using file system access control lists. The default members of the access control list include the Users and Power Users groups. Typically, neither of these groups needs access to the zone files; therefore, you should modify the access control list so that only the Administrators group, any special DNS administrative groups, and the System account have access. Remember that any dynamic updates are performed within the DNS service, and it is up to the System account to update the zone's associated file; therefore, users do not need to have access to the these files.

You should also consider moving the zone files to another partition away from the system files. Such a move would effectively reduce the chance of a zone file being compromised by a buffer over-flow and allowing an attacker to browse the files stored on the system partition. Once you move the files to another partition, make sure that you adjust the access control list so that only the appropriate DNS administrators and system have access to the files.

Lock Down Transfers

An Active Directory–integrated zone can send zone transfers to a secondary zone if the DNS server is configured to do so. You may want to review your settings to make sure that you only allow zone transfers to DNS servers that are authorized to receive the transfer. This is especially important if your zones are not Active Directory–integrated. All of the zone information will need to pass between the DNS servers as zone transfers. You should make sure that all of the DNS servers that need to receive the transfer are listed, and that no other servers are allowed to receive a transfer.

If you can be certain that all of the DNS servers that are listed within the Name Servers tab of the zone properties are valid servers, you can use the setting shown in Figure 20.7. By using the option Only To Servers Listed In The Name Servers tab, you can allow all servers that have a secondary zone configured for the namespace to receive zone transfers when a change occurs.

However, if you think you might have a rogue administrator, or someone has built a DNS server to capture records for your namespace, you may want to kick up your level of security a notch by using the Only To The Following Name Servers option. When using this setting you will need to manually enter the IP address of every valid DNS server that needs to receive a zone transfer. Of course, this will not keep a rogue administrator who has permissions to view the zone data away from your DNS records. If you have granted them the privileges, there is not much you can do besides revoke their power.

FIGURE 20.7

Allowing zone transfer to servers listed as name servers

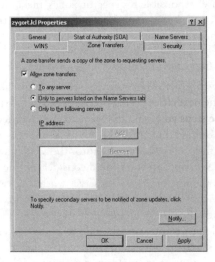

If your zones are Active Directory–integrated, you can probably use the default setting of not allowing zone transfers. This guarantees that only domain controllers hold the zone records, but limits you if there are any non–Active Directory–integrated DNS servers within your environment.

Best Practices for Securing DNS

DNS has been around for many years and its inherent open nature is easy to compromise. In order to secure your DNS infrastructure, you should consider the following:

- ◆ Use Active Directory–integrated zones. This option will secure your DNS data by allowing records to be added only by valid Active Directory members.

- ◆ Use IPSec between clients and the DNS server to restrict the systems that can resolve addresses or register records.

- ◆ Set quotas on your directory partitions so that you can limit the number of objects that accounts can create within Active Directory.

- ◆ Use Secure Dynamic Updates so that you can control the systems that are allowed to register records.

- ◆ Allow zone transfers only to authorized DNS servers. If all of your DNS server are Active Directory–integrated, turn off the ability to use zone transfers.

- ◆ Configure security on your zones within Active Directory or on the files if the zone is not Active Directory–integrated.

Next Up

With all of the different types of attacks that occur against systems and the sheer number of attackers who are salivating at the opportunity to brag to their friends about the success of their latest attempt, you need to make sure that your systems are as secure as possible. One of the most important aspects of maintaining the security of your systems is to make sure that you keep them up-to-date with the latest security patches. In the next chapter, we will look at the different methods of making sure your systems are patched and the steps you can take to make sure they have the latest and greatest security patches.

chapter21

Patch Management

AS SECURE AS YOU make your existing network, new vulnerabilities are discovered on a week by week basis. These vulnerabilities are often discovered very quickly, and patches are made available weeks, sometimes even months, before a virus is constructed to take advantage of the vulnerability. Your job in securing your network is not complete until you address the need for a quick and proper patch management plan. You could spend months tightening security on the servers in your network, only to have it come crashing down in seconds because a critical patch was not installed on your servers.

For effective patch management, you must have a plan in place. This plan should consist of many steps, including the items on this list:

- Monitor security bulletins and announcements.
- Determine if a vulnerability will affect your systems.
- Test the patch in a secured environment.
- Develop a deployment plan.
- Develop a back-out plan.
- Integrate the patch into your live environment.

Most administrators go straight to the last step in this process. Doing so could be a huge mistake if the patch has adverse effects on production systems or any applications that may run on those systems.

Monitor Security Bulletins and Announcements

Daily monitoring of security bulletins and announcements is essential in your patch management strategy. Many websites and mailing lists have this information readily available.

Microsoft's own security website, located at http://www.microsoft.com/security, is regularly updated with the latest information and should be checked daily. You can also sign up for their mailing list at http://www.microsoft.com/security/bulletins/alerts.mspx.

NTBugtraq, www.ntbugtraq.com, has a wealth of information and also has a mailing list to which you can subscribe.

You should become familiar with some of the terminology that is often used in these bulletins.

Vulnerability   A vulnerability is a weakness in software, hardware, or procedure that could be exploited during an attack. Types of vulnerabilities often include buffer overrun, privilege elevation, and validation flaw.

Attack   An attempt by a threat agent to take advantage of a vulnerability.

Attack Vector   The method or route that an attack uses to gain access to the computer system, usually by taking advantage of well-known security weaknesses.

Countermeasure   A hardware, software, or procedure put in place to lessen the risk of attack.

Threat   A threat is the source of danger.

Threat Agent   A threat agent is a person or process that is attacking your vulnerability. In most cases, the threat agent will be a virus, worm, Trojan horse, mail bomb, or an actual person attacking the system.

Regular monitoring of security bulletins and announcements is very important. Microsoft is very prompt about releasing fixes for vulnerabilities it finds. As seen in Table 21.1, many updates are available months before a threat agent can be constructed to take advantage of a vulnerability.

TABLE 21.1: PATCH AVAILABILITY

ATTACK NAME	DATE VULNERABILITY WAS DISCOVERED	DAYS PATCH WAS AVAILABLE BEFORE ATTACK
Trojan.Kaht	May 5, 2003	49
SQL Slammer	Jan 24, 2003	184
Klez-E	Jan 17, 2002	294
Nimda	Sept 18, 2001	336
Code Red	Jul 16, 2001	28

Determine Systems Affected by Vulnerability

Each security bulletin from Microsoft will be accompanied by a list of the systems affected. Know your entire environment, and know the current service pack/patch levels on all of your servers. This way you'll know which patches need to be installed in your environment. The Microsoft Baseline Security Analyzer (MBSA) utility (discussed later in this chapter) will help you gather this information.

Microsoft releases many types of updates. Understanding their terminology is important when you are assessing the need for action. Microsoft defines each of these types of updates as follows:

Security Patch A broadly released fix for a specific product that addresses a security vulnerability. A security patch is often described as having a severity, which actually refers to the MSRC severity rating of the vulnerability that the security patch addresses.

Critical Update A broadly released fix for a specific problem that addresses a critical, nonsecurity-related bug.

Update A broadly released fix for a specific problem that addresses a noncritical, nonsecurity-related bug.

Hotfix A single package composed of one or more files used to address a problem in a product. Hotfixes address a specific customer situation, are available only through a support relationship with Microsoft, and may not be distributed outside the customer organization without written legal consent from Microsoft. The terms *Quick Fix Engineering (QFE) update patch* and *update* have been used in the past as synonyms for hotfix.

Update Rollup A collection of security patches, critical updates, updates, and hotfixes that are released as a cumulative offering or targeted at a single product component, such as Microsoft Internet Information Services (IIS) or Microsoft Internet Explorer. This allows for easier deployment of multiple software updates.

Service Pack A cumulative set of hotfixes, security patches, critical updates, and updates since the release of the product; they can include solutions to many resolved problems that have not been made available through any other software updates. Service packs may also contain a limited number of customer-requested design changes or features. Service packs are broadly distributed, and they are tested by Microsoft more than any other software updates.

Integrated Service Pack The combination of a product with a service pack in one package, sometimes referred to as a slipstreamed version.

Feature Pack A new feature release for a product that adds functionality. It is usually rolled into the product at the next release.

NOTE *For more information on the MSRC, see the Microsoft website at* `http://www.microsoft.com/technet/archive/community/columns/security/essays/sectour.mspx`.

All Microsoft security bulletins are also accompanied by a security rating.

Critical A vulnerability that may result in a compromise of the system that may not require user intervention to execute.

Important A vulnerability that may result in a compromise of the system.

Moderate A vulnerability that may result in the compromise of the system, but may be difficult to exploit based on default configuration or auditing.

Low A vulnerability that may result in the compromise of a system, but is extremely difficult or the resultant impact is minimal.

After downloading a patch, verify the authenticity of the patch by checking the Authenticode and signature of the file. You can check the Authenticode before you install the patch by right-clicking on the file and viewing the properties of the file. You will still get a security popup message when you try to run the file. This is because the Windows Hardware Quality Labs (WHQL) signature for a driver file does not match what is in the catalog file. This is by design, as the new WHQL signatures are not available until after they are installed by the hotfix. Run the Sigverif utility from the Windows Resource Kit after the installation to verify the WHQL signature.

Test Patch in a Secure Environment

In a perfect world, you would have a test lab with an exact copy of all of your domain controllers, application servers, and a representation of each workstation operating system at your disposal for testing patches before they "go live." In the real world, this is not often the case.

Test environments can be very expensive, but may prove to be well worth the money. If you can afford it, you should have at least one server in the test lab to each server role in your existing network. If you have Windows 2000 and Windows 2003 domain controllers, duplicate that in your test environment so you can test the effects of the different patches that you will have to implement in your "real" network. Test from various workstations and operating systems in the lab. Test domain functionality such as group policy, etc.

If you cannot afford an extravagant lab setup, you can mimic your existing network with fewer servers by using Microsoft's Virtual PC or VMWare. You can run many virtual machines on one decent-sized server. Virtual Machine software has pretty significant hardware requirements, but the cost savings can be huge when compared to replicating your existing network server by server. Large amounts of hard disk space (to store the server images) and RAM (at least 128MB for each virtual machine) are recommended for each lab server.

Develop a Deployment Plan

When determining your deployment plan, you will be faced with a lot of decisions. How many systems need this patch? Where are they? Which tools will you use to deploy the patch? What will you do if the patch adversely affects a production server?

All Windows operating systems later than Windows 98 can use the Windows Update website to maintain their computer's operating system, software, and hardware. This site allows you to scan your computer for needed updates, select the updates you want to install from a list, and then install the updates. This must be done on a computer-by-computer basis.

An easy-to-use reporting tool available free from Microsoft is the Microsoft Baseline Security Analyzer (MBSA). MBSA allows you to scan a local or remote workstation to view possible security vulnerabilities and incorrect configurations. MBSA will scan for common incorrect configurations in the operating system, IIS, SQL, and desktop applications. It can also scan for missing security updates for Windows, IIS, SQL, and Exchange.

MBSA is available in both command line and GUI interfaces, as seen in Figure 21.1. The command-line version can be combined with the task scheduler to automate the reporting process, either during off hours or during a logon via Group Policy.

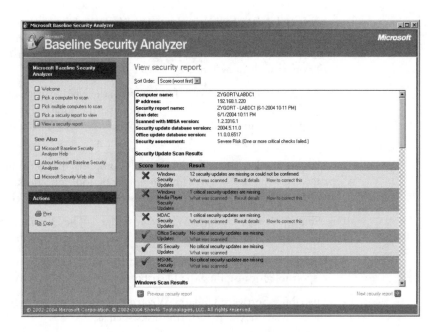

MBSA is generally considered a reporting tool only, but it does offer support for performing the security update portion of the scan when combined with a Microsoft Software Update Services (SUS) server. When an SUS is defined in the scan, either through the GUI or the command-line interface, the scan will be performed against the list of approved security updates on the local SUS server, as opposed to the complete list of security updates in the `mssecure.xml` file that is downloaded when the scan starts.

Software Update Services Software Update Services (SUS) is a local version of Windows Update that allows administrators tighter control over the patch management process. Each computer on the network can be configured to look to the local SUS server instead of going out to the Internet to find the updates. Administrators can hold the update on the server until they have sufficiently tested it; then they can approve the update, and it will then be available to the other computers. Another advantage to this solution is keeping Internet traffic to a minimum. Each server and workstation in your environment communicates with the SUS server(s) only, instead of each individual computer going out to Windows Update and downloading its own copy of the patch.

Systems Management Server 2.0 and the Software Update Services Feature Pack SMS is known for its ability to distribute any type of software. With the SUS Feature Pack, you can now use SMS to streamline your patch management process. The SUS Feature Pack adds the following three areas of functionality to SMS.

Security Update Inventory Installer The Security Update Inventory Installer consists of three components:

Security Update Inventory Installer   Creates an inventory of security updates that are either installed or applicable to client computers. The installer runs on the SMS site server and is responsible for building, packaging, collecting, and advertising the information about security on your client systems.

Security Update Inventory Tool   Using the XML parser (MSXML) and the `MSSecure.xml` file, the Security Update Inventory Tool uses the same technology as the MBSA to scan client computers for installed or applicable to those systems. This information is then converted into SMS inventory data.

Security Update Sync Tool   A single computer that is connected to the Internet that basically acts as an SUS server. This computer periodically checks the Microsoft downloads website for updates. SMS is then used to send these updates to client computers.

Distribute Software Updates Wizard Installer   The Distribute Software Updates Wizard Installer performs software update distribution tasks and contains three components:

Distribute Software Updates Wizard Installer   Installed on the SMS Site Server, this is responsible for installing the Distribute Software Updates Wizard component.

Distribute Software Updates Wizard   Responsible for software distribution tasks from the SMS site server, it performs tasks such as:

♦ Analyzes inventory information to determine update status for clients

♦ Provides a method for reviewing and authorizing suggested updates

♦ Downloads authorized updates and installation information

♦ Builds packages and advertises updates

♦ Distributes the updates to client computers by using SMS software distribution features

♦ Deploys the Software Installation Agent to client computers

Software Updates Installation Agent   The Software Updates Installation Agent checks available updates to see if they are needed on a client computer. This agent keeps unnecessary or redundant updates from being installed on the system, reducing system overhead.

Integrate Patch into Live Environment

After thorough testing and deciding on what method to use to implement the patch, you must now integrate the patch into your live environment. We will cover how to do this with the various tools at your disposal, which include Windows Update, SUS and Automatic Updates, and SMS with the SUS Feature Pack.

Windows Update

As seen in Figure 21.2, and located at `http://windowsupdate.microsoft.com`, this utility must be explicitly run from each server and client computer. Just follow these steps:

1. Launch a web browser, and go to `http://windowsupdate.microsoft.com`.

2. Accept any security popup warnings.

3. Click on the Scan For Updates link.

4. Select the option from the left under Pick Updates To Install. There will be three items to choose from: Critical Updates and Service Packs, updates specific to your operating system, and driver updates.

5. Look through the list of recommended updates, select the update from the list that you would like to install, and click the Add button.

6. Click on the Review And Install Updates link to install the selected updates.

You can see how this would be a daunting task for an administrator if all the computers and servers on a network were configured this way. The only way to avoid doing all of these updates yourself would be to let the end user perform these updates. This method would take the quality testing out of your hands though, and some of the patches could adversely affect your network.

FIGURE 21.2

Windows Update website

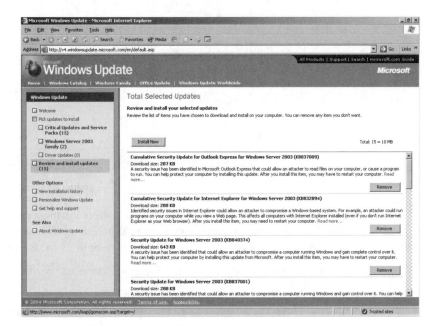

Deploying the Patch with Software Update Services

After synchronizing the server, either manually or automatically by configuring the synchronization schedule, you will have a list of new updates that are available to download. The administrator must go in and approve each update that is ready to be distributed to the client computers. After you have selected the update you want to deploy, click the Approve button at the bottom of the screen. Agree to any security warnings or license agreements that you may be prompted to read.

Configure your workstations to look to the SUS server instead of Windows Update. You can configure this by changing the Automatic Updates client. This can easily be accomplished by configuring the automatic updates portion of Group Policy.

The Group Policy area you will need to edit is Computer Configuration ➤ Administrative Templates ➤ Windows Components ➤ Windows Update, as seen in Figure 21.3.

FIGURE 21.3
Windows Update
options in a GPO

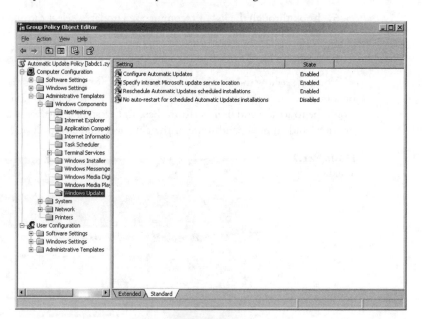

Configure Automatic Updates   Tells the computer whether it will receive downloads through the Windows automatic updating service. When enabled, as seen in Figure 21.4, you can define how the computer installs the patch. The three options are as follows:

◆   **2**   Notify before downloading any updates and notify again before installing them.

◆   **3**   Download the updates automatically and notify when they are ready to be installed. This is the default setting. The update files will be downloaded to the client computer, but they must accept the popup window telling them they have updates to install.

◆   **4**   Automatically download updates and install them on the schedule below. This setting automatically downloads the patch, but it will wait to install it until the time specified. The user cannot deny an install with this setting.

FIGURE 21.4
Configure Automatic Updates GPO setting

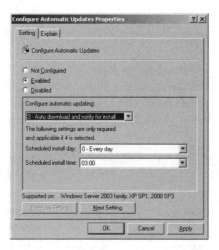

Specify Intranet Microsoft Update Service Location   Tells the client the location of the SUS server on the network. As you will note in Figure 21.5, it also has a box for a statistics server. This is the server to which the workstation will log information. This can be the same server as the SUS server.

FIGURE 21.5
Specify Intranet Microsoft Update Service Location GPO setting

Reschedule Automatic Updates Scheduled Installations   Defines the length of time for the workstation to wait before proceeding with a scheduled installation that was previously missed.

No Auto-Restart for Scheduled Automatic Updates Installations   Specifies that the computer will not automatically be rebooted, but will instead wait until the computer is manually rebooted before completing installation. If a user is on the computer, they will receive a warning. If this setting is set to Disabled, the user will get a warning and the computer will automatically reboot in 5 minutes.

As these policy changes go into effect, the Registry is modified so that the computer will now begin working with the SUS server and not Windows Update. Tables 21.2 and 21.3 show the Registry keys that are affected when a GPO is configured with settings to control automatic updates from an SUS server.

TABLE 21.2: REGISTRY SETTINGS AFFECTED BY AUTOMATIC UPDATE CLIENT
HKLM\Software\Policies\Microsoft\Windows\WindowsUpdate\AU

NAME	TYPE	VALUE	DESCRIPTION
NoAutoUpdate	Reg_DWORD	0 or 1	0=Automatic Updates enabled by default, 1=Automatic updates is disabled
AUOptions	Reg_DWORD	2, 3, or 4	2=Notify of download installation, 3=Automatically download and notify of installation, 4=Automatic download and scheduled installation
ScheduledInstallDay	Reg_DWORD	0, 1, 2, 3, 4, 5, 6, 7	0=Every day, 1 through 7=Corresponding day of the week (1=Sunday to 7=Saturday)
RescheduleWaitTim	Reg_DWORD	X	X=Number of minutes
NoAutoRebootWith-LoggedOnUsers	Reg_DWORD	0, 1	0=Computer reboots with logged-on users, 1=Logged-on users choose whether or not to reboot

TABLE 21.3: REGISTRY SETTINGS AFFECTED BY AUTOMATIC UPDATE CLIENT
HKLM\Software\Policies\Microsoft\Windows\WindowsUpdate

NAME	TYPE	VALUE	DESCRIPTION
WUServer	Reg_SZ	http://susServerName	The HTTP name of the SUS server on your network
WUStatusServer	Reg_SZ	http://susServerName	The HTTP name of the SUS server on your network

Using SMS Server with the SUS Feature Pack to Deploy the Patch

Import programs or advertisements from your test environment. Importing packages that you have already created and developed in your test lab is a best practice. Doing so will save time and help with reliability and security.

After the programs and advertisements have been imported, your next step is to assign a distribution point to make the software update available to client computers.

The next step is to stage the updates at the distribution points. After the distribution points have been assigned, verify that all files involved in the patch have been distributed to the other servers. The patch cannot be installed on client computers in that site until the software is available on the distribution point. Because SMS sends intersite information during low bandwidth times, or defined times of the day, important updates may not be available right away or exactly when you want them.

After the updates are deployed to the SMS site server, they are automatically distributed to all distribution points within the site.

Clients cannot install the updates at this time though. You must use the Distribute Software Updates Wizard to select deployment groups to distribute the update. Smart agents are deployed to each client to determine if the update is applicable or needed on that computer.

The Distribute Software Updates Wizard is used for the deployment phase of the process. During this phase, a repeating advertisement that runs the software update installation agent on the clients in the target collection is created.

Because the SMS inventory information is used for the client target list, as each computer installs the patch and is subsequently inventoried, that computer will drop off of the client target list. As new computers are added to the network and are inventoried, they will be added to the list.

Third-Party Solutions

Many third-party patch management solutions provide the same functionality as Microsoft's products, and you may find them easier to administer, easier to configure, more reliable, and more proficient than the Microsoft solutions. As with any tool you use, you will find that what you are familiar with is usually the easiest to work with. As you consider the following utilities, just remember that your mileage may vary.

Many companies offer free products to help you check for hotfixes and updates. Here are a few of them:

◆ BigFix Consumer Edition

◆ Ecora Patch Manager (Trial Edition)

◆ Gravity Storm Service Pack Manager 2000LT

◆ Shavlik HFNetChk

All of these companies also market a patch management solution that includes the ability to update client machines. Some of the more popular patch management solutions are listed here:

◆ BigFix Patch Manager

◆ Ecora Patch Manager

◆ GFI LANGuard Network Security Scanner

◆ Gravity Storm Service Pack Manager 2000

◆ LANDesk Patch Manager

◆ Shavlik HFNetChkPro

◆ St. Bernard Software UdateEXPERT

Best Practices for Patch Management

No matter which network operating system you implement, you will need to stay on top of your patch management. While this is not usually an administrator's favorite job, failure to do so could be very costly.

♦ Stay on top of security threats and vulnerabilities. Know how those threats could harm your systems.

♦ Keep an inventory of your current systems and the service pack levels and patches that are installed on them. The MBSA tool will aid you in this process.

♦ Develop a test environment to help protect your production servers; it will give you the opportunity to test the patch on replicas of your production servers so any adverse effects from the patch or update will be limited to the test environment.

♦ You can utilize VMWare and Microsoft Virtual PC software to help reduce the cost of a test environment if you do not already have one.

♦ Create a deployment plan to help distribute the patch in a timely and effective manner.

♦ Automate patch installation with the help of such tools as SUS or SMS with the SUS Feature Pack.

Next Up

Keeping all of the servers and workstations within your network infrastructure patched and secure is no easy feat. Options are available to ease your patch management woes, and Microsoft is moving in the right direction by giving administrators the tools to automate some of their updates. As we move on to the next chapter, we will build on some of the security topics that we already discussed in this unit. We will elaborate on some of the techniques that are available to make sure your Active Directory infrastructure is secure.

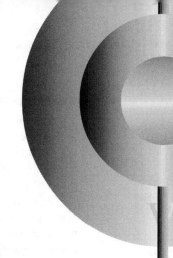

chapter 22

Securing Active Directory

THE PREVIOUS THREE CHAPTERS in this section dealt with securing your domain controllers in an attempt to make sure that they have the required prerequisites in place for the operating system and supporting services. We need to address one final piece of the security puzzle, and that is Active Directory itself. Securing the operating system and physically securing your domain controllers are good first steps in the security process. Maintaining a patch management routine to efficiently handle security updates and making sure that DNS is secure go a long way to making sure that your directory service is safe from most attacks; however, there are still some steps you should take with the directory service database itself to make sure all of your bases are covered.

Throughout this chapter, I will present some of the options you have to maintain the integrity of your Active Directory infrastructure. Many of the tools you have to work with were already covered in previous chapters.

Placement of the Active Directory Database Files

The Active Directory Database contains information about directory data, user logon processes, authentication, and directory searches. This information is stored in three files: `ntds.dit`, `edb*.log`, and `temp.edb`. I strongly recommend that you move these files from their default location when you promote the domain controller. These files should be moved if they are on the system partition in any existing domain controller. A malicious user will be very aware of where these files are located and will search that location first when looking for the files. Also, because the default location is the system partition of the domain controller, an attacker will have access to your directory service database if an attack successfully accesses the system drive.

You should also resize the active directory event log files. By default, the Directory Service and File Replication event log files are set to a maximum of 512KB. For proper auditing (which we will cover later in this chapter), the maximum size of these log files should be increased to a Microsoft-recommended 16MB. See Chapter 12, "Optimizing the Active Directory Database," for information on how to use NTDSUTIL to move the database and log files.

Guaranteeing Database Space

There are two reserve log files that are used in case the partition that holds the logs files fills to capacity. These reserve log files are 10MB each and will move along with the Active Directory log files when you move them. You should not rely on these log files to be adequate if there is an attack on your system. 10MB is not going to be enough space in case of an emergency or if you come under a denial of service attack.

You should consider creating a dummy file that will take up space on the partition where you have placed your directory database files. Create this *reserve file* so that it takes up at least 250MB of the partition. On large partitions, you can create the reserve file to be at least 1 percent of the partition size, but the minimum size should not be smaller than 250MB.

Creating reserve files becomes a good practice by guaranteeing that an attack on the database partition, or poor planning by the administrator, does not allow the database partition to become too full to efficiently recover.

To create the reserve file, you need to log on to a Windows XP or Windows Server 2003 system with an account that has domain administrator rights, and connect to the partition on the domain controller on which you want to create the reserve file. For instance, if you placed the directory database on the E: partition on the domain controller `rosebud.zygort.1cl`, you would open a command prompt and type `net use x: \\rosebud.zygort.1cl\e$`.

Once you have mapped the drive, you can open a command prompt, change to the mapped drive, and issue the command `fsutil file createnew` *ReservFileName ReserveFileSize*. The *ReserveFileSize* has to be entered in bytes. If you want to reserve 250MB on your partition and name the file `ReserveFile`, enter the command `fsutil file createnew ReserveFile 256000`.

After you create the file, make sure you set the permissions on the file so that any of the administrative staff who are responsible for the domain controller can remove the file if they need the additional room on the partition.

Auditing Domain Controllers

A very important part of securing your Active Directory Domain Controllers is enabling auditing and deciding what to audit. This section will describe in detail the objects that should be audited on a regular basis, and what to do with the audit results that you find.

If your forest is at a Windows 2003 functional level, all of these audit settings are already configured for you. If your domain has been upgraded and is still at a Windows 2000 Native or Windows 2003 Interim level, you will have to manually change these settings to the recommended level.

In a Windows 2003 Forest, Audit Directory Service Access setting is set to audit success and failure. In Windows 2000 mixed or native mode, it is set to No Auditing by default. To track access of objects that have their own system access control list, set auditing to Success and Failure. If the audit event is set to Success, each time a user successfully accesses an Active Directory object, an event will be logged. If the audit event is set for Failure, an audit entry will be recorded for each user that is unsuccessful in their attempt to access an Active Directory object.

You will need to be logged in as a Domain Administrator to use the ADSI Edit utility to enable auditing on the following items. To enable auditing on Active Directory database objects:

1. Log on to a domain controller in the root domain using an account with Domain Admins credentials, and then open the Microsoft Management Console.

2. Click File ➤ Add/Remove Snap-ins ➤ ADSI Edit ➤ Add.

3. In the console tree, right-click ADSI Edit and select Connect To.

4. In the Connection window, click on the Name dialog box, select Domain from the naming context, and then click OK.

5. Expand the console tree, right-click the *container_object* (the domain or domain controller OU where auditing will be enabled), and then click Properties.

6. On the Security tab of the Properties dialog box, click Advanced.

7. On the Auditing tab of the Access Control Settings dialog box, click Add.

AUDITING SCHEMA DIRECTORY PARTITIONS

Figure 22.1 shows ADSI Edit with the schema partition loaded. You will want to audit any additions, deletions, modifications, or attempted transfers of the Schema Operations Master role of your Active Directory Schema. You can enable auditing by setting the SACLs on the objects listed here. Table 22.1 lists the settings that Microsoft recommends for auditing the schema. Set the permissions for CN=Schema, CN=Configuration, DC=ForestRootName.

FIGURE 22.1
ADSI Edit used to control auditing of Active Directory objects

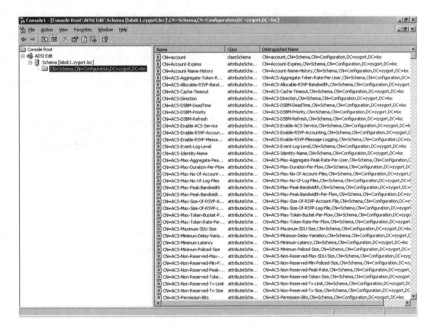

TABLE 22.1: SCHEMA AUDITING PERMISSIONS

TAB	NAME	ACCESS	TYPE	APPLY TO
Object	Everyone	Modify Permissions	Success	This Object Only
Object	Everyone	Modify Owner	Success	This Object Only
Object	Everyone	Create All Child Objects	Success	This Object Only
Object	Everyone	Delete	Success	This Object Only
Object	Everyone	Modify Permissions	Success	This Object Only
Object	Everyone	Delete Subtree	Success	This Object Only
Properties	Everyone	Write All Properties	Success	This Object And All Child Objects

AUDITING THE CONFIGURATION DIRECTORY PARTITION

You can enable auditing by setting the SACLs on the objects listed here. Table 22.2 lists the settings that Microsoft recommends for auditing the Configuration Directory Partition.

TABLE 22.2: SCHEMA AUDITING ENTRIES

TAB	NAME	ACCESS	TYPE	APPLY TO
Object	Everyone	Modify Permissions	Success	This Object Only
Object	Everyone	Modify Owner	Success	This Object Only
Object	Everyone	Write All Properties	Success	This Object Only
Object	Administrator	All Extended Rights	Success	This Object Only
Object	Domain Users	All Extended Rights	Success	This Object Only

Audit Settings for CN=Sites, CN=Configuration, DC=*ForestRootName* With the settings listed in Table 22.3, you will be able to audit all of the following directory operations:

- Add/Remove any domain controllers in the forest
- Add/Remove any Group Policy settings that are applied to a site
- Add/Remove any subnet within a site
- Any execution of the following operations on a domain controller: Do Garbage Collection, Recalculate Hierarchy, Recalculate Security Inheritance, and Check Stale Phantoms

TABLE 22.3: AUDITING SITE OBJECTS

TAB	NAME	ACCESS	TYPE	APPLY TO
Object	Everyone	Create All Child Objects	Success	This object and all child objects
Object	Everyone	Delete	Success	This object and all child objects
Object	Everyone	Delete All Child Objects	Success	This object and all child objects
Object	Everyone	Delete Subtree	Success	This object and all child objects
Object	Everyone	All Extended Rights	Success	Domain Controller Settings Objects
Properties	Everyone	: Write gPLink	Success	Site Objects
Properties	Everyone	Write gPOptions	Success	Site Objects
Properties	Everyone	siteObject	Success	Subnet Objects
Properties	Everyone	siteObject	Success	Subnet Objects
Properties	Everyone	siteObject	Success	Connection Objects

Audit Settings for CN=Partitions, CN=Configuration, DC=*ForestRootDomain*   When configuring auditing at the Partitions level, you can audit any of the following events by adding the auditing entries found in Table 22.4.

- Add/Remove any domain in the forest
- Modify any UPN suffixes in the forest
- Transfer the Domain Naming Operations Master role

TABLE 22.4: PARTITION-LEVEL AUDITING

TAB	NAME	ACCESS	TYPE	APPLY TO
Object	Everyone	Modify Permissions	Success	This Object And All Child Objects
Object	Everyone	Modify Owner	Success	This object and all child objects
Object	Everyone	Write All Properties	Success	This object and all child objects
Object	Everyone	Create All Child Objects	Success	This object and all child objects
Object	Everyone	Delete All Child Objects	Success	This object and all child objects
Object	Everyone	Delete Subtree	Success	This object and all child objects
Object	Everyone	All Extended Rights	Success	This object and all child objects

Audit settings for CN=Directory Service, CN=Windows NT, CN=Services, CN=Configuration, DC=*ForestRootDomain* Events audited by changing the settings listed in Table 22.5 include changes to the dsHeuristics attribute. The dsHeuristics attribute controls certain characteristics of forest-wide behavior of Active Directory.

TABLE 22.5: dsHeurisitcs Attribute Auditing

Tab	Name	Access	Type	Apply To
Properties	Everyone	Write dsHeuristics (property)	Success	This Object Only

Audit settings for CN=Default Query Policy, CN=Query-Policies, CN=Directory Service, CN=Windows NT, CN=Services, CN=Configuration, DC=*ForestRootDomain*. Any forest-wide changes that affect the behavior of LDAP-based queries and operations are recorded by the changes found in Table 22.6.

TABLE 22.6: Auditing Changes to LDAP

Tab	Name	Access	Type	Apply To
Properties	Everyone	Write LDAPAdminLimits	Success	This Object Only

AUDITING DOMAIN PARTITIONS

To enable auditing on the domain directory partition, follow the steps in the Tables 22.7 through 22.12. Table 22.7 is a list of settings that will allow you to audit.

◆ Add/Remove any group policy settings that are applied to the domain

◆ DNS Suffix modification of the domain

◆ Permission modification of the wellKnownObjects attribute on the Domain directory partition

◆ SID history migration

◆ PDC emulator transfer

TABLE 22.7: Audit Settings for DC=*DOMAIN*, DC=*FORESTROOTDOMAIN*

Tab	Name	Access	Type	Apply To
Object	Everyone	Modify Permissions	Success	This Object Only
Object	Everyone	Modify Owner	Success	This Object Only
Object	Everyone	Write All Properties	Success	This Object Only
Object	Administrators	All Extended Rights	Success	This Object Only
Object	Domain Users	All Extended Rights	Success	This Object Only

To audit any addition or removal of domain controllers from the domain, or modifications to the properties of the computer account of the domain controller, make the following changes to OU=Domain Controllers, DC=*Domain*, DC= *ForestRootDomain*, as seen in Table 22.8.

TABLE 22.8: AUDIT SETTINGS FOR OU=DOMAIN CONTROLLERS,DC=*DOMAIN*,DC= *FORESTROOTDOMAIN*

TAB	NAME	ACCESS	TYPE	APPLY TO
Object	Everyone	Modify Permissions	Success	This Object Only
Object	Everyone	Modify Owner	Success	This Object Only
Object	Everyone	Create All Child Objects	Success	This Object Only
Object	Everyone	Delete	Success	This Object Only
Object	Everyone	Delete All Child Objects	Success	This Object Only
Object	Everyone	Delete Subtree	Success	This Object Only
Object	Everyone	Write All Properties	Success	This Object Only And All Child Objects

To audit the transfer of the Infrastructure Operations Master role, change the auditing settings as seen in Table 22.9.

TABLE 22.9: AUDITING CHANGES TO CN=INFRASTRUCTURE, DC=*DOMAIN*,DC=*FORESTROOTDOMAIN*

TAB	NAME	ACCESS	TYPE	APPLY TO
Object	Everyone	Modify Permissions	Success	This Object Only
Object	Everyone	Write All Properties	Success	This Object Only

Table 22.10 lists the auditing settings that you should use in order to monitor changes to your GPOs. This includes any additions, deletions, or modifications of GPOs. If you want to audit all of the policies within a domain, you need to set the following auditing options on the CN=Policies,CN=System,DC=*domain*,DC=*ForestRootDomain*. If you want to audit specific GPOs, you will need to configure auditing on the individual GPO; however, you will notice that each of the GPOs is identified by its GUID beneath the Policies container.

TIP *You can locate a GPO's GUID by looking at the General tab on the GPO's properties. If the GPMC is installed, you can click on the GPO and select the Details tab.*

TABLE 22.10: RECOMMENDED SETTINGS TO AUDIT GROUP POLICY OBJECTS

TAB	NAME	ACCESS	TYPE	APPLY TO
Object	Everyone	Modify Permissions	Success	This Object Only

Continued on next page

TABLE 22.10: RECOMMENDED SETTINGS TO AUDIT GROUP POLICY OBJECTS *(continued)*

TAB	NAME	ACCESS	TYPE	APPLY TO
Object	Everyone	Modify Owner	Success	This Object Only
Object	Everyone	Create groupPolicyContainer Objects	Success	This Object Only
Object	Everyone	Delete	Success	This Object Only
Object	Everyone	Delete groupPolicyContainer Objects	Success	This Object Only
Object	Everyone	Delete Subtree	Success	This Object Only
Object	Everyone	Modify Permissions	Success	GroupPolicyContainer objects

Table 22.11 lists the settings you should put in place to audit modifications to the AdminSD-Holder role. The AdminSDHolder is a special security descriptor that is used to monitor the service administrator accounts such as Domain Admins, Administrators, Enterprise Admins, Server Operators, and any other built-in, high-priority security descriptor. The function of the AdminSDHolder role is to make sure that the rights that are granted to the Service Account Administrator roles are not changed. It runs by default every 30 minutes.

TABLE 22.11: RECOMMENDED SETTINGS TO AUDIT ANY MODIFICATIONS TO THE ADMINSDHOLDER ACCOUNT: CN=ADMINSDHOLDER,CN=SYSTEM, DC=*DOMAIN*,DC=*FORESTROOTDOMAIN*

TAB	NAME	ACCESS	TYPE	APPLY TO
Object	Everyone	Modify Permissions	Success	This Object Only
Object	Everyone	Modify Owner	Success	This Object Only
Object	Everyone	Write All Properties	Success	This Object Only

To monitor for transfers of the RID Master FSMO role, you should change the auditing entries on CN=RID Manager$,CN= System,DC=*Domain*,DC=*ForestRootDomain*.

TABLE 22.12: RECOMMENDED SETTINGS TO AUDIT THE TRANSFER OF THE RID OPERATIONS MASTER ROLE: CN=RID MANAGER$,CN=SYSTEM,DC=*DOMAIN*, DC=*FORESTROOTDOMAIN*.

TAB	NAME	ACCESS	TYPE	APPLY TO
Object	Everyone	All Extended Rights	Success	This Object Only
Object	Everyone	Write All Properties	Success	This Object Only

Maintaining the Service Account Administrators

In Table 22.11, the auditing options for the AdminSDHolder object were set so that you could audit any changes made to this object. You may also want to make sure that you have protected the Service Account Admin accounts by controlling membership in the Enterprise Admins, Domain Admins, and Administrators groups. These groups have a high level of authority within the forest/domain and should be monitored closely. Remember that any account that is a member of the Domain Admins group from the forest root will be able to add themselves into the Enterprise Admins and Schema Admins group. For this reason alone, many companies have implemented empty forest root domains so that they do not have to worry about these forest-wide administrative accounts.

Turn on auditing for account management so that you can track when changes to group membership occur. In order to do so, modify an audit policy within the domain or OU where you want to monitor the groups. Using the Group Policy Object editor, open the Audit Policy container and check the Success and Failure boxes of Audit Account Management policy, as seen in Figure 22.2.

To monitor the changes, you should open the Security Log within Event Viewer and look for event ID 641, which denotes that a security group has been changed. You can then search for event ID 632, which specifies that an account has been added to a security group, or 633, which indicates that an account has been removed from a security group.

FIGURE 22.2

Auditing Account Management

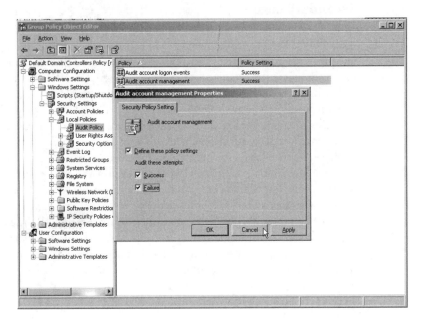

Creating a Baseline

Just as you would when you are preparing for performance monitoring, you should create an Active Directory baseline that includes all of the settings that you have made during the configuration of your domain controller. You should document all your settings so that you can pull out the documentation and review it whenever you want to review the settings.

Make sure you double-check the auditing settings as well as all of the directory service permissions and service account administrator group memberships. Documenting these items will give you a starting point when you are trying to determine what has changed within your environment.

Updating the documentation after you make a change to the system is just as important as creating a baseline for your systems. If you don't update the documentation, you might find yourself thinking the change is a problem instead of part of the solution!

Using Secure Administrative Methods

There are some measures that you can take that will allow you to enhance the security of your systems. Some of these tips are built into the operating system. Others are practices you should consider implementing to keep special functions locked away from attackers or rogue administrators.

Secondary Logon

All of your domain controllers are important systems, as are any of the member servers you have in your Active Directory environment. You will need to use an account that has special rights and permissions to perform some of the administrative tasks on these systems. However, you do not want to use an administrative account for typical day-to-day activities such as reading e-mail and researching problems on the Internet. Doing so could introduce problems within your network. If you are logged on with an administrative account and a virus finds its way past your defenses, it could attack your systems with administrative level privileges. For just this reason, Windows 2000, Windows Server 2003, and Windows XP allow the use of a secondary logon.

Whenever you log on to your workstation, you should authenticate as a standard user account that does not have special system privileges. You can then use the runas command to launch your administrative tools. This allows you to authenticate as another account for the purpose of using that utility, but the operating system will still use the typical user account for all other applications.

With Windows Server 2003, you can use a smart card with the runas command. The secondary logon protects the operating system from attacks, and the administrative functions can be limited to users who use smart cards to authenticate. Just make sure you have not disabled the Secondary Logon service when you were trying to harden your servers.

Trustworthy Personnel

You should make sure that the personnel you hire can be trusted with your organization's data. One company I worked with has a solid administrative staff that the management completely trusts. Their secret to success is that they would rather hire someone trustworthy over someone with glowing credentials and a sketchy background. They can afford to teach someone some required skills; they can't afford to teach them character. This is not to say that every company needs to spend the money to perform a full background check on all of their employees, but you should be careful and thorough when you are hiring personnel.

Two-Person Authentication

This practice is used by high-security installations when they want to make sure that it takes two people to perform a specific task. You have probably seen movies where it takes two people, each with their own key, to open a safety deposit box, or where it takes two people to activate a missile that is going to rain destruction on an enemy.

The same theory applies here. You could use an account to change the schema for your organization, and you can associate that account a smart card. Don't give the PIN used to authenticate to the user who holds the smart card. Give the PIN for the smart card to another user, but don't give that user the smart card. Under this scenario, both users are required to authenticate the account so that the schema can be modified.

You do not have to limit this type of two-person authentication to schema changes, you can use it whenever you want to restrict enterprise-level administrative management. You should consider what steps to take if one of the users is not available when a change needs to be made; however, for the most part, this is a very secure method of controlling your environment.

Controlling Cached Credentials

Any time a workstation is used by administrative staff, you should consider turning off the use of cached credentials when the system is activated from a screen saver. By default, when a system is awakened from a screen saver, the cached credentials of the logged-on user are used to access resources. You can use a Group Policy setting to change the behavior of the system when it comes back from a screen saver so that the user is authenticated by a domain controller before they are allowed to access the system. Figure 22.3 shows the policy option Interactive Logon: Require Domain Controller Authentication To Unlock Workstation. Enable this policy setting so that you can force reauthentication of the user's account.

Best Practices for Securing Active Directory

The following practices should be followed by anyone who wants to keep their directory service safe and secure.

◆ Do not install the directory service database on the system partition so that any attacks against the system partition do not leave the database vulnerable.

◆ Create a reserve file on the partition where the directory database is located so that you have the ability to quickly reclaim space in case the partition becomes full.

◆ Turn on auditing for important Active Directory objects so that you can monitor when they are modified.

◆ Secure the service account administrators so that you have control over the high-level accounts.

FIGURE 22.3
Controlling locked
workstation
authentication

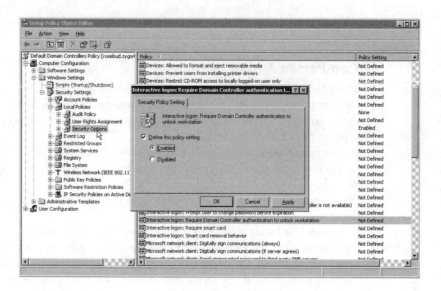

◆ When performing administration of Active Directory, use a secondary logon instead of logging on to a system as an administrator.

◆ Do not allow an administrator to use cached credentials when unlocking a workstation.

◆ Limit the number of users that you allow to have high-level administrative privileges. You will need to have a few users who have a lot of power within your forest, but you will want to make sure you keep the number of administrators to a minimum.

Next Up

That's it. You have made it through the book. This is where you take the information that I have disseminated and use it within your organization. If you follow the best practices and work with the utilities that we have covered, you will find that your Active Directory infrastructure will run silently and efficiently. Remember that proactive administration is far better than reactive, and if this book helps you get into a proactive mode, then my job here is complete!

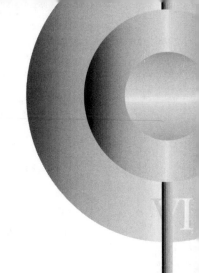

Scripting Resources

WITH THE INTRODUCTION OF Windows 2000, Microsoft started allowing far more access to the inner workings of the operating system through the use of scripting. Immediately, administrators started devising their own administrative scripts to ease their workloads and make their jobs easier. Although Microsoft boasted that an administrator could script nearly anything, there were still limitations to the access an administrator had.

Windows Server 2003 has upped the ante by allowing access to every configurable option within the operating system. If you know how to write scripts using VBScript, XML, or any of the popular scripting languages, you can devise administrative scripts that will allow you to manage your organization from the convenience of your living room. Okay, maybe that was a stretch, but you get the idea. Scripts can automate many of the mundane tasks that you need to perform, and they will perform them quickly and efficiently.

If you are interested in learning about administrative scripting, Microsoft offers courses that are presented through Microsoft Certified Partner for Learning Solutions (CPLS), formerly known as Microsoft Certified Technical Education Centers (CTEC). Course MS2433, Visual Basic Script and Windows Script Host Essentials, and course MS2439, Scripting Microsoft Windows Management Instrumentation (WMI), can help you out if you are just starting with scripting, and they can also give someone who is proficient at scripting a good insight into how the WMI can work for you.

For more information about scripting, check out some of the following resources.

From Microsoft

Script Center   This is the home of Scriptomatic and Tweakomatic. This site contains a wealth of administrative scripting solutions for Windows environments. If nothing else, these guys have a good sense of humor and will keep you entertained.

```
http://www.microsoft.com/technet/community/scriptcenter/default.mspx
```

Scripting Newsgroup   This is a good place to interact with other developers who are probably trying to figure out the same things you are, plus it's a place to go to have some of the experts help you out.

```
http://www.microsoft.com/technet/community/newsgroups/dgbrowser/en-us/default
.mspx?dg=microsoft.public.windows.server.scripting
```

MSDN Windows Script   This is a good starting place to find information on creating scripts and locating some stock scripts.

```
http://msdn.microsoft.com/library/default.asp?url=/nhp/default.asp?contentid=28001169
```

MSN Scripting Group   Join this group to learn scripting from the beginner stage through advanced topics.

```
http://groups.msn.com/windowsscript/_homepage.msnw?pgmarket=en-us
```

From Third-Party Vendors

Clarence Washington Script Repository   This is one of the best websites to start your search for coding examples and solutions.

```
http://cwashington.netreach.net/
```

Windows Scripting Newsletter   This is a rather expensive but valuable newsletter that contains concisely written articles and no advertisements. The website contains information from past newsletters that you may find helpful.

```
http://www.winnetmag.com/WindowsScripting/
```

Devx.com   This is a popular website that covers all aspects of writing code, including the scripting languages.

```
http://www.devx.com/
```

```
http://www.freevbcode.com/
```

Experts Exchange   This site covers many aspects of IT and not just scripting. Although they do not cover scripting in detail, many of the solutions that they present are scripts that will help solve a problem.

```
http://www.experts-exchange.com/Programming/
```

Index

Note to the Reader: Throughout this index **boldfaced** page numbers indicate primary discussions of a topic. *Italicized* page numbers indicate illustrations.

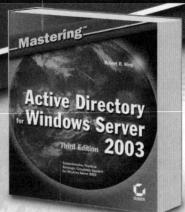

TELL US WHAT YOU THINK!

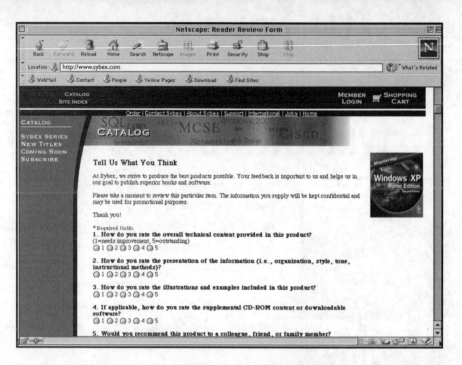

Your feedback is critical to our efforts to provide you with the best books and software on the market. Tell us what you think about the products you've purchased. It's simple:

1. Go to the Sybex website.
2. Find your book by typing the ISBN or title into the Search field.
3. Click on the book title when it appears.
4. Click **Submit a Review.**
5. Fill out the questionnaire and comments.
6. Click **Submit.**

With your feedback, we can continue to publish the highest quality computer books and software products that today's busy IT professionals deserve.

www.sybex.com

SYBEX Inc. • 1151 Marina Village Parkway, Alameda, CA 94501 • 510-523-8233